THE LAW OF
THE HARVEST

THE LAW OF
THE HARVEST

by

STERLING W. SILL

"Be not deceived; God is not mocked: for whatsoever a man soweth, that shall he also reap."
(Galatians 6:7)

INTERNATIONAL STANDARD BOOK NUMBER
0-88290-142-7

Printed in the
United States of America
by

**Horizon Publishers
& Distributors
P.O. Box 490
50 South 500 West
Bountiful, Utah 84010**

FOREWORD

O<small>N JULY</small> 4, 1776, a great new nation was born into the world. On that day, the men chosen to stand in the forefront of our national life, proclaimed the adoption of the American Declaration of Independence. It said in part:

"We hold these truths to be self-evident that all men are created equal; that they are endowed by their Creator with certain inalienable rights; that among these are life, liberty, and the pursuit of happiness."

The Founding Fathers breathed into this declaration, and the constitution that followed it, the spirit of the magnificent accomplishment destined to flourish in this great new nation. Then after filling in the details of their ambition, they indicated that they were willing to invest everything they had, including themselves, in bringing about the inspired purposes to which they had dedicated their lives. Before signing they wrote:

"And for the support of this declaration, with a firm reliance on the protection of Divine Providence, we mutually pledge to each other our lives, our fortunes, and our sacred honor."

Down through the years the great ideals embodied in the American way of life have been held constantly before our minds. We have greatly cherished the God-given privileges of sustaining and improving our lives and our opportunities, in this divinely favored land. We are grateful for our freedom, our right to own property and enjoy the lawful fruits of our own labors. We cling vigorously to our rights to promote life and liberty, and to engage further in the pursuit of happiness. We hope and pray that we shall not fail in our efforts.

During recent years we have run a kind of check on ourselves by making a number of public surveys, and taking a series of private opinion polls. We have asked our own generation what it is that we want from life. The returns tell us that we still desire those things for which our fathers sought. We want to be free. We desire health and strength, including both spiritual and mental vigor. We want a long life. We hope to bring about the greatest possible development of ourselves, and achieve a substantial measure of material success. We want to feel that we ourselves are worthwhile, and that we have earned the right to the honest esteem of good people. We desire a high degree of intelligence, good judgment and a sense of social well-being, both for ourselves and our families. Fundamentally we have always been a religious people. Our Pilgrim Forefathers came to this continent for spiritual reasons, and we desire to build upon their foundation, and further develop our religious faith and general well-being. Long before our Pilgrim Forefathers knelt at Plymouth Rock, God had implanted in the soul of man an instinct to reach upward, and an earnest desire to serve the best interests of his fellow man. In many ways, including the sacred scripture and the offices of the Church, God has made available his own program for helping us to make the most and the best of our lives. In that spirit, the fifty-two religious discussions recorded on the following pages have been prepared, and during the year just past they have been delivered to a radio audience over the air.

They are now being presented in book form in the hope that they may make some contribution to those who may read them.

The important "law of consequences" points out that everything we think or do completes itself in us. We are directly responsible for that particular 50 per cent of an action which is "cause," and then nothing can prevent us from receiving that other 50 per cent, which is "consequence."

There is an old proverb that says, "What a lion eats becomes lion, but what a serpent eats becomes serpent." And the kind of thoughtful consideration that we may give to the important questions of life will determine our own accomplishment both here and hereafter. The successful development of our lives, was the purpose for which our ancestors established us in this favored land; that has also been the theme of the prophets since time began; and it is the primary interest of God himself. As we make our own pledge to bring that purpose about, we need to have our values clearly in mind. And everywhere we turn, we come face to face with the short, blunt, powerful question of Jesus, asking "What doth it profit?" No matter what department of life is under consideration, that is one of the most important questions needing to be answered. What is the supreme good to which our life's effort should be directed and how can we bring accomplishment about. We sometimes run a considerable risk, when we imagine ourselves living under what we have referred to as "the profit system." We are on much safer ground when we apply its full title and remind ourselves that we actually live under "the profit and loss system." The possibility of loss presents a challenge equal to our opportunity for gain, and we need to keep an eye on both sides of the balance sheet of our lives. It is hoped that a consideration of these humble messages may encourage the formation of motives and ambitions strong enough to draw our lives a little further into the profit column, as well as to contribute something to our satisfaction, as we make our interesting way in quest of our God-given rights, among which are life, liberty and the pursuit of happiness.

CONTENTS

The Law of the Harvest

ONE OF THE distinguishing characteristics of our world is that it is a
place of law and order, and the basic law of creation is God's
fundamental law of compensation. It says that all work must
be paid for, that we can no more do a good thing without
sometime, in some way receiving a reward, than we can do an
evil thing without suffering a penalty. In everything that we
do, including the very thoughts that we think, we are subject
to this interesting, undeviating eternal law. It is just as universal in its operation as are the laws of gravity, electricity, light
or heat. It is never set aside, it is never suspended or restricted, and it governs in every department of human activity.
Nothing is ever denied to well-directed effort and nothing is
ever achieved without it.

The Lord himself gave this law its clearest expression
when he said, "There is a law, irrevocably decreed in heaven
before the foundations of this world, upon which all blessings
are predicated—and when we obtain any blessing from God,
it is by obedience to that law upon which it is predicated."
(D&C 130:20-21) It is a thrilling challenge, that we may
have any blessing that we are willing to live for. And the
primary law of the universe is this immutable, inexorable,
irrevocable law of the harvest that says, "Whatsoever a man
soweth, that shall he also reap." (Gala. 6:7)

One of our most serious problems is that so frequently
we fail to comprehend the application of this law to our personal, social and religious lives. It is fairly easy to understand
that those individuals working in agriculture, mining, manu-
facturing or transportation, should rightly share in the benefits
they help to create. It is perfectly proper for businessmen

to realize some return to themselves from the vision, planning, forethought and industry which they have expended.

But we do not always apply this fundamental principle to the most important enterprise ever undertaken upon this earth which Jesus referred to as "My Father's business." As we have our work to do, so God has his work to do. He has said "This is my work and my glory—to bring to pass the immortality and eternal life of man." (Moses 1:39) It is his business to build honesty, integrity, godliness and eternal happiness into the lives of his children. And he has endowed us with some basic, natural motivations to help us to help ourselves. This process of uplifting human life is not just the most important business in the universe, it is also the most profitable to engage in. All of the important values in the world are human values, and the greatest rewards are reserved for those who help to bring them about. To make our own lives more interesting and profitable, God has invited us to have a part with him in this most important of all undertakings.

Some time ago, I talked with a farmer who has a family of five boys. As his sons become old enough to assume a share of the responsibility of the farm, he allows them to obtain a little piece of land to till, or to acquire some farm animals to raise. This wise father understands the power underlying the important reward motivations, and he helps his children to use them to bring about their own accomplishments. And certainly the Father of our spirits is not less wise, nor less just, than this thoughtful farmer. God wants every human being to attain a maximum of development and personal righteousness. This can best be brought about by sharing his own responsibility with us. Therefore, God has invited the members of his own family to join him in the family firm, so to speak. In this position we can assist in building industry, honesty and eternal life into each other. We are not only permitted to share in God's work but we may also share in his glory. For it is the law, that "Those who do God's work shall get God's pay."

We have had something of a controversy going on in the world for some time about the comparative merits of the capitalistic system as compared with the various philosophies of communism and socialism. In the first instance, the wealth and means of production are privately owned and operated, whereas in the second case the people become the tools of autocratic power. The record proves that more than about anything else, God is committed to freedom, individual initiative and free enterprise. He wants everyone to enjoy the fruits of his own labor.

The war in heaven was fought to determine whether or not men and women would be free, and God himself is the greatest of all of the creators of wealth, abundance and beauty. And he has promised possession of all of these things to his faithful children by saying, "Inasmuch as ye do these things . . the fullness of the earth is yours . . . . And it pleaseth God that he hath given all these things unto man; for unto this end were they made to be used, with judgment, not to excess, neither by extortion." (D&C 59:16-20) If we effectively develop the highest values of life, God has promised to make us great in our own right, and he offers us the same rewards for our labors that he himself receives. We must not fail to understand and take advantage of this important opportunity.

Some time ago I heard a very interesting discussion at a ward officers and teachers' meeting between the bishop and the ward Sunday School superintendent. It appears that there was a Sunday School teacher in this ward who had not been as vigorous as he might have been in his assignment, and the bishop was suggesting that maybe the Sunday School superintendent should sit down with him and try and work out some basis for a more effective accomplishment. The Sunday School superintendent said to the bishop, "If this man worked for me in my business, I would feel perfectly free in doing exactly as you have suggested, but," he said, "inasmuch as we don't get paid for what we do in the Church, I think we should accept whatever contribution this man may feel like making and let it go at that."

There are far too many people who for lack of understanding incline themselves to the point of view that the things of the spirit are of minor importance, to match the material rewards usually associated with spiritual activity.

Just what do we mean when we say, "We don't get paid for what we do in the Church?" Think what benefits would be lost to any other accomplishment if we removed the provision for compensation. But we may settle our minds as to that for just as surely as we can count on the law of gravity, we can count on God's law of compensation. In one of the thrilling scriptures we read as follows:

"And also they who receive this priesthood receive me, saith the Lord. For he that receiveth my servants receiveth me; and he that receiveth me receiveth my Father; and he that receiveth my Father receiveth my Father's kingdom; therefore, all that my Father hath shall be given unto him." (D&C 84:35-38)

God is a very wealthy personage. We all like to inherit from a wealthy parent. And what could be more exciting than to inherit from God, who has promised to give his faithful children everything that he himself has. Then what do we mean when we say that we don't get paid for what we do in the Church? To help us understand this important idea, just think how lavishly Nature rewards us for the things that we do in a material way. If we plant a bushel of seed potatoes in good soil, Nature gives us 60 bushels back. One potato carried to England by Sir Walter Raleigh in the 16th Century multiplied itself into food for millions. One tomato seed will multiply itself a million times in a single year. A few pounds of onion seed gives us a return of 50 tons of onions. Ten forests can grow from one acorn. Now who can imagine that the God of Nature, who is also the God of our souls, will pay more for planting tomato seeds and onions and acorns than he will for planting the seeds of faith and honor and eternal life in the lives of his children! Out of his great intelligence, God has organized helpful uplifting laws to govern our lives. He has included in his Church every requirement necessary to get us into the Celestial Kingdom. In fact, every ordinance of the gospel has to do with the Celestial Kingdom.

If one is not interested in this highest glory, it is unnecessary for him to be baptized or establish his family relationship for eternity, or even to obey the sacred, religious covenants that God has asked us to make. Just suppose we try to figure out how much it would be worth to live forever in the Celestial Kingdom. The Celestial Kingdom is the highest. It is the one described by Paul as "The glory of the sun." It is the place of the celestial order of beings to which God himself belongs, and as we seek membership therein we need to understand something about it.

We have formed the habit of measuring most things by the yardstick of the dollar. Then how much is the Celestial Kingdom worth in American money? It is interesting to remember that of the thirty-eight parables of Jesus, nearly one-half of them were related to money. Jesus talked of the 10 talents, the tribute money, the tax money, the lost coin, the pearl of great price, etc., etc. He probably used money as a basis for his comparisons because that is the thing that we probably understand better than any other thing. There isn't any six-year-old who doesn't understand all about a five-dollar bill. Then suppose we figure out how much it would be worth in our money to qualify as Celestial beings with the highest possible standard of living, the highest possible standard of thinking, and the highest possible standard of being.

There are no greater values than that of the human soul and the human personality. Jesus compared the value of the soul to the value of the entire earth. Sometime ago I saw a newspaper statement that said that the assessed valuation of

the United States alone was well over a trillion dollars.   How
many hours of devoted, capable labor "in our Father's business" would be necessary to start a trillion-dollar soul along
the pathway toward eternal exaltation?   We know how many
bricks a good bricklayer can put in place in a day, and how
much should be paid for such a service.   We know what a
good bank president or a good doctor or a good Governor is
worth.   But how much integrity and godliness can a good
workman build into human lives, and how much is it worth
to save a soul from death?   With effective work in this area
one might discover a profit situation going far beyond the
present ability of our limited comprehension.

In its best meaning, wealth is not so much what one has,
as what he is.   We don't work merely to acquire, we work to
become.   Success in life isn't measured by what we can get
out of it, but rather by what we can become by it.   The
greatest possible accomplishment, is what we can help ourselves or someone else to *become*.   The most valuable workman is the one who understands these all-important values
and learns to practice the laws of God under which they can
best be produced.   And our greatest motivation logically
comes from finding out what it is really worth to live forever
in the Celestial Kingdom.

We may be able to get some ideas about this by determining what it would cost to live in the best hotel that this
earth affords. For example, there is a hotel in Southern Florida
used as a club that was built by some wealthy men from the
north and east as a place to spend their winters.   I don't know
how many millions of dollars it cost, but it is a lavish, luxurious
elegant, beautiful place.   It is located on the beautiful beach
of a beautiful ocean in the warm Florida sunshine.   It is surrounded by flower gardens, orange groves and golf courses.
There is yachting, fishing and swimming.   Every conceivable
kind of food has been provided from every corner of the earth.
There is every pleasure, service and convenience that the most

thoughtful ingenuity of man can devise. No expense has been spared to make this the most pleasant comfortable possible place. If you occupied the best accommodations in this hotel your expenses would be a hundred dollars a day. Of course, you would have your wife with you, that would mean $200 a day. If you took your seven children it would cost you $900 a day. But your children would be much happier if they had their playmates with them; you may also want to have some of your friends to share this luxury with you. Suppose you took along a company of 50 friends and stayed for a month in the finest hotel. How much would it cost? Of course, you would not want to spend such a limited period in such a place and then come back to less desirable surroundings. So just suppose that you determined the cost of spending an eternity with your family and friends in the best hotel. Of course, no hotel could conceivably compare with the Celestial Kingdom, because no matter what the luxury and elegance of the best hotel may be, you would still have the problems of sin, disease, old age, sickness, trouble, war and death to contend with. But if you once determined the total cost of staying in the best hotel, you might then magnify the amount by a few million times as a means of approximating the value of the Celestial Kingdom. If one would actually require himself to get a definite answer to this important question, it might help him to overcome the bad habit of vagueness that we sometimes assume as we think about accomplishment in the important work of human uplift and eternal exaltation.

Our personal growth, our spiritual development, our material welfare, our honor and every other thing comes under this immutable law of the harvest that says, "Whatsoever a man soweth, that shall he also reap." We have become too much accustomed to thinking of avoiding the consequences of law. We may violate the traffic regulations and never get caught. If we are caught we may get off without a penalty or we may be able to get the ticket "fixed" afterwards. But as regards our own eternal welfare, we had better not plan to

get too far away from what it says in the book, for this immutable law of God always has stood and always must stand
unchanged and unchangeable.   Jesus himself said, "It is
easier for heaven and earth to pass, than one tittle of the law
to fail." (Luke 16:17)   Ignorance or disregard of the law
does not excuse us.   And we need to study our situation and
ourselves from every possible point of view.   We must understand our possibilities on both their negative and their positive sides.   We need to be able to appraise our own traits of
good and bad and what can best be done about each.   We
need to know how to apply the commandments, and how to
make the most of every situation.

When John Bunyan's Pilgrim came within the range of
the Celestial City, he was permitted to look at it from a
distance through a field glass, but as he put the glass to his
eye he became excited, his hand shook and blurred his vision.
Then because he couldn't see it clearly his motive power failed
and Pilgrim turned away.

It is most important that our vision does not blur nor our
motives lose their strength.   For a stimulating future view in
our own interests we might profitably borrow the field glasses
of John the Revelator, and see what he saw as he looked down
the stream of time to the final judgment.   About this important event the Revelator said:

"And I saw the dead, small and great, stand before God;
and the books were opened and another book was opened,
which is the book of life: and the dead were judged out of
those things which were written in the books, according to
their works. And the sea gave up the dead which were in it;
and death and hell delivered up the dead which were in them:
and they were judged every man according to their works."
(Revelations 20:12-13)

Ahab and Jezebel

IT HAS frequently been said that behind every great man stands
some great woman who is responsible for his success, but
history also tells of many other men, great and otherwise,
whose downfall has also been brought about by a woman.

We remember that it was the daughter of Herodias who
demanded that the head of John the Baptist be brought to
her on a platter. One of Shakespeare's great tragedies centers in the account of Goneril and Regan, the selfish daughters of King Lear, who tread unfeelingly upon the broken
heart of their sire. It was the unholy ambition of Lady Mac-
beth that urged her husband to plunge a dagger into the
heart of the sleeping King Duncan while he was a guest in
their home. Lucretia is remembered for her dagger thrust,
Borgia for her poison, and we cannot forget the great Bible
classic of Samson and Delilah. Delilah centered her efforts
and resources in learning the secret by which she could rob
Samson of his strength, and her greatest triumph was in bringing about his blindness, imprisonment and death.

Many a woman is the chief support of her husband's
success. She is the well spring of his courage and the source
of the faith and industry by which he climbs the heights of
righteous accomplishment. Then there are those women
who, Delilah-like, rob their husbands of whatever strength
they may already have. It is probably even more true that
many women are dragged down by the men in their lives.
One of the marital teams that will live in history because of
the evil they brought upon each other, and upon the society
in which they lived, was King Ahab and Queen Jezebel,
whose history is recounted in the Old Testament. If one
could properly use the term, "Pure wickedness," it would

undoubtedly be the phrase that would best describe this unholy pair. However, such great extremes, even in wickedness, sometimes carry with them a kind of fascination and opportunity for learning. Certainly if Ahab and Jezebel were not extremes they were nothing. In fact the Bible says that, "Ahab did more to provoke the Lord God of Israel to anger than all the kings of Israel that were before him." The record says, "There was none like unto Ahab, which did sell himself to work wickedness in the sight of the Lord."

And what a mate Ahab found in Jezebel! Her name not only blasted the name of her husband with wickedness, but it left a dark blasphemous stain upon the annals of Israel's history which survived to the very last chapter of the New Testament. In the Book of Revelation, the name of Jezebel is used as a symbol of female depravity and impiety. She represents that influence bringing the greatest possible ruin to the Church. To this day she stands without a peer as a symbol of colorful wickedness. Jezebel achieved her high place through her husband's power. It was she who stirred up Ahab to commit his abominations.

Omri, the father of Ahab, had also been King of Israel. He had been very successful in his military conquests and in killing off his rivals. He founded the national capital of Israel at Samaria. For reasons of politics, trade and national strength, Omri desired an alliance with the King of Tyre. For this reason he encouraged his son, Ahab, to marry Princess Jezebel, who was the daughter of Tyre's king. It was customary in those days that when an alliance was made between two countries, each participating nation accepted the Gods of the other. But, because Jezebel was extreme in worshiping the heathen Gods of Baal, she went far beyond what the custom intended. She brought with her to Israel, hundreds of heathen priests and prophets, and supported by Ahab she was instrumental in establishing the idol worship of the Phoenician Gods in her new homeland. And for a time under the leadership of Ahab and Jezebel, Baal threatened to displace Jehovah as the God of Israel.

Upon the death of Omri in 874 B. C., Ahab ascended Israel's throne and with Jezebel by his side they ruled for 22 years. And what a pair they were to govern in the promised land which Jehovah had given to Abraham, Isaac and Jacob! They represent a striking picture of the amount of degradation that one person can bring upon another or even upon a nation. We are aware of the problems that sometimes arise when someone marries outside of his own kind. We know of the harm that can come even from an unfortunate social association. But here we see the evil of a wicked influence at its height. The names of Ahab and Jezebel stand out among the individuals of the world as Babylon does among nations. Jesus symbolized the name of Babylon to denote corrupt Rome, apostate Jerusalem and the entire empire of Satan. Wherever the powers of men are wholeheartedly antagonistic to the Kingdom of God there is Babylon, and there also are Ahab and Jezebel. In their perfume scented court, reeking with corruption, Jezebel decided that the worship of Jehovah should be stopped and accordingly she ordered that all of the prophets of Jehovah should be put to death. This was in part accomplished, and Ahab built temples for the idol gods that Jezebel had brought from her homeland to take their places.

The records indicate that from some points of view Ahab was extremely capable and with more righteousness might have been a great king. He seemed to have inherited all of the abilities of his father with some besides. Among a certain element of the people he was very popular. However, from the priestly point of view he was a very bad man and an even worse monarch. Certainly one of the greatest misfortunes of his life was his marriage to the evil princess of Tyre. For more than any other single event this marriage threatened and partially brought about the downfall of the

entire northern kingdom of Israel. Jezebel caused terrible
scenes of blood and death as she went about killing the
prophets of Jehovah and establishing the worst forms of
Phoenician worship where Jehovah had hoped to establish a
righteous nation. Jezebel herself was forceful and cruel and
she encouraged Ahab in every kind of wrong doing.

Her upbringing had been quite at variance with the
ideals in vogue in her adopted land of Israel. Her father was
an autocrat who had himself gained his throne by assassina-
tion. When he wanted anything he took it, and in this respect
Jezebel proved to be a worthy daughter of her father. How
well she followed in his footsteps is told in the Bible account
of their dealings with one of their subjects.

Samaria was the official capital of Israel but it was
situated in the colder, central hills, so Ahab and Jezebel
established a winter capital for themselves in Jezreel, which
lay at the junction of two important roads. Jezreel had
beautiful surroundings, a mild climate and a fertile soil. These
made Jezreel an ideal location for the royal winter residence.
A small land owner by the name of Naboth owned a vineyard near the royal palace and Ahab was desirous of acquiring it as a garden to provide the royal table with choice
products. Ahab asked Naboth to sell him the property; but
this land was Naboth's inheritance from his fathers and he
declined to part with it.

Then the record says, "And Ahab came into his house
heavy and displeased because of the word which Naboth
. . . had spoken to him . . . and he laid him down upon his
bed, and turned away his face, and would eat no bread."
But Jezebel his wife came to him, and said, "Why is thy
spirit so sad, that thou eatest no bread? And he said to
her, because I spake unto Naboth the Jezreelite and said unto
him, 'give me thy vineyard for money; or else if it please
thee, I will give thee another vineyard for it: and he answered,
'I will not give thee my vineyard.' And Jezebel his wife said
unto him, 'Dost thou not govern the kingdom of Israel?

Arise, and eat bread, and let thine heart be merry: I will give thee the vineyard of Naboth the Jezreelite.' "

And so Jezebel wrote letters in Ahab's name and sealed them with a state seal and sent the letters to the elders and nobles who governed the city where Naboth lived. She had them arrange for a fast at which false witnesses were asked to swear that Naboth had cursed God and the king. Jezebel's plan worked perfectly and inasmuch as the alleged crime was punishable by death, Naboth was taken on the spot and put to death by the prescribed penalty of stoning.

Then Jezebel said to Ahab, "Arise, take possession of the vineyard of Naboth the Jezreelite, . . . for Naboth is . . . dead." It was the law that the king inherited the property of all felons executed for blasphemy and sedition. Accordingly, Ahab prepared to take over the vineyard of Naboth. However there was one who objected to this procedure and that was Jehovah, who sent the prophet Elijah to meet Ahab as he took over the vineyard of Naboth. Elijah roundly condemned Ahab and Jezebel and foretold the tragic ending of their dynasty. Elijah said to Ahab, "Hast thou killed, and also taken possession?" Then speaking for Jehovah, Elijah said that, "In the place where dogs licked the blood of Naboth shall dogs lick thy blood . . ." Because Ahab had sold himself to do evil in the sight of the Lord, Elijah said God would bring evil upon him and utterly sweep him away for he had provoked God to anger and had made Israel sin. Then through Elijah the Lord gave his final sentence when he said, "The dogs shall eat Jezebel by the ramparts of Jezreel." (I Kings 21)

The contest between Jezebel and the fiery old prophet Elijah lasted over a long period. On one occasion Elijah came to the court of the wicked king and queen and told them that the Lord's anger would be evidenced in a prolonged drought. Elijah said, "As the Lord God of Israel liveth, before whom I stand, there shall not be dew nor rain these years, but according to my word." This made the king and queen very angry and they would have killed Elijah had he not escaped.

Then the Lord had Elijah go into hiding by the brook Cherith where he was miraculously fed by the ravens. Finally the brook dried up because of the drought and Elijah was sent to Zarephath where he was fed by a widow from her handful of meal in the barrel and her small supply of oil in the cruse.

Only after three years did Elijah return to the kingdom of Ahab and Jezebel. On the occasion of his return he matched his strength and ability as a prophet against the prophets of Baal in the famous and dramatic contest of Mount Carmel. Elijah won and the priests of Baal were all put to death. The destruction of her priests aroused the proud consort of Ahab to a murderous fury and Elijah was again forced to flee from Israel. Ahab finally met his death when in one of his battles a chance arrow struck him in the joint of his armor which was one of the vulnerable spots in the protective covering of the ancients. Gravely wounded as he was Ahab knew that if he fell, his army would break and run, so he kept himself on his feet until the last. He bled to death in his chariot while still facing the enemy and after his death the dogs licked up his blood. Later when Jezebel heard that the new ruler was coming to Jezreel she painted her face and otherwise adorned herself to meet him. As Jehu the new king approached, Jezebel stood by an upper window, which was the usual procedure for receiving royal company in those days. Jehu looked up to Jezebel at the window and said, "who is on my side?" And the record says, "And there looked out to him two or three eunuchs and he said to them, throw her down." So they threw her down: and some of her blood was sprinkled on the wall and on the horses and he trod her under foot, and left her body for the dogs to eat. The record recites that at a later time when the dogs had finished their job, parts of Jezebel still remained unburied. Thus was fulfilled the word of the Lord, which he spake by his servant Elijah saying, "The dogs shall eat Jezebel by the ramparts of Jezreel." (II Kings 9:36)

After the death of Ahab, Jezebel and all seventy descendents of the royal family were put to death by Jehu. The record says that Jehu wrote letters to the rulers in Samaria and gave them just one day to cut off the heads of the seventy members of the royal family and bring them to him in Jezreel, and the record says: "And it came to pass, when the letter came to them, that they took the king's sons, and slew 70 persons, and put their heads in baskets, and sent them to Jehu in Jezreel . . . so Jehu slew all that remained of the house of Ahab in Jezreel, and all his great men, and his kinfolks, and his priests, until he left him none remaining." (II Kings 10:7, 11)

And thus the awful scenes of blood and death were returned upon Jezebel and all of the members of the royal house which she had condemned to death by her evil.

Again we see a demonstration of the important truth, that evil and wickedness always brings unhappiness and suffering. And we may be able to increase our own understanding by occasionally getting into our minds a picture of the awful visage of sin, and thereby be inspired to more nearly conform our own lives to righteousness.

Amnesia

ONE OF the serious problems of our world has always been that of ill health. Disease has many forms and a multitude of physical, mental and spiritual manifestations. In one way or another it cuts down our effectiveness, kills our accomplishment and makes our lives miserable and unprofitable. Some diseases are more to be dreaded than others because of their greater ability to maim, disable and destroy.

Ranked in order of number of fatalities, the diseases of the heart stand at the head of the list. The awful scourge of cancer comes second in breaking up our homes and wrecking our happiness. Polio, muscular dystrophy and kindred ills strike down the young and robs them of the use of their limbs and the exercise of their opportunities. Disease leaves in its awful wake a host of dead and a vast multitude consigned to be cripples for the rest of their days.

In the Bible we read of the frightful plague of leprosy which made life an experience of horror to many of the ancients. Jesus lived in the very midst of this serious problem and when he was referred to as the great physician, it was not only because he cured the bodies of people; he also helped to restore the health of those with sick souls.

And one of the most common of all the causes of soul sickness is forgetfulness. This is one of the problems that is frequently referred to in the holy scriptures. In *Cruden's Concordance* there are over two hundred references to our need for remembering. But still in our day there are probably few things that so adversely affect our lives here and hereafter as the fact that we don't remember. It is our history that since the beginning of time, men and women have largely forgotten God. They have forgotten obedience.

They have forgotten righteousness. The result is that they have lost the way to their eternal exaltation.

Isn't it interesting that everyone complains of a poor memory. We can't remember names, we can't remember faces, we can't remember ideas, we can't remember New Year's resolutions, we can't remember our own ambitions and ideals. Sometimes we can't remember the promises we have made to our creditors, we can't remember the promises we have made to our families or the covenants that we have made with God. Certainly one of the worst of all of the dread diseases goes by the name of amnesia or the loss of memory. Like paralysis or stroke or heart disease, this malady may be total or it may possess us in some damaging fraction, with mental, spiritual or physical implications. There are many people every month who actually forget who they themselves are. They can't remember their own names, they can't remember their past, their families, their standards or their ambitions. Polio robbed Franklin D. Roosevelt of the use of his legs, but amnesia robs one of his ability, his family, his friends and his sense of responsibility. Amnesia takes away our very experience which was one of the important reasons we came to the earth in the first place.

Amnesia may be caused by some injury to the brain or some severe nervous shock or fever. The dictionary mentions several classes of amnesia. There is infantile amnesia, which is the lack of the memory of early childhood; there is a retrograde amnesia, which is the loss of memory of the period just preceding a blow on the head or some other kind of shock. The dictionary also describes what it calls systematic amnesia, which is the loss of memory of a certain system or class of experiences. There is a verbal amnesia which is the inability to recall certain words. And there are several other manifestations of this dread disease.

I have probably been more than ordinarily impressed with the unpleasant possibilities of this idea, because of the

disturbing personal experiences that I have had with some
varieties of forgetfulness. For example, I am subject to the
recurrence about every six months of an unpleasant dream.
The outstanding characteristic of which is that I can't remember. In my most recent dream experience, I had forgotten where I had parked my automobile. Not only had I
forgotten the street on which it had been left, but I had also
forgotten the city, the state and the nation in which I had
used it last. I can vividly recall my emotion of confused helplessness as in my dream I hopelessly tried to recall even the
faintest memory of where I had left my automobile. To make
matters worse, I was reminded in my dream that I had not
only lost one car, but three in close succession. It seemed that
I tried unsuccessfully for hours to stimulate a reluctant mind
to remember. This predicament produced in me a dismal
feeling of hopelessness, frustration and regret. The loss of
the automobile was bad enough, but the terrible, addled
blankness and awful frustration that possessed my brain was
far worse.

In another of these semiannual dreams, I was back in
my school days and had forgotten my lessons. I was taking
part in a written examination and hadn't the slightest idea
of what the answers were, and to my confused mind there
was no way of finding out. In one of these awful experiences,
I was aware of a part I had been given in a school play.
It seemed that it was time for me to go on the stage, but
I couldn't remember my cues, and all mental traces of my
lines had been completely erased. I had a terrible feeling
of self-consciousness and regret that I was holding up the
whole performance and disappointing everybody including
myself.

When I wake up after such a dream, it takes some time
to clean this frustration and unhappiness out of my mind
and get back my composure. Then I can easily imagine
what it might be like to have a nervous breakdown or some

other kind of real mental or religious disintegration. My experience also helps me to understand this serious sin of spiritual amnesia.

The Bible is a long, unpleasant record of forgetfulness. It seems that God's biggest problem is not to create and organize worlds, but to keep the minds of people properly focused on those things that will prevent them from losing their eternal exaltation. Very frequently God has been forced to give us a kind of shock treatment, to help us to remember to be humble and obedient. He has often sent wars, floods, famines, depressions and plagues upon us to help us to remember. But, even after some dreadful chastisement, it usually isn't very long before we are back at it again, forgetting our promises, forgetting our obligations and even forgetting the purposes of our own lives. Many people have no difficulty remembering certain material or pleasurable interests, but find it almost impossible to remember truth and God and righteousness.

Many people forget the most easy rules of simple English grammar who never forget their long, bloodcurdling list of profane, immoral and blasphemous words and ideas. James compares those who hear the word but fail to *do* it, to a man who beholds himself in a glass and straightway forgets what manner of man he is. To forget the manner of men we ought to be is one of these special kinds of amnesia where we lose memory for certain classes of ideas. Unless eternal life is to be lost, there are some things that we *must* remember, and there are ways to strengthen our minds for that important job.

During the Babylonian captivity, because the Jews so deeply longed for their homeland, they thought about it continually. They used to sing, ". . . If I forget thee O Jerusalem, let my right hand forget her cunning. If I do not remember thee, let my tongue cleave to the roof of my mouth." (Psalm 137:5, 6)

Isaiah also sang a song about remembering.   He said, "Can a woman forget her sucking child, that she should not have compassion on the son of her womb?"   Then Isaiah said, "Yea, *they* may forget, yet I will not forget.   Behold, I have graven thee upon the palms of my hands; and thy walls are continually before my face." (Isaiah 49:15, 16)   *We* need some similar system. For *our* success, as well as Isaiah's depends largely on which things we remember, and which things we forget.

It is an interesting fact that a creditor always has a better memory than a debtor.   It is far easier to remember our anticipated pleasures than it is to remember our anticipated duties.   Many people cannot remember their responsibilities, yet they seldom forget their smoking or their drunkenness or their immoralities or their Sabbath Day violations.   Sometimes while we are remembering trifles we forget our souls. Through Jeremiah the Lord said, "Can a maid forget her ornaments, or a bride her attire? yet my people have forgotten me days without number." (Jeremiah 2:32)

To forget God and his righteousness is an error that no one can afford.   Out of the fire and smoke covering the sacred top of Mount Sinai, the Lord gave ten commandments.   Probably to make them more memorable they were given to the accompaniment of lightnings and thunders, while among other things God said, "Remember the sabbath day, to keep it holy.   Thou shalt not take the name of the Lord thy God in vain; . . . Thou shalt not steal.   Thou shalt not kill.   Thou shalt not commit adultery.   Thou shalt not bear false witness. . . ."

How difficult our lives become if we forget these important commandments!   How impossible our success is, if we forget God!   We must remember to be obedient. If we forget the laws of God, eternal life and eternal glory become impossible for us.   A lost soul is much harder to recover than a lost automobile.   And the forgotten man is the man who forgets God, whereas our eternal lives depend upon how well we remember to obey and keep his commandments.

It might stimulate our memories if we tried to imagine what it would be like if *God* should forget *us*. Through Jeremiah, the Lord makes a terrifying declaration about some who had forgotten their covenants. He said, ". . . therefore, behold I, even I, will utterly forget you, and I will forsake you and the cities that I gave to you and to your fathers, and I will cast you out of my presence. And I will bring an everlasting reproach upon you with a perpetual shame which shall never be forgotten." With this possibility in mind, Rudyard Kipling composed his great prayer, in which he repeated over and over again, "Lord God of Hosts be with us yet, lest we forget, lest we forget."

One of the most important parts of religion is in learning to remember. God said, ". . . remember the sabbath day, . . . remember the Lord thy God." The sacrament was instituted to help us to remember him. (I Corinthians 11:24) The office of the Holy Ghost is to bring all things past to our remembrance. (John 14:26)

During one long period, God tried to stimulate the memory of ancient Israel by commanding them to make bright colored fringes and attach them to their clothing to help them to remember. God said, "And it shall be unto you for a fringe, that ye may look upon it, and *remember* all the commandments of the Lord, and do them; . . ." (Numbers 15:39) This seems like a permanent adaptation of that idea where we sometimes tie a string on our finger to help us remember some particular thing. The scriptures themselves serve primarily as a prod to our memory. Strange though it may seem, our greatest need is not to be taught but to be reminded.

In his address to the elders of Ephesus, Paul said, ". . . remember the words of the Lord Jesus. . . ." (Acts 20:35) To the Galatians, he said, ". . . remember the poor; . . ."

(Galatians 2:10) To the Thessalonians, he said, "Remember
. . . that . . . I told you these things." (II Thess. 2:5); and
in the last letter of his life addressed to Timothy, Paul said,
"Remember that Jesus Christ . . . was raised from the dead
. . ." (II Timothy 2:8) How terrible it must be for those who
forget these things, even temporarily. On one occasion Job
said that when he remembered he was afraid and he said
that trembling took hold of his flesh. (Job 21:6) If sometimes it frightens us to remember and trembling takes hold
of our flesh when we think of our responsibilities, what
trembling must finally take hold of those who eternally forget!

On one occasion when the Holy Ghost fell upon Peter
he said, "Then remembered I the word of the Lord, . . ."
(Acts 11:16)   What a wonderful ability!

Physical amnesia can be caused by injury or disease, but
spiritual amnesia can be brought about in practically the same
way, and when we begin getting spiritually or morally sick, we
should be particularly aware of the possibility of forgetfulness, for when we forget our objectives, our duties and God;
then, more or less automatically, we lose our greatest possibilities. Every time we forget to say our prayers, or forget to go
to church, or forget to be honest, or forget God's standards
of morality, priceless blessings are lost. Forgetfulness causes
our lives to be overrun by ignorance, indecision and indifference, and no man can be saved in *any* of these. It is primarily
our forgetfulness that causes the second death. Then we die
as to things pertaining to righteousness and live on in the
misery and torment of our sins. The greatest opportunity in
the universe is to remember God and his righteousness and
his holiness and to put every one of his teachings in force
in our individual lives.

Angels

IT HAS BEEN said that the greatest discovery ever made is when man discovers God. God is the center of the universe, the Creator of worlds, the Father of spirits. As John says, "All things were made by him; and without him was not any thing made that was made. In him was life; and the life was the light of men." (John 1:3-5)

God enlightens our minds and quickens our understandings. Every day he sends us energy, light and food from the sun. He is the author of law and the designer of our eternal exaltation. To really discover God is not merely to believe that he exists. We need to know the kind of being he is and what his purposes are.

Daniel Webster once said that the greatest thought that can ever enter the mind of any man is the consciousness of his individual relationship and responsibility to God. But man's discovery of God helps him to make the second greatest discovery, and that is to discover himself. Because we are the children of God, created in his image and endowed with his attributes, God and man can best be studied together.

Isn't it interesting that the thing that we know less about than almost anything else in the world is our own individual selves? You can ask a man questions about science, invention or history and he will answer you. But if you ask him to write out an analysis of himself and tell you about his mind and soul qualities, you may not get a very good answer. Or ask a man where he came from, or why he is here, or what his eternal possibilities are. Before these questions he becomes confused and uncertain.

What a strange paradox that our age, known for its wonders and enlightenment, should also be noted for its disbelief in God and its confusion about man. The most thrilling of all research is that devoted to understanding the family of our eternal Father, not only in their present, but we should also know something about their past and their future as well. Nothing in the scriptures could be plainer than the fact that the life of Jesus did not begin at Bethlehem, nor did it end on Calvary. The scriptures are equally plain that our lives did not begin at our mortal birth neither do they end at death. We had a long and important life before our mortality began. Many are still in the spirit world awaiting mortal experience. Billions of others have already returned to God from whom they came. We should also know something about them, as they are now, what we ourselves have been and will be.

The scriptures tell of a great group of beings called angels. The Apostle Paul speaks of an innumerable company of angels. (Heb. 12:22) A multitude of the heavenly host appeared upon the hills of Bethlehem over nineteen centuries ago. The scripture teaches the interesting and important fact that God, angels and men are all of the same species and together make up the eternal family.

In April, 1843, the Prophet Joseph Smith received a revelation to the effect that all angels who minister to this earth are beings who do belong or have belonged to it. The revelation says, "The angels do not reside on a planet like this earth; But they reside in the presence of God, on a globe like a sea of glass and fire, where all things for their glory are manifest, past, present and future, and are continually before the Lord." (D&C 130:6-7)

When God placed Adam upon the earth, angels were sent from God's presence to instruct him. Angels have continued to minister to man upon the earth ever since. But we fail to believe in God, so we also fail to believe in angels, and our own past and our own future. It is fairly simple to believe that angels appeared on the Judean hills in that long ago Christmas night. It is easy to believe that there were angels in the days of Adam, Isaiah, and Abraham. But it is a little more difficult to believe in angels in the present or in the future. If we don't presently believe in angels, how are we going to explain what happened to those who lived in other ages? If they have ever existed, they must still exist, and make up an important part of our universe.

The word angel comes from a Greek word meaning "messenger." For example, St. Luke records the announcement of the birth of Jesus as follows:

". . . the angel Gabriel was sent from God unto a city of Galilee, named Nazareth, to a virgin espoused to a man whose name was Joseph. . . . And the angel . . . said unto her, The Holy Ghost shall come upon thee, and the power of the Highest shall overshadow thee; therefore also that holy thing which shall be born of thee shall be called the Son of God."

The personal pronouns "he" and "him" are used in referring to this angel. Angels are not things or birds. Angels do not have wings any more than we do. Like all other angels this particular angel was an individual eternal being. He had a personality and a name. His name was Gabriel. He was a personage of great importance who had come from the presence of God. Some 2500 years previously, he himself had lived upon the earth. He could speak, hear, understand and be understood.

A few months later an angel appeared to the shepherds who were watching their flocks upon the Judean hills. The angel said to the shepherds: "Fear not: for, behold, I bring you good tidings of great joy, which shall be to all people. For unto you is born this day in the city of David a Saviour, which is Christ the Lord. And this shall be a sign unto you; Ye shall find the babe wrapped in swaddling clothes, lying in a manger. And suddenly there was with the angel a multitude of the heavenly host praising God, and saying, Glory to God in the highest, and on earth peace, good will toward men. And it came to pass, as the angels were gone away from them into heaven, the shepherds said one to another, Let us now go even unto Bethlehem and see this thing which is come to pass, which the Lord hath made known unto us."

Apparently these angels knew a great deal about space travel, and many other things that we do not yet understand. The birth of the Savior of the world was just as important to those who had previously lived upon the earth, and to those who would yet live upon it, as it was to those who were then tabernacled in the flesh. These heavenly beings lived with God who is the source of all intelligence and power, and they themselves are clothed in his authority.

While Jesus was being arrested, he declared that he could command twelve legions of angels to fight in his behalf. Just previous to the arrest an angel had been with Jesus in Gethsemane to comfort him during his awful agony. Angels are not mere shadows. They are as definite in form and as real as mortals. Angels attended Jesus at the tomb, they rolled away the stone that was too heavy for the women. They also made the announcement that Christ had broken the bonds of death.

Then when Jesus was ready to ascend to heaven, Luke records as follows: "And when he had spoken these things, while they beheld, he was taken up; and a cloud received him out of their sight. And while they looked stedfastly toward heaven as he went up, behold, two men stood by them in white apparel; Which also said, Ye men of Galilee, why stand ye gazing up into heaven? this same Jesus, which is taken up from you into heaven, shall so come in like manner as ye have seen him go into heaven." (Acts 1:9-11)

These angels were called men, and they were men. They were in the form of men, with the features, bodily characteristics and personality traits of men.

During the exile of John the Revelator on the Isle of Patmos he had a vision of an angel coming to the earth in our day. He said, "And I saw another angel fly in the midst of heaven, having the everlasting gospel to preach unto them that dwell on the earth, and to every nation, and kindred, and tongue, and people, Saying with a loud voice, Fear God, and give glory to him; for the hour of his judgment is come." (Rev. 14:6-7)

In 1823 this angel appeared to the Prophet Joseph Smith in fulfillment of the revelator's prophecy. *His* name was Moroni. He had been a soldier and prophet, and had lived upon the Western Continent 1400 years previously. Joseph Smith said, "While I was thus in the act of calling upon God, I discovered a light appearing in my room, which continued to increase until the room was lighter than at noonday, when immediately a personage appeared at my bedside, standing in the air, for his feet did not touch the floor. He had on a loose robe of most exquisite whiteness. It was whiteness beyond anything earthly I had ever seen; nor do I believe that any earthly thing could be made to appear so exceedingly white and brilliant. His hands were naked, and his arms also, a little above the wrist; so, also, were his feet naked, as were his legs, a little above the ankles. His head and neck was also bare. I could discover that he had no other clothing on but this robe, as it was open, so that I could see into his bosom. Not only was his robe exceedingly white, but his whole person was glorious beyond description, and his countenance truly like lightning. The room was exceedingly light, but not so very bright as immediately around his person. When I first looked upon him, I was afraid; but the fear soon left me. He called me by name, and said unto me that he was a messenger sent forth from the presence of God to me, and that his name was Moroni; that God had a work for me to do; and that my name should be had for good and evil . . . among all people." (Joseph Smith 2:30-33)

Then Moroni proceeded to give Joseph Smith instruction about a volume of sacred scripture containing the everlasting gospel, and the Church presently has some 12,000 full-time missionaries throughout the world, working without pay, teaching the gospel brought by Moroni in fulfillment of the prophecy of John the Revelator. Some may say that they do not believe, but if the angel spoken of by John did not come to Joseph Smith, then who did he come to, as the scriptures say that he *must* come? If Moroni was not a fulfillment of John's prophecy, then we must look for another.

Other angels have ministered upon the earth in our own day, including Elijah the prophet, who was taken into heaven without tasting death. Through Malachi the Lord had said, "Behold, I will send you Elijah the prophet before the coming of the great and dreadful day of the Lord." There are many who believe the Bible account that Elijah was taken into heaven without tasting death who could not believe that he could come back the same way.

On February 9, 1843 the Lord gave another interesting revelation to Joseph Smith saying, "There are two kinds of beings in heaven, namely: Angels who are resurrected personages, having bodies of flesh and bones—For instance, Jesus said, *Handle me and see, for a spirit hath not flesh and bones, as ye see me have.* Secondly: The spirits of just men made perfect, they who are not resurrected, but inherit the same glory." (D&C 129:1-3) The scriptures are literally full of prophecies having to do with the future ministrations of angels upon the earth. The work of the Lord is not yet finished, and God has not gone out of business, and we are destined to see many wonderful things take place in the future.

The angels at the ascension promised that *this same Jesus* should come again in the manner in which the apostles had seen him go into heaven. That is, his body did not evaporate after his resurrection, nor did it expand to fill the immensity of space, nor did it change to some other form.

The Prophet Joseph Smith said, "When the Savior shall appear we shall see him as he is. We shall see that he is a man like ourselves." Other heavenly personages are also beings like ourselves. The Prophet said, "That same sociality which exists among us here will exist among us there, only it will be coupled with eternal glory, which glory we do not now enjoy." (D&C 130:1-2)

The angel showed John the Revelator many wonderful things which were to come in the future. Then John said, "And I, John, saw these things, and heard them. And when I had heard and seen, I fell down to worship before the feet of the angel which showed me these things. Then saith he unto me, See thou do it not: for I am thy fellow servant, and of thy brethren the prophets, and of them which keep the sayings of this book: worship God."

John mistook the angel for God because the angel was of the same order and also had great glory.

What a thrilling thought that we may work at this greatest of all discoveries and discover our Heavenly Father, our own future destiny, and what we should do in our own eternal interests.

Antonio Stradivari

ONE OF THE most important parts of our success frequently comes through our study of biography. We seem to learn faster from people than from things or abstract ideas. In people we have an important visual aid, an actual working model where we can see success and failure ready-made. Fortunately for us everyone has something to teach us. Jesus used the lives of people both good and bad to illustrate the great lessons of life. With substantial profit to ourselves, we can build on his example.

The man whose name provides our present title was the master violin maker of the world. But once developed, excellence can be made to carry over into every other part of life. The traits that will forever identify the name of Stradivari and make it a household word were his love of his job and his painstaking effort to give superiority to every work that his hands touched. If practiced that will also bring greatness, happiness and success to our own lives.

Antonio was born in Cremona, Italy in 1644. He loved music, but he couldn't sing, and he couldn't play. But as a young boy someone made him a present of a jackknife, and because he had to do something, he whittled. Because Antonio loved music his whittling was directed to producing little wooden violins. There have been a lot of whittlers in the world and some may have even whittled violins, but it was different with Antonio because he whittled *perfect* violins. To him whittling had a purpose far more important than a mere pastime, and every violin that his jackknife touched had to be completely finished before he laid it down.

It just happened that Cremona was also the home of the famous violin maker, Nicholas Amati. Then one day, one of Antonio's toy violins fell into Amati's hands. Nicholas knew that some extraordinary person had made it, for the man who loves his job always leaves distinguishing marks on whatever he does. As soon as Amati could find Antonio, Antonio began carving violins for the master.

From the very beginning he was destined to be famous, for while Antonio was making violins, the violins were making Antonio. What one does and the way he does it, builds his character and forms in him a priceless philosophy of life that will distinguish him forever. Good work is important for many reasons. One is that it soon gets into the worker's muscles and attitudes and determines the kind of man he himself will be.

The immortal football player Red Grange gave the reason for *his* success in five words. He said, "I practice like I play." Grange allowed no inferiority even during practice, for he knew that imperfections permitted during practice might reappear during the most important game. That was also the philosophy of Antonio. Even though he was making violins for someone else, yet he made them with his whole heart. He utilized to the full his God-given urge to excel. Antonio felt that he must make better violins than anyone else even including Amati himself, and that is exactly what he did.

It has been said that in over 300 years not one of Stradivari's violins has ever been known to come to pieces or break because of poor workmanship. When Stradivari began working for himself he needed no patent for his violins, for no other violin maker would pay as great a price for excellence as did Antonio. There was no point in writing his name on his work for it was already stamped in the superiority of every part of every instrument. And every Stradivarius now in existence is worth many times its weight in gold.

Whatever our own work may be, we might well memorize Antonio's philosophy of life. He said:

When any master holds
Twixt hand and chin a violin of mine.
He will be glad that Stradivari lived
Made violins, and made them of the best.

The masters only know whose work is good;
They will choose mine,
And while God gives them skill,
I give them instruments to play upon,
God choosing me to help him,
For God could not make Antonio Stradivari's violins
Without Antonio.

A philosophy of excellence underlines and determines one of the most important principles of any success. Nicholas Latena has said, "One may possibly be better than his reputation, but no one will ever be better than his principles." Life will grant us any desire that is built upon a sufficient love of what we are doing and supported by a firm determination to do it well. This philosophy not only produces excellence in every accomplishment, but it also does away with worker fatigue and gives vigor and grace to life itself.

By way of contrast we might look at the other side of the picture and take the measure of the man who doesn't love his job and consequently does it poorly. It has been said that some men looking for work quit looking the minute they find it. Instead of making love to what they are doing many people fight their jobs.

Some time ago *Look Magazine* made a survey which disclosed that 75 per cent of all workers hate their jobs. Many of them hate the companies they work for. They hate the people they work with. Many men hate their wives, and even hate God. Subconsciously this trait of hate becomes the distinguishing part of many lives. No matter what job or company or wife they select, it will not be long before dislike will be their dominant motive. This defect like all others is more in the hater than in the thing hated. When a hater changes jobs or wives or companies, he usually transfers his hates to a new location.

Jesus pointed to love as the greatest of the commandments, and to hate as one of the worst of the sins. When this ugly trait once gets a foothold in our lives, it is carried over into everything we do. Sometimes we live with it for a lifetime without being aware of the terrible things it does to us.

There are many people who consciously or subconsciously adjust their lives so that they cannot escape the natural by-products of hate. There are some people who can't be happy with any job for more than a short time and so when they change jobs they merely repeat the process of dislike in a new location. In an unfamiliar situation it takes one's hate a little time to again build up to its full strength and then another move is made necessary.

There are, of course, all degrees of this evil from open hostility down to mere boredom, but even in the smallest doses hate causes failure, unhappiness and sin.

When one's love is not properly nourished, adjusted and focused, it causes him to go stale on the job. Then he becomes like a child who can only maintain his interest in new toys, and he must be constantly changing playthings if he is to keep himself amused. Antonio worked only with wood and strings and glue, and yet he was never bored in making violins, and his job never lost its freshness nor its challenge.

It has been said that the soul of the lover lives in the body of the object loved. When someone fails to develop a great love centered in something outside himself, then offense and hate grow quickly and tend to turn the hater sour and unsuccessful.

I know a fine young man who worked for an excellent company. He was very enthusiastic and very successful for a few years. But his love became too much focused on himself. At first this trait went unrecognized. Then a combination of circumstances, including a little over-confidence, a little unscheduled relaxation of his effort and a little failure in his interest brought about a weakening in his effort. He subconsciously began to blame others for his decline. He made himself feel that his company and his friends delighted in opposing him. He hopelessly exaggerated in his own mind every unfavorable situation.

Soon he was entertaining a most ridiculous set of untruths. He took every occasion to dislike the company officers, and seemed to get a kind of sadistic pleasure out of his own hate, while all of the time he was the one being most seriously injured. Curses always recoil upon the head of him who set them in motion.

Sometime ago a friend of mine was stung by a bee, and the bee left his stinger in my friend's arm. The sting hurt my friend but it killed the bee. Hate is always harder on the hater than on the hated. When we allow any amount of the poison of hate to be generated by us, it soon fills up our system until we can't take it any longer.

We can solve almost every one of our problems by learning to love—to love our jobs, to love the company we work for, to love the people we work with, to love life, to love excellence, to love God. No one can fail to encounter problems and differences of opinion who works with other people. But all of these problems can be solved. Of course we need to recognize that there are no perfect people in the world. Ever since time began, the work of the world has been done by imperfect men in an imperfect way, and will continue to be so done until time ends. If someone makes a mistake, it can usually be corrected if we maintain our love at proper strength. But if we get angry and allow our hate glands to start pumping poison, then we are lost. We increase this poisonous output by thinking about it, agitating its causes, giving voice to our unfavorable opinions about it, and trying to justify it. By these processes we can soon completely destroy our confidence in the best people, or in the best company, or in the government, or in the Church, or even in God himself, but the hater is always the one that is hurt most.

How can anyone do good work for a company that he hates, or for leaders in whom he has lost confidence, or for associates for whom he has no regard, or for God whom he believes to be unfair. And one of the best ways to learn to love one's work is to follow the formula of Stradivari and do it the best that it can be done. The other is to follow Jesus' formula of love given in the two greatest commandments. It was Stradivari's business to build better violins. It is God's business to build better men and women with greater character qualities, more determined faith, and more unwavering righteousness. And then he has invited us to have a part in the work in which he himself spends his entire time. What a tremendous advantage it would give us if we could develop a little better philosophy of life!

In his inaugural address President John F. Kennedy said, "Never ask what your country can do for you, but rather what you can do for your country." That man loves his country best who serves it most. That man loves God most who puts his own life in harmony with him, and who serves his fellow men as though his life depended upon it, as indeed it does. Antonio learned to love his job by doing superior work and that is the best way for anyone to bring about his own success. Instead of making so many prayers asking God to do things for us, we ought to make more of our prayers about the things that we can do for God, and then we ought to do those things with the same skill and enthusiasm that characterized Antonio Stradivari. We should turn out no shoddy work.

The loafer in business or in the Church is always tired, and never very much in love with what he's doing. The one who cuts the corners of integrity or tries to cheat others never thinks very well of his company. The man who gets married and then gives his attention to other heart interests will never be very successful as a husband. And the man who joins the Church and then spends his time in a lot of little sins will never be very successful in his quest for eternal life.

Stradivari's friend Naldo once tried to induce Antonio to try to make more money by turning out a greater number of violins. He argued that Antonio's painstaking efforts were undesirable. Naldo said, "Why work with such a painful nicety?" And Stradivari replied:

> My work is mine;
> If my hand slackend, I should rob God.
> I am one best
> Here in Cremona, using sunlight well
> To fashion finest maple till it serve
> More cunningly than throats for harmony,
> 'Tis rare delight; I would not change my skill
> To be an Emporer with bungling hands,
> And lose my work which comes as natural
> As self at waking.

We might all well say, "Hurrah for Stradivari!" We should then take a leaf out of his book and get his philosophy of life into our blood stream by making it a part of our own philosophy of life. Stradivari said that his violins were made for eternity, and that is exactly the period for which our lives are being fashioned. It is our business to make great lives, and that includes our own.

Ballistics

THERE is a very interesting science called *ballistics*. It deals with the motion and impact of projectiles, especially those discharged from fire arms. One part of this science is very important in crime detection. Because each gun barrel is different, those bullets shot through it will be given a set of characteristic markings which may lead to the criminal.

But this science of ballistics is not limited to the motion and impact of projectiles. It also has an application to the motion and impact of ideas and ideals. Out of this fact is born a kind of science, that we might call "mental ballistics," or "spiritual ballistics." Minds are like guns and fingerprints in that they also have a set of characteristic markings. Whenever an idea is passed through the mind, the idea is marked by the mind, but the mind is also marked by the idea. Psychologists says that every time an idea passes through the brain, it forms a particular groove or engram. When the same idea passes through the brain again, the groove is made a little deeper and more permanent. And our total mental development can be judged by the number and character of these engrams or wrinkles that our thinking process makes on the brain. Someone has challenged us by saying, "How would you like to create your own mind?" But isn't that just exactly what everyone is doing? William James said, "The mind is made up by what it feeds upon." If we feed our minds with the same kind of ideas that fed the minds of Emerson, Apostle Paul or Jesus then we might expect our minds to respond as did the minds of Emerson, Apostle Paul or Jesus. The traitor, the sinner, the ignorant, and the degenerate are all creating their own minds, just as do the patriots, the scholars, the workers and the saints.

Someone has said that, "The mind, like the dyer's hand, is colored by what it holds." That is, if I hold in my hand a sponge full of purple dye, my hand becomes purple, and if I hold in my mind and heart great ideas of faith, devotion and righteousness, my whole personality is colored accordingly. On the other hand, if I hold in my mind thoughts of spite, dishonesty, idleness, and lust, my personality will take the color of what it holds.

In the operation of this law we see some of our worst dangers as well as some of our greatest opportunities. The one who practices this science of ballistics is called a ballistician. An expert mental ballistician might be described as one skilled in devising effective programs of mind development by regularly passing the right kind of ideas through his own brain. The results of this science are certain. One cannot think big and be little. One cannot think righteously and be evil. When good ideas are run through the mind, the person will soon be distinguished for his goodness. Even when we rethink the great ideas of someone else, we will soon resemble the greatness of the man whose thoughts we are rethinking. The mind of a student soon assumes the characteristics of the mind of the teacher. Socrates left his marks upon Plato. Jesus stamped his impress upon Simon Peter. The operation of this law not only makes people think alike but it can even make them sound alike in their talk or even look alike. Children develop the family characteristics of speech and behavior. A mother and father who live together harmoniously may grow to resemble each other physically, mentally, socially and spiritually.

We know of no greater rewards than those received by an expert ballistician whose program of reading, thinking and action makes the right kind of engrams in his mind. Therefore, to help ourselves become expert in this important field, suppose that in our mind's eye we place ourselves on an elevated balcony from which we can get a good view and exercise a firm control of everything that comes into our minds. Suppose that we not only carefully select the kind of ideas that will be admitted, but rigidly control their use thereafter. Our idea supply should come only from books, people and other sources of the highest quality; and there is plenty of raw material, for all of the ideas that have been well thought by others become our property. And the best mind is not necessarily the one who first discovers the greatest truth but rather the one who puts it to its most effective use. Truth shows itself in its best form only when it is being lived. An expert ballistician first acquires truth and then makes it a part of his blood stream by thoroughly memorizing and practicing it. Thus the pathway of uplifting ideals and powerful ideas becomes so easy to follow that a characteristic response on the highest level is more or less automatic. Solomon referred to this law when he said, "As a man thinketh, . . . so is he." However, that is not true of those thoughts that touch our minds so lightly as to leave no imprint. Some ideas wear a kind of snowshoe and leave a trail too indistinct for other ideas to follow.

One way to give our ideas greater influence by getting good, deep engrams into our brains is to put our plans and thoughts down on paper. Before we write our ideas down we must think them through and get them more definitely organized in some usable form. Francis Bacon pointed out that "Reading makes a full man, . . . but writing makes an exact man." Too much of our thinking is done on the same level that we use for our New Year's resolutions. They are usually so poorly prepared that only a few hazy ideas skate lightly across our polished brains, making almost no impression. If we would thoroughly work out the details of our plans, then make a permanent written record with an accomplishment time table attached, we would find our New Year's resolutions and all other resolutions assuming a far greater importance. When we write our ideas down, it is like putting a bridle on them so as to make their intelligent guidance and direction possible.

We can also greatly increase our thought control by memorizing. The constructive ideas, uplifting philosophies and great scriptural passages that we memorize make up our mental substance just as bricks make up the substance of a wall. And if we become effective in this important construction process we can build our lives to any specification. But action always follows the trail of a thought, and when we have a regular program of right thinking in sufficient depth, we can control the results of our lives. But when even the best ideas are allowed to skim too lightly over our minds, no path is left and confusion reigns. Without a good bridle even the best ideas may go in several directions. Then there is no central path to establish a main purpose in life. To bring the highest price, ideas, like anything else, must be sorted, graded, organized, harnessed, and utilized. Even good ideas need direction, for while they may all start out with good intentions, they are bound to cross the scent of some conflicting thoughts going in another direction, and any idea can be misled. A mind filled with unbridled thoughts might be compared to the inside of an atom where a large number of electrons are bouncing against each other and going in all directions. When we fail to hold a tight rein on our thoughts, they may easily jump the track or go in circles or go down some dead end street. Sometimes one impulse tries to follow the scent of a half a dozen ideas at once.

An interesting study in thought direction is illustrated when a number of people get together for a group conversation. The course of the discussion may run smoothly for a time, but soon it may be jumping rapidly from one subject to another so that no particular progress is being made. Lacking thought guidance a kind of barbed-wire entanglement of our engrams results and we get nowhere. Of course, it is very important that our ideas themselves are not indefinite, fractional, immature, infirm or unrighteous. But by constant planning and good mind management we may become more and more effective in the development and control of our thoughts. This can be brought about by a definite regular program of reading, writing, memorizing and practicing so that we get the pathways through our minds clear enough and definite enough that our lives can be brought under our control.

Of course, a good ballistician should make sure that the mind does not shirk its responsibility or engage in the questionable practices of rationalizing, offering excuses, or indulging in negative thinking. At the first sign of any mental trickery the reins should be tightened and the whip should be brought into play if necessary.

As a young man on the farm I had a kind of demonstration of this ballistics idea in irrigating a field of tomato plants where the furrows ran from east to west with the gradual slope of the land. But the field had its greatest grade from north to south. And because water always seeks out the path of least resistance, the water in one row would sometimes find a weak place in the banks of its furrow and run at right angles to its prescribed course to join the water in the row next to it on its downhill side. The double amount of water thus accumulated in the second row could then more easily break its banks and both run into the third row. If someone were not on hand with a shovel to keep the ditch banks repaired and insist on each stream of water remaining in its proper channel, the individual small streams would soon gang up and run crosslots down through the field washing a gully as they went. Of course, this downhill channel would make it impossible to get the water to do its assigned job in the rows, and consequently the plants beyond the gully would die for lack of nourishment.

But our minds also have some of these same characteristics. When they are not given proper attention and supervision, they frequently center on the wrong things and soon the gullies caused by wrong thinking habits cut off all nourishment from the important areas that should be served by the mind. When the mind is short-circuited by a surge of contrary thoughts, it soon gets out of control. Then instead of resembling a well-irrigated, productive field, the irresponsible gullies use the mind's power for destructive ends.

What a wonderful thing it would be if we could get the same control over our thoughts and feelings that we have over our body members. That is, if I tell my finger to bend, it bends. If I tell my foot to move, it moves. My legs can be depended upon to carry me to about any destination almost automatically. But I don't have that kind of control over my will nor my enthusiasm nor my faith. I have a great deal more trouble managing my thoughts than I do managing my fingers. One of the probable reasons for this lack of mental control is that we improperly humor our minds and gratify those thoughts that clamor most loudly for our attention, rather than those that serve the most important ends. Too often our thoughts are subject to the destructive cross-currents of our fears, doubts, negative thinking and evil imaginations. Then when too many of these harmful gullies are running in the wrong direction, we lose control of the personality. An effective ballistician, like a good irrigator should keep things under sufficient control that he can use his thoughts to vitalize the useful plants at the very end of the mental row.

Food can be purchased at the grocery store, but there is no central market place for self-control nor the attainment of effective idea management. Of course, the right kind of ideas do not come easily nor automatically. They have to be ensnared, impounded and preserved. Then each good idea that we capture and domesticate will introduce us to its friends and relatives. If you examine one idea closely you will usually find that it is holding another idea by the hand, and thus through one idea you may get acquainted with a whole family of interesting thoughts.

One gold mine for great ideas is the holy scriptures. These are the ideas that an all-wise Heavenly Father has prescribed to serve our best interests. These especially should be loved, memorized, kept in good working condition and practiced. God wants us to become as he is. This requires that we should think as he thinks, and do as he does. We should live by every word that proceeds from the mouth of God. We should never allow doubts and fears to stampede our ideas out of their proper channels. But by organizing our thinking and by putting our ideas to work we may get the same discipline over our minds that we get over our body members.

Then week after week as we sit on our mental balconies and direct our thought in the right kind of mental grooves, we may give our lives purpose as we stamp them with the characteristics of productivity and godliness.

Be Ye Therefore Perfect

THE greatest sermon ever delivered is almost universally identified as the one given by Jesus called "The Sermon on the Mount." For some time previously Jesus had been going about the countryside teaching in the synagogues and healing all manner of diseases among the people. The number of his followers had become very great. A vast multitude had gathered from Galilee, Decapolis, Jerusalem, Judea and even from beyond the Jordan, and then Jesus led them up into the Mount where he taught them the great truths contained in this most important of all discourses.

This sermon probably reached its highest point when Jesus said to the people, "Be ye therefore perfect, even as your Father which is in heaven is perfect." When carefully considered, this statement has always had an important impact upon human thought and personality. In fact, ever since this statement was made, it has been a source of great wonder among thoughtful men and women. The people to whom it was spoken were aware even as we are aware of the poor, weak, sinful natures of most mortals. As the Apostle Paul reminded the Romans "All have sinned, and come short of the glory of God." (Romans 3:23)

The people who listened to Jesus on the mountainside that day knew that their lives were far below the standard of perfection maintained by their Father in heaven. There had been a continual demonstration of weakness and sin even among the closest disciples of Jesus. Even Peter was weak and possessed those traits that on the very eve of the crucifixion would cause him to deny the Master. Thomas was a doubter and other disciples had done things of which they were not very proud. There were dishonesties, disloyalties and immoralities in many hearts. Matthew says that many sinners sat at meat with Jesus. (Matthew 9:10) And it was a matter of public inquiry as to why Jesus associated so freely with publicans and sinners. (Matthew 9:11) Certainly this association with imperfect people was not accidental, as the mission of Jesus was to save sinners. And on the mount it was an ordinary group of weak, ignorant, sinful, though well-meaning men and women, who heard Jesus say, "Be ye therefore perfect, even as your Father which is in heaven is perfect."

This statement must have been something of a shock to them, as it is something of a shock to us when we understand the importance of the tremendous standard set up by the Savior. Yet this high goal must always be the final objective of our lives. Our Father in heaven is the most intelligent and the most righteous being in the universe. He is a member of the highest order of existence. He has the highest sense of values, the best personality development, and the greatest capability for happiness. Jesus was saying that we, the offspring, should be like God the parent. God himself has been trying to bring us to this place since "the beginning," and anyone who in eternity attains the highest degree of glory must qualify to live in God's presence. No other goal could possibly equal this.

The most thrilling idea in the world is that we are the literal children of God, created in his image and endowed with his potentialities. The laws of inheritance indicate that if we are faithful, we may some time hope to become even as God is. We should cling to our birthright. There is everything in remembering our heritage and constantly reaffirming it in our lives. Jesus held this goal up before us, that we might take appropriate action. However, he probably did not intend that this goal should be fully reached in this life. But there is much more to life as God knows it than the three score years and ten that belong to mortality.

But even in this life we may reach a state of near perfection in some areas. For example, anyone can be perfect in abstaining from tea and coffee. We can be perfect in freeing ourselves from the use of tobacco and intoxicating liquor. We can be perfect in the payment of our tithing. We can be perfect in our attendance at sacrament meeting. We can be perfect in our punctuality. We can be perfectly honest, and perfectly dependable and perfectly moral.

Suppose that we make up a list of those things in which we can reach near perfection today. Then as we achieve perfection in these goals, new possibilities will present themselves. As our accomplishment grows, our nearness to perfection will increase.

It has been said that making our way toward perfection is like climbing a mountain. We master them both in sections. How well I remember the first mountain I climbed as a boy. As I stood at its foot, the top of the first steep ascent seemed to me to be the top of the mountain. I could see nothing beyond, as the second section was completely hidden behind the first. However, when I reached the top of the first section, I saw a new expanse of mountain stretching out before me. This process was repeated several times before the top of the mountain was finally attained. But all success has some of these characteristics. Success has a kind of extension ladder arrangement. When you reach the top of one section, another section is pushed up to be climbed. Later in life when I read Alexander Pope's essay in which he referred to climbing the Alps, I knew exactly what he was talking about. He said:

> So pleas'd at first the tow'ring Alps we try,
> Mount o'er the vales, and seem to tread the sky,
> Th' eternal snows appear already past,
> And the first clouds and mountains seem the last:
> But, those attained, we tremble to survey
> The growing labors of the lengthen'd way;
> Th' increasing prospect tires our wand'ring eyes,
> Hills peep o'er hills, and Alps on Alps arise!

That process also bears some similarity to our lives. President Joseph F. Smith gives us this interesting account of his own spiritual progress. He said, "When I as a boy first started out in the ministry, I would frequently ask the Lord to show me some marvelous thing, in order that I might receive a testimony. But the Lord withheld marvels from me, and showed me the truth, line upon line, precept upon precept, here a little and there a little, until he made me to know the truth from the crown of my head to the soles of my feet, and until doubt and fear had been absolutely purged from me. He did not have to send an angel from the heavens to do this. . . . By the whisperings of the still small voice of the Spirit of the living God, he gave to me the testimony which I now possess." (*Gospel Doctrine*, 1928 ed., page 9)

During the Golden Age of Greece, Pericles said that no one had a right to fill an important office until he had first served with distinction in a number of smaller offices. Too frequently we want to so some great thing before we have perfected ourselves in doing little things well.

One prize fighter said to another, "If I were a great big man like you, I would become the champion heavyweight prize fighter of the world." His friend said, "If I were a little man like you, I would become the champion lightweight prize fighter of the world." Before we apply for admittance to any heavyweight championship bouts in life, we should have won a few lightweight championships. We should make ourselves worthy of our opportunities. The best way to become a great soul in heaven is to practice being a great soul here. If one believes that honesty is better than dishonesty, then he should immediately begin practicing it, not just in big things but also in little things. And it will not be long before new fields of opportunity will have opened up before him. Emerson said, "Do the thing and you shall have the power."

Jesus said, "He that doeth my will shall know of the doctrine." Only as we live the principles of the gospel can we really know of their truthfulness. It is the person who pays his tithing who believes in tithing. It is the one who observes the Word of Wisdom who knows the value of the Word of Wisdom. It is the person who keeps the Sabbath day holy who champions it. And it is the person who gives service who knows the joys of serving. As we climb the mountain, one section after another presents itself to be mastered. If we can live one gospel principle perfectly today we can live two principles perfectly tomorrow. Perfection in one thing will act as a steppingstone to perfection in something else.

The famous "as if" principle of William James might supply us with some good supplementary reading for the Sermon on the Mount. Mr. James said that if you want a quality, act "as if" you already had it. That is, if you want to be friendly, act "as if" you were already friendly. If you want to be courageous, act "as if" you were already courageous. Don't go around imitating cowards or indulging in negative, unchristian thinking. If you want to be faithful, act "as if" you are already faithful. Do the things that faithful people do. Go to church, say your prayers, study the scriptures, be honest with yourself, and everyone else. Act "as if" you were a true-blue follower of Christ. Near perfection is very easy once we really get the spirit of it.

There are some people who maintain that it is difficult to live the religion of Christ. And to live their religion is next to impossible for some people. But what kind of a person would you expect to have difficulty in abstaining from liquor? Or what kind of a person would you expect to be tempted by dishonesty or immorality or the use of profanity? One who experiences the greatest temptation from evil would likely be the one most familiar with evil. We are not paying ourselves compliments when we confess how difficult it is for us to live the simple principles of our religion, any more than we would be paying ourselves compliments to say we were having difficulties in restraining ourselves from robbing banks or being disloyal to our country. It is very difficult for an unfaithful person to be faithful. It is very hard to live one's religion if he has never lived it before. It is very difficult to be a non-smoker this week if you have always been a smoker previously. It is extremely difficult for an alcoholic to be a non-drinker. It is very difficult to be moral if you have always been immoral.

But it is just as easy for an industrious man to be industrious as it is for a lazy man to be lazy. We become godly or industrious or obedient just as we become anything else— by practice. That is what Jesus was recommending when he said "Be ye therefore perfect even as your Father which is in heaven is perfect." It is very easy for God to live his religion, anything else would be difficult or impossible for God. And if we want to follow his pattern and obey God, we should act "as if" we were already obedient. Then we will think obedience and love obedience and allow no exceptions to obedience. The fewer exceptions to perfection, the nearer we get to perfection.

It is interesting to know that there have been many perfect and near perfect people live upon the earth. Of course, Jesus is the great example of perfection. But the Book of Genesis says "that Noah was a just man and perfect in his generation." It also says, "And Noah walked with God." Noah practiced perfection. The scriptures tell us that Enoch was also a perfect man. In fact, he was so perfect that he and his entire city were translated and taken up from the earth. The record says, "And Enoch walked with God: and he was not; for God took him." (Gen. 5:18-24) Modern-day revelation tells us that Enoch's great city was called "the city of holiness." The record says, "And the Lord called his people Zion, because they were of one heart and one mind, and dwelt in righteousness; and there was no poor among them." (Moses 7:18)

The scriptures not only tell us that the city of Enoch was taken up into heaven, but that when the earth is restored to its perfect state, Enoch and his translated city will rejoin us upon the earth with great rejoicing. The Lord said unto Enoch, ". . . Then shalt thou and all thy city meet them there, and we will receive them into our bosom, and they shall see us, and we will fall upon their necks, and they shall fall upon our necks, and we will kiss each other." (Moses 7:63)

It is important to work for perfection here, but life continues its prescribed course beyond the boundaries of this life. We know that we take our abilities, our records, and our personalities with us into eternity, and the good lives that we have lived here may be continued there. Our knowledge, our loves, and our abilities to learn and to enjoy also go with us beyond the grave.

Death is also a step in our progress and is as much a part of God's program for our perfection as is life, and there are some things looking toward perfection that can best be done while the spirit and the body are temporarily separated. As the finishing school for our perfection our spirits will be cleansed, purified, educated, and glorified in such a way as to be fully qualified for God's presence. With him the faithful children of God will realize that final objective of life held up before us by Jesus in the greatest of all sermons wherein he said, "Be ye therefore perfect, even as your Father which is in heaven is perfect."

The Chance World

MANY YEARS ago someone wrote an interesting book with the fascinating title of *The Chance World*. It described a world in which everything happened by chance. The sun might come up in the morning or it might not. If it did not come up, it might appear at any hour of the day or night, or the moon might show up instead. If you jumped up into the air, you might come down, or you might keep on going, and there was no way of telling what would happen beforehand.

If you planted a field of wheat, it might come up wheat, or it might come up barley, or asparagus, or rose bushes or apples trees. You might be born with one head or a dozen; and they might be located on your shoulders or in some other place. What happened yesterday would be no indication of what might happen under the same circumstances today. There was no reaction pattern for anything that could be depended upon. Gravitation, electricity, light and heat were free to change their performance from hour to hour. Today the weight of a man's body might be so light that it would be impossible to get it down to the ground. But tomorrow some unexpected force might drive it into the center of the earth. In this chance world, cause and effect were unknown, and law had never been established. To the inhabitants of such a world, order would be unknown and reason would be impossible. It would be a lunatic world with a population of lunatics.

This situation may seem very strange, and yet there are people who in many ways claim to believe in a chance world. They believe that even human life itself is a result of blind chance; that man's great brain just happened to grow in such a way that it could solve the problems of the world.

That his eyes gained their miraculous power of vision as a result of chance, and that the wonders of hearing, thinking and understanding all just happened.

Try to imagine the billions of worlds hurtling through space at different rates of speed, going in different directions; all maintaining perfect order with nothing in control. We know that if the earth should deviate in its rotation by just a few degrees, the polar icecap would be on top of us. Or if the variation should be in the other direction, or if the earth should spin around for a few days with one side always toward the sun, the earth would catch fire. What a universal pile-up we would have if we had only chance at the steering wheel of the universe!

Probably the most important lesson that we ever need to learn in life is that we do not live in a chance world. We live in a world governed by laws, all of which may be known in advance. What a wonderful satisfaction that we live in a world where no one will ever have his intellect insulted or his conscience abused because of a capricious nature. The acts of nature are bound by law from which they cannot deviate. If you release your hold on a heavy suspended object, it will fall. It has no other choice. It must strictly obey the law ordained to govern its existence. Water will freeze at 32° Fahrenheit and boil at 212° and it cannot do otherwise. We may know that the great forces of gravitation, electricity, light, cause and effect, rewards and punishments, growth and decay, progress and retrogression will never be out of date. Man is a rational being, and has been given a pledge by creation that he may depend upon nature for the exact result that nature has previously led him to expect. Man is also a moral being, and he may know that the God of nature and physical law is also the God of heaven and spiritual law, that law and order obtains in the spiritual realm with the same fidelity as it does in the physical and mental worlds. We know that God will continue to be the same yesterday, today and forever, and that any man willing to learn, and obey the rules can bring about any desired blessing. And we also bring our own woes upon ourselves when we fail to understand and be governed by law. This is one of the most important ideas in life.

It is fairly simple to understand that if we jump over the cliff, we may expect to go down and not up. We know what will happen if we throw ourselves into a vat of boiling steel, or put our bodies in contact with high tension electric power lines. But we do not always have the same respect for the spiritual laws, because the rewards and penalties may be deferred, but they are not a bit less certain. That is, we can absolutely depend on the mental law that says, "As a man thinketh in his heart, so is he." Though the changes are more gradual, yet from this law there can be no deviation, nor is there any way for anyone to set it aside.

Paul made an excellent statement of fact to the Galatians when he said, "Be not deceived; God is not mocked: for whatsoever a man soweth, that shall he also reap. For he that soweth to his flesh shall of the flesh reap corruption; but he that soweth to the Spirit shall of the Spirit reap life everlasting." (Gal. 6:7-8)

Jesus had the same idea in mind when he said, ". . . For of thorns men do not gather figs, nor of a bramble bush gather they grapes." (Luke 6:44) The application of this law is just as dependable in the spiritual realm as in the physical. In neither place do these laws change. James says, "Every good gift and every perfect gift is from above, and cometh down from the Father of lights, with whom is no variableness, neither shadow of turning." (James 1:17)

But to hope that some capricious chance will start grapes growing on bramble bushes is no more unlikely than to hope that chance can create intelligence or bring harmony and order in the world.

The story is told of a guide who was conducting an atheist through the great St. Paul's cathedral. During the tour the atheist asked the guide who the builder of the cathedral was. The guide, hoping to teach the atheist a lesson said, "One of the very strange things about this cathedral is that there was no builder. I just awoke one morning and found the cathedral standing here." Is it any easier to believe that a cathedral of brick and cement, stained glass windows and steeples, altars and pews could come into existence by itself than to believe that the great miracle of flesh and blood, vision and energy, voice and understanding, intelligence and personality that we call a human being could form itself out of nothing with no one to give it direction?

Anciently it was believed that life generated spontaneously. Now we know that to be untrue. We now know that all life must come from some life already in existence. We also know that our life came from God, that he is our Father, and according to the natural laws of procreation, the offspring may ultimately hope to become like the parent. We also know that it requires time, sunshine, moisture and plant food to develop an oak from an acorn. It also requires time and understanding to use effectively the laws of chemistry, engineering or medicine. An investment of effort and study, faith and righteous conduct are required to bring our own eternal possibilities up to their maximum. However, we do not need to know all of the reasons why something is so in order to get its benefits.

Someone has pointed out that Newton did not discover gravity. Actually gravity has not yet been discovered. All that Newton discovered were some of the laws of gravity, indicating how gravity might be profitably used. These laws tell us nothing about the origin, cause or nature of this mysterious power of gravity.

We don't need to know everything about electricity in order to have light and heat in our homes. Neither do we need to understand all about electricity in order to electrocute ourselves. We don't understand very much about sunlight, and yet we are able to harness its benefits merely by understanding and obeying its laws.

Neither do we know all about why or how God carries out the divine program, but we can understand his laws of faith, repentance, baptism, prayer, eternal marriage, honesty, and the results that come from obedience to these great laws. Someone said, "I will not believe anything that I do not understand." If we did not believe anything unless we fully understood it, our lists of beliefs would be extremely short, for we don't understand birth, or life, or death, or vision, or how the grass grows, or what heat or light or coal or fire is. We don't understand how we breathe, how our nervous system works, nor what makes our heart beat. We didn't even discover the circulation of our own blood until Harvey's time, a little over 300 years ago. Certainly we do not understand all of the spiritual laws, yet we can readily know what they are, and we can use them to develop character and spirituality and thereby bring about our eternal exaltation. We know that if we jump off a high cliff, or hug a million volts of electricity, or drink poison, or put fire into the gasoline tank, we can be fairly sure of trouble. It is just as certain that by a violation of the spiritual laws, we can bring eternal damnation upon ourselves.

Every child knows that if he wants a harvest of wheat, he must plant wheat; not rye nor barley nor oats. If we want to become like God we must follow the law designed to make us like God. If we expect to live in the Celestial Kingdom, we must abide the laws of the Celestial Kingdom. We must not expect that our world will be changed into a chance world to enable us to evade the natural penalties of our deeds. Neither should we expect that God will make his own laws inoperative merely because we have disregarded them.

The great lesson we must learn in life is that we do not live in a chance world. Almost more than anything else we need to learn that God is not the author of confusion. God is unalterably opposed to sin, which is the transgression of law. God cannot look upon sin with the least degree of allowance. He knows that unhappiness and degradation always come to the life that tolerates evil in any of its forms. The universe and everything in it is governed by law and our success in every field is determined by how well we understand and obey the eternal principles regulating each particular accomplishment.

A successful farmer works in harmony with the laws of God which says that there must be a proper seed bed, good seed, sufficient moisture and fertility if a good crop is to be expected. If a farmer violates the law and plants his corn in the chill of a December blizzard, he may expect failure because the laws of successful farming are working against him. If a child of God violates the Ten Commandments and orders his life in opposition to the Sermon on the Mount, he may similarly expect failure.

The books of every individual life must be balanced and the greatest mistake that anyone can make is to imagine that in our spiritual affairs the laws and the records will be done away with. We cannot sow tares and reap wheat. The wages of sin is death. We cannot sow evil and reap good. We cannot devote ourselves to evil and hope that a chance world will provide a happy ending. God's law abideth forever. It is the perfect plan for our eternal exaltation. It involves a faithful obedience to the great laws of repentance, baptism, and the gift of the Holy Ghost. It includes the development of faith, honesty, character and godliness. It requires the proper care of our bodies, minds and spirits, obedience to the laws of eternal marriage, and all of the other important principles and ordinances given by God for our benefit. If we will take the pains to be informed, and then obey the rules, a glorious destiny will be a certainty.

Covenant Makers

THE DICTIONARY gives some interesting meanings for the word "covenant." A covenant is primarily an agreement between two or more persons or parties aimed at accomplishing a certain end. A covenant may also have legal, social, business or religious significance.

The Bible tells of a covenant of friendship made between David and Jonathan. (I Sam. 18:3) Shakespeare said, "Let there be covenants drawn between us." There are marriage covenants and political covenants. The charter of the United Nations is a covenant with a great many articles describing the rules and procedures for the conduct of that organization's affairs. In its religious meaning a covenant pertains primarily to the promises of God contained in the holy scriptures and based on a condition of man's faithfulness. Those entering into covenants bind themselves by contracts, promises, oaths or vows to carry out the course previously agreed upon.

One of the most effective ways for our improvement is to become better covenant makers and better covenant keepers. In a religious sense we need what those in law school might call a good course in contracts. No one lives by himself or for himself alone. The activities of every individual are so involved with that of the Creator and other people that confusion would reign unless we had an understanding with an agreement, that each should perform in good faith what had previously been agreed upon.

Some time ago the chairman of the board of one of our most successful national business organizations said that 40% of the time of their executive officers was spent in what he called communication. They were trying to make sure that all concerned had a clear understanding of the ambitions, procedures and objectives for which this company was organized. This corporation also had skilled supervisors and trainers to help each one to successfully carry his share of the responsibility.

About this same procedure is involved in having a good government. Since the beginning of time, tribes and nations have made treaties outlining the conditions under which they hoped to live peaceably and successfully together. When no clear understanding exists or when treaties are not kept, serious trouble always follows.

Some time ago an article in the *U. S. News and World Report* described 52 agreements that had been made by the Russians in the previous 22 years. Fifty of these had already been broken. It was expected that the other two would be broken as soon as it served communist interest to do so. Such a lack of dependability on either side of an agreement makes any success impossible. To make agreements in bad faith or to go back on one's word is a serious violation of honor, and lies at the root of almost all of the troubles of nations, families and individuals. Utopia would be just around the corner if unquestioned integrity always existed between seller and buyer, teacher and student, friend and friend, neighbor and neighbor, nation and nation, God and man. All success is primarily a matter of making and then honoring the right kind of covenants. For example, if one entering military service or becoming a citizen of the United States hopes to be successful, he first finds out what his duties, privileges, authority and responsibilities are. Then he takes the oath of office or the Pledge of Allegiance or is sworn in as a citizen. And both sides have a right to know in advance what the purpose and performances of the other will be.

When two people decide to enter the marriage relationship, certain promises are made which are based on the right and the mutual welfare of both. The parties agree to love, honor and serve each other. Each accepts the responsibilities as well as the privileges covered by their agreement. The marriage contract requires that children must be fed, clothed, taught and prepared for their life's work and eternal happiness. No one under covenant is irresponsibly free to go his own way or to do as he pleases. His personal activities must thereafter be restricted. For example, when one is sworn in as President of the United States he takes an oath of office. He commits himself to loyalty, truth and faithfulness and thereafter he must do and refrain from doing certain things.

But anyone who aspires to any accomplishment must also make commitments. Without commitments life loses much of its meaning. An uncommitted life is comparatively shallow, empty and unfruitful. For how could one hope to be a good citizen or a successful father or a profitable child of God who refused to commit himself? What would it mean to remain forever uncommitted to truth, family, country, self and God? It takes careful thought and wise planning to make a covenant, and once made these commitments are sacred and must be kept. A covenant breaker is called by the unpleasant names of traitor, betrayer, falsifier, or son of perdition.

Our final success depends upon the commitments we make to honor, and the integrity with which they are carried out. The greatest conception of freedom is the acceptance of individual responsibility and an affirmation and devotion to our covenants and our self-imposed limitations. To this end we make sacred pledges, take holy vows and make promises of faithfulness. We also need the supporting comradeship of other vow makers. Someone has said that this world is too dark and cold to remain indefinitely on lonely picket duty by ourselves. We need what William Adams Brown calls the fellowship of the hopeful. But we also need individually to commit ourselves to truth, our families, our fellow men and our God.

A firm commitment is the highest expression of Americanism. It is the highest expression of success. It is the highest expression of religion. The most important question is not, can we trust the Russians or can we trust the Chinese or the Cubans, but, "Can we trust ourselves?" and can God trust us. Of course, before we make a commitment we need to make up our minds about our goals in life. Then we make a covenant which is a kind of performance bond that we will be faithful to our partners, our customers, our family, our country and most important of all to our Creator and the provider of our blessings. God also has a right to hear our commitments. More than anyone else he is involved in our lives. He is our Father. He created us. He enlightens our minds and quickens our understandings. It is his work to bring to pass our immortality and eternal life.

To make a successful religious covenant it is necessary that we believe in God. It is also helpful if God believes in us. Long ago God committed himself to those eternal principles of right from which he does not deviate. Because of the limitations he has placed upon his own acts, he cannot lie or cheat or engage in evil or go back on his word. He makes no compromises with wrong and cannot look upon sin with the least degree of allowance. What a wonderful situation we would place ourselves in if we would always carry out *our* vows with a similar determination.

Of course this life is not the beginning of our association with our Heavenly Father and we made some important covenants with God before this world began. Nothing in the scriptures could be plainer than the fact that the life of Christ did not begin at Bethlehem, nor did it end on Calvary. It is equally plain in the scriptures that *we* lived for a long period before our mortality began. Our present lives were planned under God's direction in the pre-earth life. Then we walked by sight. Now we must learn to walk a little way by faith. It was known in advance that because of free agency many would sin and that this life would be a place of sickness, and death, sorrow and disease, bloodshed and heartbreak. We knew that in some degree all would come short of the glory of God. Therefore a Redeemer was provided for us who Peter says, "was foreordained before the foundation of the world." (I Peter 1:20) We not only had a part in the Savior's appointment as the mediator of the new and everlasting covenant (Hebrews 12:24), but with him we also made a covenant of faithfulness.

There is an old tradition that has been handed down to the effect that in the pre-earth life we made a covenant with each other that if we were successful in finding the straight and narrow way to eternal life, we would do all in our power to make it known to our brothers and sisters. As soon as man was placed upon the earth God renewed the heavenly covenant. Adam and Eve and their posterity were taught the importance of living those eternal principles of truth which had already been established and accepted in heaven.

This eternal covenant has been re-established at various times from Adam until now. Sometimes the people have been true to their agreements but sometimes their violations have brought wars, floods, sickness, poverty, confusions and spiritual darkness upon themselves.

When the Son of God came into the world in the meridian of time to atone for our sins, he also established the new and everlasting covenant. Then in order to bring its importance to the attention of everyone, Jesus sent out his missionaries, saying to them, "Go ye into all the world and preach the gospel to every creature. He that believeth and is baptized shall be saved; but he that believeth not shall be damned." By this process every individual is given the opportunity to make a personal covenant with God.

In the interests of our covenants, God has given us in our own day one of the most unusual of all books called the Doctrine and Covenants. It is a modern volume of scripture containing revelations given specifically for our day. A "doctrine" is a statement of one of the fundamental principles on which our eternal exaltation rests. It is something for us to understand, believe in, live by, and make commitments about. A "covenant" is an *agreement* with God in which the opportunities and responsibilities of each party are made clear and accepted. This book is filled with the most wonderful promises made for our acceptance and leading to our eventual exaltation.

We frequently speak of being born under the covenant. Of course everyone is born under that covenant made in our pre-earth life. But those born to parents who have made certain important vows in this life are in a special way born heirs to God's blessings on condition of obedience. These parents are committed to start their children out with an advantage by teaching them righteousness in their youth. Then as the child reaches the age of accountability, he reaffirms the covenant and makes an individual commitment of his own. He enters the waters of baptism and covenants with the Lord to be faithful throughout his life. We make covenants at the Sacrament table. We make covenants when we receive the priesthood. There is a wonderful statement recorded in the Doctrine and Covenants in which it is said, "And . . . all they who receive this priesthood receive me, saith the Lord; For he that receiveth my servants receiveth me; And he that receiveth me receiveth my Father; And he that receiveth my Father receiveth my Father's kingdom; therefore all that my Father hath shall be given unto him. And this is according to the oath and covenant which belongeth to the priesthood. Therefore all those who receive the priesthood, receive this oath and covenant of my Father, which he cannot break, neither can it be moved. But whoso breaketh this covenant after he hath received it, and altogether turneth therefrom, shall not have forgiveness of sins in this world nor in the world to come. . . . And I now give unto you a commandment to beware concerning your-

selves, to give diligent heed to the words of eternal life."
(D&C 84:35-43)

In the Lord's instruction on eternal marriage he said:
"For behold, I reveal unto you a new and everlasting covenant; and if ye abide not that covenant, then are ye damned;
for no one can reject this covenant and be permitted to enter
into my glory. For all who will have a blessing at my hands
shall abide the law which was appointed for that blessing,
and the conditions thereof, as were instituted from before
the foundation of the world. And as pertaining to the new
and everlasting covenant, it was instituted for the fulness of
my glory; and he that receiveth a fulness thereof must and
shall abide the law, or he shall be damned, saith the Lord
God." (D&C 132:4-6)

That sounds as though the Lord is in dead earnest about
his covenants, and we pray that he may help us to realize the
importance of making and keeping ours.

Damon and Pythias

WE HAVE often been reminded of the advantages of filling our minds with good ideas. As we read the world's great literature, we tend to absorb the best from the lives of others and use it for our own uplift. We ought to put on our magnifying glasses occasionally and then very earnestly read the great success stories of the world, such a course would fill our minds with the spirit of real achievement.

The quality of our lives would also be greatly increased if we read the world's great love stories more frequently. Who could fail to be thrilled by recalling the experiences that ripened the love between David and Jonathan? Their common bond of friendship and trust strikes one of the high notes of the scriptures. The Bible says "The soul of Jonathan was knit with the soul of David, and Jonathan loved him as his own soul." (I Samuel 18:1)

Many people have had their lives lifted above the ordinary by a recital of the Bible story of Ruth and Naomi. After Ruth's husband had died, her widowed mother-in-law tried to get her to return to her own people, and begin life anew with them. But Ruth said to Naomi, ". . . Intreat me not to leave thee, or to return from following after thee: for whither thou goest, I will go; and where thou lodgest, I will lodge: thy people shall be my people, and thy God my God . . . the Lord do so to me and more also, if ought but death part thee and me." (Ruth 1:16-17)

We can find other great vicarious experiences to fill our various needs. One of the most worthwhile satisfactions that ever comes to any human being is the feeling of absolute confidence in the integrity and ability of someone he loves. And to get this feeling vicariously is second only to the real experience.

There is a stimulating old Roman legend about two famous friends who lived in the ancient city of Syracuse in Sicily, about 400 B.C. Their names were Damon and Pythias. The tyrant King Dionysius, who ruled Syracuse at the time, unjustly condemned Damon to death because he had been falsely accused of plotting against the king. Damon begged for three days of time in which to put his affairs in order before his death. He also desired to attend the wedding of his sister, who lived at a considerable distance away.

The cynical old king had heard of the unusual friendship existing between Damon and Pythias, but he did not believe that such a love and loyalty could exist between two friends as that which was reported to be binding Damon and Pythias together. The king decided that this would be a good opportunity to test their feelings for each other, and so he told Damon that he would grant the three-day stay of execution if Pythias would stand as his surety, and agree to die in his place if Damon did not return.

Damon told Pythias what the king said, and Pythias promptly presented himself at court to be bound in Damon's stead.

In attending to his affairs Damon had to travel over some very rough country, but by the morning of the third day he had wound up his business and was returning to his doom when some unforeseen difficulties began blocking his way. A poem recounting some of these problems was written by William Peter entitled "True Friendship." He said:

> The heavens interposed by bringing up a great tempest.
> And Damon had a roaring river to cross.

And Mr. Peter said:

> And when the poor pilgrim arrived at the shore
> Swollen to torrents the rills
> Rushed in foam from the hills.
> And crash went the bridge in the whirlpool's wild roar.

An impassable flood now blocked Damon's way, and his time was running short. He was unable to get aid, so in desperation Damon threw himself into the wild, roaring flood waters and swam with superhuman strength, not to save his own life, but to save his friend Pythias. Damon sank, then rose, then swam again. By the greatest efforts he struggled on until at length "the shore was won." He had hardly escaped from the perils of the flood when as the poet says:

> A band of fierce robbers encompassed his way,
> "What would ye?" he cried, "my life I have nought;
> Nay, my life is the king's." — then swift having caught
> A club from the nearest, and swinging it round
> With might more than man's, he laid three on the ground,
> While the rest hurried off in dismay.

But dispersing the robbers didn't end his troubles. He also had a desert to cross, and the poet said:

> As the noon's scorching flame
> Shoots through his frame,
> He turns, faint and way-worn to Heaven on High
> From the flood and the foe,
> Thou'st redeemed me, and oh!
> Thus, by thirst overcome, must I effortless lie,
> And leave him, the beloved of my bosom to die?"

But still Damon didn't stop. He made his way against every kind of obstacle in his Herculean effort to save his friend Pythias. Overcoming flood, robbers, fatigue, heat and thirst, he finally came within sight of Syracuse. On the outskirts he was met by his own servant who advised him to flee and save himself because Pythias had already been executed, and the king was now seeking Damon to put him to death also. The servant said of Pythias:

> "No; nothing can save his dear head from the tomb;
> So think of preserving thine own.
> Myself, I beheld him led forth to his doom;
> Ere this, his brave spirit has flown!

With confident soul he stood, hour after hour,
Thy return never doubting to see;
No sneers of the tyrant, that faith could o'erpower,
Or shake his assurance in thee!"

Then Damon replied to the servant:

And is it too late? and can I not save
His dear life? Then, at least, let me share in his grave,
Yes, death shall unite us! no tyrant shall say,
That friend to his friend proved untrue; he may slay,—
May torture,—may mock at all mercy and ruth,
But ne'er shall he doubt of our friendship and truth."

Damon continued to go forward as fast as he could,
only to find that the servant himself had been untruthful.

Tis sunset: and Damon arrives at the gate,
Sees the scaffold, and multitudes gazing up from below;
Already the victim is bared for his fate,
Already the deathsman stands armed for the blow;
When hark! a wild voice which is echoed around,
Shouts, "Stay!—'tis I—it is Damon, for whom he was bound."

And now they sink in each other's embrace,
And are weeping for joy and despair,
Not a soul, among thousands, but melts at their case,
Which swift to the monarch they bear;
Even he, too, is moved—feels for once as he ought—
And commands, that they both to his throne shall be brought.

Then alternately gazing on each gallant youth,
With looks of awe, wonder, and shame: —
"Ye have conquered!" he cried, "Yes, I see now the truth—
That friendship is not a mere name.
Go;—you're free; but, while life's dearest blessings you prove
Let one prayer of your monarch be heard,
That — his past sins forgot — in this union of love
And of virtue — you make him the third.

When King Dionysius saw real trust and friendship in
operation he wanted these qualities for himself and asked
to be included with Damon and Pythias as the third member
of this alliance devoted to true loyalty and friendship.

To experience love and confidence in someone is one of the most priceless virtues in life. Using a little different name, Jesus put these qualities under the title of the second great commandment. There are very few things in the world that are more pleasant than to believe in someone, or to be believed in by someone. What a thrilling experience to have a feeling of absolute confidence in the integrity and ability of one you love, and to believe that no matter what may happen he will prove faithful to every trust. Solomon says that many people are called pious, but there are not many who can be called loyal.

Of course, one of the important ingredients in this situation is to make ourselves worthy of that trust. Then we may know within ourselves that we can and will fully support with our actions the faith and good opinions of our friends. And what greater compliment could anyone pay us than to trust us? Or think of the pleasure that we can give to others by merely making ourselves deserving of their wholehearted confidence. Carried to its ultimate this delightful quality is very closely allied to worship. There is an article of our faith in which we say, "We believe in God . . ." That not only means that we believe God exists, it also means that we know the kind of being that he is, that we were created in his image and endowed with his potentialities; but it also means that we believe in him, that we trust him, that we believe that he knows his business, and that our affairs are safe in his hands.

Job had this kind of belief in God. In his sorest trials and afflictions he said: "Though he slay me, yet will I trust in him." But to be complete, this Damon and Pythias kind of relationship must go in both directions. So let's look at the other side of the picture and see how God felt about Job. On one occasion God said to Satan, "Hast thou considered my servant Job, that there is none like him in the earth, a perfect and an upright man, one that feareth God, and escheweth evil? and still he holdest fast his integrity, although thou movedst me against him, to destroy him without cause." (Job 2:3) How would you like to have God say that about you?

One-half of the greatest idea that I know of in the world is to believe in God. The other half of that idea is to conduct our lives so that God will believe in us. This idea does not belong only to religion, it is the most important idea in business, in the professions, in government, or in our social relationships. Everything that is right and good makes us better citizens and more worthwhile individuals. What quality could help us more before God or with our fellow men than this ability to get ourselves believed in and trusted by others?

By contrast we might look at this trait on the negative side. What can be more unpleasant than to be continually disappointed by someone you want to believe in. You may even love him, but because he lacks in basic character you cannot trust him. Such a one may borrow money but must be forced to pay it back. If you try to help him he will misinterpret your action. Give him information and you will be misquoted. Give him your confidence and he will betray you. Depend on him and you will be double-crossed. Give him employment and he will let you down. On every occasion he meets you with excuses, alibis, untruths, worthless promises, laziness, irresponsibility, and a low grade of accomplishment. What a great prayer someone uttered when he said:

> Great God, I ask thee for no meaner pelf
> Than that I may not disappoint myself.

One of the most cherished blessings in life, or in business success, or in religious worship, is to have something solid for your faith to cling to. A climbing vine needs a non-crumbling brick wall to climb. Damon and Pythias were each a brick wall for the other. If you want to be a really great human being, be the kind of person that anyone can cling to without fear, climb up on with confidence, and trust and believe in with love.

We can help develop these qualities in ourselves by a closer association with such great stories as Damon and Pythias, David and Jonathan, Ruth and Naomi. But then at the very top of the list we have the most inspiring of all of the accounts of love and trust in the experience and association of God the Father and his Son Jesus Christ. On at least four different occasions the Father has introduced the Son to the world and said, "This is my Beloved Son, in whom I am well pleased." What a great ambition, if, like Dionysius, we determined to qualify as a third member of this alliance, fully devoted to true loyalty and friendship!

For we are also the sons of God and are entitled to give our Heavenly Father the same pleasure in our association that he gets from his most prominent Son. No one can reach his maximum accomplishments who cannot say, "We believe in God." But then to make the picture complete our lives must be such that God can say that he believes in us.

The Family

ONE OF THE distinguishing characteristics of our day is the very in-
teresting problems we have to solve. In many ways our
standards are higher than they have ever been, but the size
of our problems have also increased. We have gigantic educational problems. The problems of government are becoming more and more difficult. We have ever increasing
needs in our technological fields, and our human relationships
are loudly calling for an upgrading in effectiveness.

All improvements are best brought about when people
work closely together in groups. Our progress depends on
the effective functioning of nations, states, counties, cities,
business organizations, social, political and religious groups.
But the basic unit of society and the group on which most of
our success depends is the family. The family is the very
foundation of civilization. It is the most important organization in the world. It exerts the determining influence in
economics, government, business, social relations, and religion. It is from the family that we get our heredity, and
that is where much of our environment, education, love, opportunity and happiness have their origin.

The greatest of all creations took place when God formed
man in his own image. But God was not satisfied, and he said,
"It is not good that man should be alone." And so man was
made complete by the creation of a woman, and God ordained that they two should be one flesh. God himself
established the marriage relationship and ordained that it
should be eternal. God gave to this pair the miraculous joint
power of procreation. He ordained that the family should be
bound together by the power of the priesthood for time and
for all eternity. (This sealing power was given to his servants

when he said, "Whatsoever you shall bind on earth shall be bound in heaven.") After the marriage had been completed, God said, "Be fruitwul and multiply and replenish the earth." Thus God gave to man the privilege of establishing his own family, to be the basic unit throughout all of eternity.

Men and women were not only created in God's image, but they were endowed with his attributes. As one of God's attributes the scriptures say, "God is love," but God has also given to the family a substantial measure of this trait by which he himself is characterized. Love is the strongest power in the world. It is the primary emotion in life. For example, who has not wondered at the marvel of mother love born out of the miracle of motherhood! We see an ordinary human being transformed by mother love and made willing to give everything, including life itself, for the welfare of her offspring.

Mothers and fathers often forget themselves and spend their lives in toil and hardship that their children might have more of the opportunities of life. Outside of God himself, the greatest manifestation of this wonderful emotion is in the keeping of the family. By this love attraction men and women are brought together in marriage by a power that cannot be denied. Then under the right circumstances this love becomes sweeter and more holy as the years go by. Real love may sometimes be blind, but it is never weak. It can induce people to give up everything else to devote themselves to spouse, parents, or children, and the greatest of all joys comes from an exercise of true love.

Abraham Lincoln's mother died when he was nine years old. But throughout his life his relationship to her was held in the highest reverence and adoration. He said of her, "All that I am or ever hope to be, I owe to my angel mother." This godly virtue sometimes shows itself at its best when functioning between brothers and sisters. We cannot express greater feeling than to say, "I love him like a brother."

God ordained the home as the place where family members could get together and feel the closeness and affection of each other, as each supported and upheld the other family members. Just suppose that you had no family and no home to go to. The home is also the fundamental teacher training institution of the world. Here people without academic degrees or training in pedagogy can acquire an excellence in guiding others equaling the untaught perfection of the mother of Abraham Lincoln. The home is the center of the most important public relations operation. It is the citadel of religion. It is the basis of morality. It supplies the chief ingredient of morale. It is the fountain from which all blessings flow.

During World War II War Correspondent Ernie Pyle lived among the soldiers. He saw important history in the making and men fighting and dying for what they believed. Mr. Pyle pointed out that nine-tenths of morale came from "pride in your outfit and confidence in your leaders." When a soldier is fighting for his life, few things can give him greater satisfaction than to know that he is supported on all sides by associates sharing his objectives, with courage, ability and ideals to match his own. He also likes to know that standing at his head are honest, capable leaders who know their business and are worthy of his greatest confidence and admiration.

But life itself has been compared to a kind of war, and the primary battle unit is the family. What a thrilling experience and what a tremendous advantage to belong to a loving family where parents are united in the same vital religious convictions and where all of the members are happy, faithful, righteous, capable, true-blue members of their basic unit.

It might help us to understand family importance by asking what a good father is worth, or what price would you place on a mother's faith, love and loyalty. We might be able to answer this question if we could understand what the love of God is worth, or how the value of his loyalty and honor could be measured and appraised. God has given to the family an extra amount of love for each other member. And he has given to the family itself an added significance in the eyes of each member.

It might help us to place a proper value upon the individual members of the family if we were to determine how much we would be willing to pay to get one back once he were lost? We have often had this question answered in a very real way. For example, in the fall of 1953 some evil people kidnapped little Bobby Greenlease of Kansas City, Missouri. The next day the kidnappers wrote his parents a letter and said, "We will let you have him back for $600,000." The money was furnished and if possible they would have been willing to pay $600 million or $600 billion to get Robert back unharmed. If a mortal life is worth so much, how much would an eternal life be worth, and what would we be willing to pay to get it back once it were lost? Or what should we be willing to do to prevent it from getting lost?

We are told that the worth of souls is great in the sight of God, and it is certain that they would be worth a great deal more in our own sight if we had a proper understanding of our true situation.

Some years ago Ethel Lynn Beers wrote some stimulating verses involving two brothers. One had great wealth but no children. The other was very poor and had a large family. The wealthy man wrote a letter offering to exchange a large part of his goods for any one of his brother's seven children. The question to be decided by the parents was

WHICH SHALL IT BE?

Mrs. Beers says —

> Which shall it be? Which shall it be?
> I looked at John; John looked at me,
> And when I found that I must speak,

My voice seemed strangely low and weak:
"Tell me again what Robert said;"
And then I, listening, bent my head.
        This is his letter: "I will give
A house and land while you shall live,
If in return, from out your seven,
One child to me for aye is given."

I looked at John's old garments worn:
I thought of all that he had borne
Of poverty, and work, and care,
Which I, though willing, could not share;
I thought of seven young mouths to feed,
Of seven little children's need.
        And then of this.
        "Come, John," said I;
"We'll choose among them as they lie
Asleep." So walking hand in hand,
Dear John and I survey our band:
First to the cradle lightly stepped,
While Lilian, the baby, slept.
Softly the father stopped to lay
His rough hand down in a loving way,
When dream or whisper made her stir,
And huskily he said, "Not her."

We stooped beside the trundle bed
And one long ray of lamplight shed
Athwart the boyish faces there,
In sleep so beautiful and fair.
I saw on James' rough, red cheek
A tear undried. Ere John could speak
"He's but a baby, too," said I,
And we kissed him as we hurried by.
Pale, patient Robbie's angel face
Still in his sleep bore suffering's trace;
"No, not for a thousand crowns not him,"
He whispered, while our eyes were dim.

Poor Dick, bad Dick, our wayward son—
The turbulent, restless, idle one—
Could he be spared? Nay, he who gave
Bade us befriend him to the grave;
Only a mother's heart could be
Patient enough for such as he:
"And so," said John, "I would not dare
To take him from her bedside prayer."

Then stole we softly up above,
And knelt by Mary, child of love,
"Perhaps for her 'twould better be,"
I said to John. Quite silently
He lifted up a curl that lay
Across her cheek in a wilful way,
And shook his head: "Nay, love, not thee"
The while my heart beat audibly.

Only one more, our eldest lad;
Trusty and truthful, good and glad;
So like his father, "No, John, no,
I cannot, will not let him go."
And so we wrote, in a courteous way,
We could not give one child away;
And afterward, toil lighter seemed,
Thinking of that of which we dreamed,
Happy in truth that not one face
Was missed from its accustomed place;
Thankful to work for all the seven,
Trusting the rest to the One in Heaven.

But one of the most important facts in the universe is that God did not design our lives merely for this vale of tears alone. Not only is life eternal, but love is eternal, and we have the sure word of God that under certain conditions the family unit may be eternal also. It was intended by God to go on unbroken forever. The scriptures say, "Whatsoever God doeth, it shall last forever." Mortality is but a period of preparation, a rehearsal for the real thing. We know that God himself has a family. He has already made us acquainted with his Only Begotten Son in the flesh. But Jesus was also the spirit offspring of God in heaven. Paul calls him the firstborn among many brethren. (Romans 8:29) We know that we are also the children of God. A great latter-day poet has written:

In the heavens are parents single?
No, the thought makes reason stare.
Truth is reason, truth eternal
Tells me I've a mother there.

One of the greatest concepts of the religion of Christ is the eternal continuance and eternal glory of the family. It is just as inconceivable that God intended our family relationship to end after a few years of mortality, as that he intended his own relationship with his son Jesus Christ to end, after the son's thirty-three years of mortal life. Of that relationship Jesus said, "And now, O Father, glorify thou me with thine own self with the glory which I had with thee before the world was." This wonderful relationship also indicates our own possibility. People and particularly the sexes are incomplete singly, and individuals cannot be perfected alone. Speaking of the fathers, the Apostle Paul said, "That they without us should not be made perfect." (Heb. 11:40) Neither can we be made perfect without our families.

One of the most destructive of the doctrines of Satan is his philosophy of marriage that says, "Until death do us part." Andrew Jackson said, "Heaven would not be heaven to me without my wife." And you can depend upon it that heaven will not be heaven to you without your wife, or without your children. Neither will it be complete without having the family bound together exactly as God has ordained. It is not good for man to be alone in this life, but it would be many times worse to be alone throughout eternity. Someone has said, "I desire no future that will break the ties of the past." We know that Jesus clung to his family association.

Just before his death he said, "I came forth from the Father, and am come into the world: again, I leave the world, and go to the Father." (John 17:28) Certainly Jesus here shows no inclination to be a part of this damaging philosophy of "until death do us part." God has ordained marriage "for time and eternity." Some of the important purposes of this life are to get our bodies, form our families, develop our personalities, and qualify for eternal life by proving our righteousness. Then our ultimate destiny is that we may become as our Heavenly Father, with quickened senses, amplified powers of perception, and vastly increased capacity for understanding, godliness, happiness and love.   Without our bodies we could never have a fulness of joy either here or hereafter.   Neither can we have a fulness of joy without our families.

We love our children in this life and get great happiness from their success and righteousness.   We can only imagine what that love will be like when we are glorified and joined together according to the plan of our Heavenly Father, endowed with his pure love to live throughout eternity with a perfect body, a perfect mind, and a perfect love.   Only then can the scripture be fulfilled wherein we are commanded, "Be ye therefore perfect, even as your Father which is in heaven is perfect."

The Fiery Serpents

THE HOLY BIBLE is filled with many interesting accounts of the great experiences of the past. From these accounts we can learn a great many things, and get some helpful patterns by which to guide our lives. I have often felt very sorry for those who lived before printing made it possible for us to share in the interesting experiences of those living in other lands and in ages past.

The Old Testament centers around God's attempt to mold a great nation out of a group of people who for hundreds of years had lived as Egyptian slaves. In order to teach obedience and self-control, God gave the Israelites work to do and obstacles to overcome. He gave them eternal success principles to live by, and he tried to make clear to their minds the important differences between right and wrong.

On one occasion as the Israelites were making their difficult way toward their promised land, they became discouraged and rebellious. They were passing through a barren country with very little water to supplement their monotonous diet of manna. In their discouragement they did what people frequently do when in difficulty. They began speaking against their leaders and criticizing God.

But one of the universal laws on which all progress is based involves correction, and punishment for wrong doing. Sooner or later we must all learn that sometime the books must be balanced. The Old Testament itself is a long series of rewards for good and punishment for transgression. As a part of the schooling that the Lord was giving to the chosen people, it had to be understood by them that disobedience could never go unpunished; otherwise the spirit of irresponsibility and lawlessness would completely take over. The lives of children or adults can easily be spoiled when tantrums are honored and wrongs 'rewarded. It always has a detrimental effect upon us to get wealth without effort, to receive opportunity without responsibility, or to commit transgression without blame.

Before they began their journey, the Lord made an agreement with the Israelites that he would make them a favored people if they would obey his commandments. We know the troubles that both nations and individuals get into when covenants and promises are not kept. A judge in San Francisco recently said that very few people who appear before him ever honor their oaths. Even after men and women have been sworn in to important government positions, many of them have given out valuable secrets to those who would destroy the very country they have promised to protect. Others use their sacred office to further their own selfish ambitions. In the presence of moral decay, graft and corruption always flourish.

However, the most important covenants are broken in our dealings with God. And when any wrongs are allowed to go unnoticed and unpunished more serious violations are bound to follow, and even eternal life may eventually be lost as a consequence.

Therefore, following the rebellion and disobedience of the children of Israel, the Lord imposed their punishment by sending fiery serpents among the people. Many were bitten and over three thousand died. Other thousands suffered severe discomfort and unpleasantness because of the bites and their fear of the serpents. The serpent has always been the symbol of evil. It has been the special symbol of the evil of disobedience. These particular serpents were probably called "fiery" serpents because of the intense burning pain caused by their bite which was often severe enough to be fatal. Snakes are always particularly repulsive. The

scriptures say that the serpent was cursed "above all cattle."
The mere presence of a snake produces a feeling of hatred
and dread in most people. What a difficult ordeal it must
have been therefore for the Israelites to be forced to live
with these hateful fiery serpents among them. The heat,
hunger and fatigue of the desert were bad enough, but *these*
difficulties must have been minor compared to the unpleasantness, tension, dread and fear of attack, caused by these
loathsome, deadly serpents crawling everywhere and striking from every ambush.

In any event, it was not long before the Israelites had
had their fill of fiery serpents. Then they were very sorry
for the sins that had brought the snakes upon them. They
now decided to try and undo their wrong in order to get rid
of the serpents. Accordingly the people went to Moses
and said. "We have sinned, for we have spoken against the
Lord and against thee; pray unto the Lord, that he may take
away the serpents from us." Moses did as the people re-
quested, but the Lord was not quite ready to recall their
punishment. It is not always as easy to terminate the effects
of evil, as it is to set it in motion. All diseases are more
easily contracted than cured. Anyway, the Lord declined to
remove the serpents. It may be that he felt it necessary to
keep the Israelites reminded that punishment was always
close at hand. It might also help *us* to keep out of trouble
if we knew that a dozen loathsome, fiery serpents were always
on duty and were looking in our direction.

However, the Lord did offer the Israelites a compromise
solution for their problem. He instructed Moses to mold a
fiery serpent out of brass, and lift it up on a pole where all
the people could see it. Then the Lord said, "And it shall
come to pass that everyone that is bitten, when he looketh
upon the brazen serpent shall live." Obediently Moses made
a serpent of brass and put it up on a pole. Its polished surface shone like fire, and whosoever was bitten could save

his life by looking upon the serpent of brass. (Nu. 21:4-8)
Of course, the people were still not freed from the burning
pain and the inconvenience of being bitten, nor could they
get away from the fear and dreadful loathing they felt in
the presence of their evil, unwelcome, disgusting guests.

The brazen serpent that was made by Moses under the
command of God continued in Israel until the time of Heze-
kiah, by which time it had become an object of worship
because of its power to save people from death. (II Kings
18:4)

Jesus himself gave this idea of the brazen serpent its
greatest significance however when some 1500 years after
this experience in the wilderness, he used the brazen serpent as a symbol of his own power and said, "As Moses lifted
up the serpent in the wilderness, even so must the Son of
man be lifted up: that whosoever believeth in him should
not perish, but have eternal life." (John 3:14) It would
probably be very difficult to find a more helpful idea in our
own interests. Like the Israelites we are surrounded on every
side by sin and trouble. We are being continually bitten
by the evils that we bring upon ourselves. And whether
we fully realize it or not, we are still subject to the law that
requires us to pay the penalty of every wrong. As no one
can do a good deed without sooner or later receiving a reward, so no one can do an evil deed without sometime suffering a penalty. The consequences of evil may not always
be as immediate as a serpent bite, and yet sooner or later a
satisfactory settlement must be made, and it is still as though
some fiery serpents were awaiting behind every bush of
wrong doing to sink their hot, poisonous fangs into our
sensitive flesh.

The effect of sin upon the spirit, is also very similar to
that of a bite on the body by a poisonous serpent. Certainly
sin causes us much greater unhappiness than snake bite, and
its consequences of spiritual death are far more serious. The

damaging effect of sin was known even before this earth was created. Lucifer was banished from heaven because of his own evil. And God himself cannot look upon sin with the least degree of allowance. His aversion to sin is undoubtedly far greater than would be our loathing of ugly, poisonous serpents crawling over us. God knows the unhappiness and destruction that always comes from sin, and he wants to protect us from it, just as we would want to protect our children from a group of rattlesnakes making their nest in the living room. Yet to remove sin from the world and make it impossible for us to do wrong would also make it impossible for us to see good and evil side by side and would thereby destroy the free agency and the opportunity for personal development that God so much desires us to have.

God is very anxious that our lives become something of which he can be proud, and we must climb to glory by our own choices. The opportunity for growth must not be denied us, and God has fully provided for our relief when we are bitten by the deadly thing called sin. Jesus took our evil upon himself. He suffered severely for our transgressions, but as Moses lifted up the serpent in the wilderness to save the lives of the Israelites, so was our Redeemer lifted up upon the cross to save us from suffering and death. And if we look up to him in faith, and if we repent of our sins and follow divine instruction, we can free ourselves from the harmful effects of the fiery serpents of our own transgressions.

It is an interesting fact, however, that even after Moses had lifted up the brazen serpent in the wilderness, with God's sure promise of relief, there were some Israelites who chose to die rather than to look upon it. I suppose they must have felt a little bit embarrassed to run the risk of having anyone think that they were gullible enough to believe that by looking upon a brass image they could cure themselves of snake bite. Therefore, even after the solution of their problem had been provided, many still lost their lives, not because death was inevitable, but because they would not believe and obey God's commandments.

We have many of the same problems in our own day. Christ has made us offers of peace, happiness and prosperity, if we will only live the principles of the gospel. By centering our minds on him and following his instruction we can save ourselves from death, and live with God forever in eternal happiness and glory. Whereas if we follow our own devices we may die from the serpent bites of our own sins. Most people have always refused to follow divine directions, and even now as a result of *our* present rebellion and disobedience, the world is teetering back and forth on the very brink of disaster. It looks as though many of us will *personally* go to destruction because we will not look to God.

How foolish to refuse to believe in God! How foolish to disobey the little easy, simple commandments required to bring about our eternal salvation and happiness! When the Prophet Elisha gave Naaman the opportunity of curing himself of his leprosy by washing himself seven times in the river Jordan, Naaman became angry and said, "Are not Abana and Pharpar, rivers of Damascas, better than all the waters of Israel?" (II Kings 5:10-12) And that may have been so. But it was only after he had done as he was commanded that he was cleansed of his leprosy.

In the United States we have also set up a standard for ourselves by writing on our coins "In God we trust." But again we don't look, and our actions indicate that we actually put our trust in other things.

On one occasion when Alexander the Great was ill he received an anonymous letter warning him that his physician intended to poison him while pretending to give him medicine. The physician came to see Alexander as the letter had predicted. The physician poured out some medicine and handed it to Alexander. The Emporer, looking his friend full in the face, drank the contents of the goblet and then handed the doctor the letter. Alexander trusted his friend because he knew him. He knew of his skill as a physician, of his integrity as a man, and of his devotion as a friend. The seeds of doubt planted in the letter, intended to incite Alexander's mistrust, found no root.

Certainly we should have enough confidence in God to take his medicine. Emerson once said, "All that I have seen teaches me to trust God for that which I have not seen." We should remember that God is still trying to get us to keep our covenants and become a royal priesthood and a holy nation. But our progress is very slow. Rebellion, disobedience and the fiery serpents of sin are still taking their toll among us. The resulting loss of blessings is not because such a loss is inevitable, but because we do not take advantage of the means provided for our deliverance.

Faith in God is the basic principle of the gospel. Obedience to his law is the divine order of the universe. All blessings are available to us if we will only look up to him who is our Savior and Redeemer. "For God so loved the world, that he gave his only begotten Son, that whosoever believeth in him should not perish, but have everlasting life." John 3:16)

A Fighting Heart

THE DICTIONARY describes the heart as a hollow, muscular organ, which by contracting rhythmically, keeps up the circulation of the blood. In human adults this little engine is about five inches long and 3½ inches broad. It has a conical form, placed obliquely in the chest, with the base or broad end upward and to the right.

In the last few years there has been introduced into the world enough marvels and wonders to stagger the most vivid imagination, but none of them have yet come close to equaling this magnificent little invention called the human heart.

Sometime ago I woke up in the middle of the night and listened to my heart as it worked away at its job. I thought how much I owed to this two and one-half pounds of muscular dependability. My heart pumps a full load about 70 times per minute, and has kept up that pace hour after hour and month after month for well over half a century. It doesn't matter whether I am standing up or lying down or standing on my head. It doesn't matter whether I am asleep or awake, running or walking, working or resting, it keeps itself regulated at exactly the right speed for every occasion. Sometimes it pounds like a sledgehammer, and sometimes it purrs like a kitten, but the most scientific timing device in the world couldn't make it any more accurate or efficient. It has never once had to be cleaned, repaired, regulated or have its valves ground. So far as I know my heart has never missed a single stroke in 60 years.

Some of my other personal equipment is a little faulty. Because I have not properly trained my brain it is inclined to be disturbingly forgetful at times. And I thought about the trouble I would be in if my heart should forget to beat for just a few minutes. But I go to sleep each night with a reasonable assurance that *it will not forget,* but will stay on the job throughout the night. And I hope its dependability will continue for a good while into the future. The heart itself goes without sleep, without rest and without any outside supervision or food supply. It not only keeps the pumps going but it also makes sure that the temperature controls, the disease fighting forces, and all of its other subsidiary duties are always in full operation, assuring me that in the morning I will still be in business. Yet with all of this responsibility it doesn't have to be reminded, compensated or stimulated to do its work.

I don't understand just how my heart got its job or its ability in the first place. I don't understand when it started to work, or why it keeps going. I don't know from what source it gets it devotion, its motivation, or its seemingly perpetual motion, but I am very grateful for all of this wonder and dependability.

But pumping blood is not the heart's only job. It is also the headquarters for life itself. In a little different way it is the seat of the emotions. It is also the power plant of success, for when one puts his heart into what he is doing, every accomplishment is assured.

Solomon said, "Keep thy heart with all diligence; for out of it are the issues of life." (Prov. 4:23) When the heart isn't on our side, failure is just around the corner, then we start developing faint hearts or tired hearts or hard hearts. A fearful person is said to carry his heart in his mouth. If a person is seriously discouraged his heart is said to sink into his boots. Sometimes we get weary, unenthusiastic, lazy hearts or allow wickedness to take over its operation and control.

The Bible says, "Blessed are the pure in heart." Impurities in the heart can easily kill all of our chances for success.

We know of the harm that can be done by allowing frustrations, heartaches, disappointments, or sin to get into this control center of our lives. The Bible speaks of "faint hearts," "deceitful hearts" and "perverse hearts." It calls one man a "backslider" in his heart. These degrading emotions, unworthy ambitions or destructive thoughts in our hearts always cause a severe deterioration to take place in our conduct.

On the other hand, there are a lot of ways we can help the heart. We have a common expression in which we say, "This will do your heart good." Solomon said, "A merry heart doeth good like a medicine." (Prov. 17:22) The Bible speaks of "a willing heart," "an understanding heart," and a heart filled with wisdom and righteousness.

The roadside billboard of an oil company proclaims that, "A clean engine produces power." But so does a clean heart. Lord Tennyson tells Sir Galahad's secret of success by saying, "His strength was as the strength of ten because his heart was pure." This is always true. Probably next in importance to a pure heart is a valiant heart, one that is filled with courage and determination. We sometimes call such a heart "a fighting heart." It is an interesting fact that like a good soldier, everyone is constantly waging war; not a war against anyone, but a war for everyone. Everyone should constantly be fighting a war for his family, his country and his God. He is fighting for peace, respectability, righteousness, security, and happiness. Life itself has often been compared to a battle and our antagonists come in many shapes and sizes. We need to wage a constant war against lethargy, sloth, sin and ignorance, especially in ourselves.

Abraham Lincoln fought against melancholy and despair all of his days. When anyone lays down his arms, his troubles immediately begin to increase.

There is nothing that failure, error or sin loves quite so much as peace. For years Hitler, the assassin and troublemaker, cried out to the nations, "Let us alone, we want peace." The communist dictators are continually pleading for peace. They want to be let alone while they carry out their announced purpose of enslaving the world and murdering helpless peoples. Evan Satan wants peace. In the synagogue at Capernaum, the spirit of the unclean devil cried out with a loud voice, "Saying, Let us alone; what have we to do with thee, thou Jesus of Nazareth? Art thou come to destroy us? . . ." (Luke 4:34) Sloth and lethargy also cry out, "Let us alone. We want peace." Ignorance wants nothing quite so much as merely to be let alone. The loudest plea of idleness is that it does not want to be disturbed. The chief cry of every criminal and every sinner and every delinquent is to be let alone. They all want peace. But every righteous man, every seeker after success, everyone ambitious for righteousness, or devoted to happiness, or in quest of freedom, everyone in search of justice and truth, every scholar and every leader, every thinker and every prophet must be a warrior continually engaged in war. The moment we relax our fighting effort we are in danger.

In his novel, *The Citadel*, A. J. Cronin has the faithful young wife say to her slipping husband, "Don't you remember how you used to speak about the future, that it was an attack upon the unknown, that it was an assault up the hill, as though you must take the castle on the hilltop?" The failing, half-hearted husband replied, "I was young and foolish then." When the spirit quits fighting, the mind is soon taken captive. When enthusiasm is lost for the fight, the battle of the mind soon ends in failure and defeat.

But it is always a thrilling thing to contemplate a truly great fighter, whether he functions as an individual or stands at the head of a great nation. A real fighter is one who has his mind centered on righteousness and his blood filled with a passion for victory. A great fighter counts it a pleasure always to be on his feet going the second mile. He has the ability to make long marches on short rations, and he is able to hold his ground in the face of the most severe difficulties. He welcomes challenging problems to solve. In our lives we too frequently become what Emerson calls "parlor soldiers," we like to dine nicely and sleep warm, but we shun the vigorous battle of life where strength and accomplishment are born. We pray for ease and peace and prosperity, we think of comfort, enjoyment and rest; and in the process we become sluggish, soft, lethargic, sinful and lose the spirit of our own success.

One of the great success stories of all time centers around the lion-hearted King Richard who ruled England in the latter part of the 12th century. Richard organized a crusade to go to the Holy Land to dispossess the Turks of the Sepulcher. However, the expedition was unsuccessful and Richard himself was captured and confined to a foreign prison.

During his absence, traitors at home took over the government, and when Richard finally effected his escape and returned to England, it was necessary for reasons of his own personal security that he come disguised in plain, unmarked armor. Then quietly he gathered about him a few of his faithful followers, with the idea of putting England back in the hands of its rightful rulers.

One of his first moves after this little battle group had been assembled was to attack the castle at Torkelstone, a stronghold of the enemy in which Ivanhoe, the friend and follower of the King, was wounded and imprisoned.

When Ivanhoe heard the noises of assault beginning to take place outside the castle, and because of wounds and loss of blood he was unable to raise himself from his couch, he asked his nurse, Rebecca, to stand by the window and tell him what was taking place outside. And the first thing that he wanted to know was who the leader was. Of course, that is the first thing that anyone wants to know about any undertaking.

Ivanhoe asked Rebecca to describe the insignia or other marks of identification on the armor of the leader so that he would know who he was, and what their chances of rescue were. But Rebecca reported back that the leader fought in plain, unmarked armor and that he had no insignia or marks of identification. Then Ivanhoe said, "Then describe how he fights, and then I will know who he is." That is, everyone has a set of activities about as characteristic as his fingerprints. So Rebecca tried to describe this great warrior clad in plain, unmarked armor as he swung this ponderous ax with thunderous blows, assaulting this castle stronghold almost single-handed. Rebecca said, "Stones and beams are hurled down from the castle walls upon him, but he regards them no more than if they were thistledown or feathers." She said, "He fights as if there were twenty men's strength in his single arm." Again she said, "It is fearful, yet magnificent, to behold how the arm and heart of one man can triumph over hundreds."

Ivanhoe could think of no one but the King. He said, "I thought there was but one man in England who might do such deeds." But he believed the King to be a prisoner in an Austrian dungeon. I suppose that Richard's arm wasn't really any stronger than many other warrior's arm, but that is not where strength comes from. Rebecca had said, "The arm and heart of one man." Richard was fighting with his heart. He was fighting for England, and when anyone begins fighting with his heart, then things really begin to happen.

Then Ivanhoe paid this tribute to an unknown leader. He didn't know who this man was but he knew the qualities and always characterized great accomplishment, and he said to Rebecca, "I swear by the honor of my house, I would endure ten years of captivity to fight a single day by that great man's side in such a quarrel as this." Captivity would have been the greatest punishment to which Ivanhoe could have been subjected, and yet he said in substance, I would gladly languish ten years in a dungeon cell for the privilege of fighting by the side and under the banner of a great man in a great cause.

We who engage in the work of human betterment are also fighting in a great cause, and the only other question that we need to ask ourselves is, "How will we fight?" And in one of the greatest scriptural passages, the Lord himself has given us the answer. He said, "Oh ye that embark in the service of God, see that ye serve him with all your heart, might, mind and strength, that ye may stand blameless before God at the last day." (D&C4:2) That commandment makes us all warriors; and the adoption of that attitude will make every accomplishment easy and every victory certain. We do not read our futures in the stars. We read them in our own hearts. Therein is the center of every success. Therefore, may we keep our hearts with all diligence and be valiant fighters for righteousness.

A Four-Square Life

WE HAVE many interesting words and ideas that always bring us a profit when we adequately think about them. Some of these interesting thoughts are connected with the idea of a "square." The dictionary says that a square is a "parallelogram having four sides of equal length and four right angles." For an example of a square we might think of a checkerboard, or the squares into which our cities are divided.

But one of the most challenging uses of this interesting word is found in its application to people. One of the greatest compliments that we could receive, would be to have it truthfully said of us, that we were always on the square. When we have an important job to do, we square our lives with the fundamental principles of achievement, and then we square our shoulders to bring the accomplishment about.

One great man said that no accomplishment could ever have real acceptance that did not square with the word of the Lord as found in the Holy Scriptures. The plan of salvation itself has on occasions been referred to as the four-square gospel. Certainly the Lord wants four-square men and four-square women who can fit his four-square program. Life itself is a four-sided affair, and a four-square life must be one that has all of its sides in proper balance. Certainly life loses much that is worthwhile when it becomes lopsided.

In living a four-square life as in other worthwhile things, Jesus is our finest example. In recording the progress of Jesus, Luke gives us this stimulating line. He said, "And Jesus increased in wisdom and in stature, and in favor with God and man." (Luke 2:52) Jesus increased along all of these important fronts at the same time. He increased in wisdom; that is, he increased the mental side of life. He increased in stature; that indicates his physical progress. He increased in favor with God; that represents his spiritual attainment. And he increased in favor with man; that points out his social advancement.

Suppose we use this as a pattern for our own growth. It was with this scripture in mind that Mr. W. H. Danforth, the founder of the Ralston-Purina Company, adopted the checkerboard has his company trademark. Then Mr. Danforth wrote a stimulating little book about his own four-square program called I DARE YOU, in which he challenges others to follow the formula of Jesus.

Just suppose that we think of these four sides of our own lives as the four sides of a square checker. We might think of the horizontal line forming the top of the checker as representing our own mental development. The right hand vertical side stands for our physical development. The base of the checker represents our spiritual development. And the left hand vertical side shows our social development. Actually we have four lives to live instead of just one. We live physically, mentally, socially and spiritually. And this gives us a four-fold opportunity to make progress.

We also have four major instruments of accomplishment —a body, a mind, a heart and a spirit. These are the tools of our progress and represent the greatest of our life's opportunities.

Jesus gave outstanding emphasis to two sides of the square by making them the two greatest of all of his commandments. He said, "And thou shalt love the Lord thy God with all thy heart, and with all thy soul, and with all thy might, and thou shalt serve him with all thy strength." This relationship with God must always be the base of a four-square life. Then Jesus named the social side of the square as being next in importance. He said "And thou shalt love thy neighbor as thyself." John Locke helped to make the square complete by saying "a sound mind in a sound body is a short but full description of a happy state in this world."

Man was designed by God as the masterpiece of all creation and our greatest human concept might well be that of a perfect development in each of these four main departments of life. It might help us to borrow the scout oath with one phrase added, and then take our own pledge to make ourselves physically strong, mentally awake, morally straight, and socially useful.

Suppose that one at a time we hold our four lives up for review and consideration as to how they may be improved. One of the greatest wonders of the world is a beautiful, well-developed human body without which we could never have a fulness of joy, either here or hereafter. Greece reached her golden age only after her people had developed strong, vigorous, healthy bodies. That was the basis for all of their other accomplishments. The Spartans thought of themselves as children of Hercules and they trained themselves accordingly. A healthy body is the dwelling place best suited for a clear mind, a pure heart, and an enthusiastic spirit.

The Apostle Paul referred to the human body as the "temple of God" and indicated its importance by saying, "If any man defile this temple, him shall God destroy. For the temple of God is holy, which temple ye are." Man's body was designed for an eternal life. God did not intend us to be physical weaklings with ailing bodies filled with sickness and disease. In our age tending toward soft living, we sometimes let this wonderful body lose its Spartan qualities and become flabby and unfit. What a terrible distortion of a four-square life to saturate our tissues with alcohol, poison our bodies with nicotine, or weaken them with sin, so that the lines of this wonderful image fashioned after God's own likeness becomes blurred and indistinct. We should have bodies sufficiently strong to bear the weight of an eternal life.

Even if we were merely trying to be effective athletes, we would eat only wholesome food, recommended for the training table. We would get regular hours of sleep and undergo a vigorous, body-building program that would make us alert, resistant to disease, and ready for every test, and any accomplishment. But life is much bigger than a football or basketball game and if we are to be successful in life, we must maintain a high physical score by always being fit and full of energy and healthful enthusiasm.

Many years ago the great British Prime Minister Disraeli declared that, "The health of the people is the foundation upon which all of their happiness as well as the power of the state depends." He said, "The health of the people is the first duty of a statesman." Physical, mental, spiritual and social health is also the first duty of every individual. To discharge this duty effectively we must square our shoulders and be at our best physically, mentally, spiritually and socially.

In George Bernard Shaw's play "Pygmalion" the professor assumed the task of taking a flower girl from the slums and making her into the finest lady. In his instructions he said to her, "Think like a duchess, act like a duchess, talk like a duchess." Gutter language keeps one in the gutter. Gutter thoughts keep one in the gutter. The mind of a lady makes one a lady. The mind of a general makes one a general. "As a man thinketh, so is he."

The human mind was designed to be man's presiding officer to draw the blueprint for his success, and to build the roadway of his accomplishment. God gave man dominion over everything upon the earth, including himself. The appetites, passions, urges, fears, emotions, hopes and ambitions must be stimulated, guided and controlled by the mind. The first and greatest victory of every man should be his victory over himself. A great philosopher once said, "To be conquered by one's self is of all things most shameful and vile.

This conquering and direction of ourselves is the field of our greatest responsibility and opportunity.

Most of the far regions of the earth have now been discovered, but there is still plenty of room for some mental Columbus's and some thinking Peary's, and some planning Admiral Byrd's. Someone has said that the biggest room in the world is the room for self-improvement. Mental adventure can provide twice the thrill that ever comes from physical adventure. We can feed the mind on the greatest ideas. We may even nourish our mental selves with the word of God himself as it is found preserved for us in the Holy Scriptures.

Theodore Roosevelt died with a book under his pillow. He was consuming the greatest ideas of others until the very last. There are many treasures and wonders on the bookshelf that are waiting to give us pleasure if we will only discover them. Robert Louis Stevenson always kept two books handy—one to read from and one to write in. Early in everyone's life he ought to get the notebook habit, as one of the best ways to strengthen the mental side of his life.

Then we come to the social side of our life's square. That is the side that regulates our relations with other people. That is the "service to our fellow men" side of life. The scouts have a very substantial idea of doing a good turn to someone every day. How can we better fulfill the instruction of Jesus to love our fellow men than to serve them? Just suppose that you select five new people this month to show a real friendship for. Just suppose that you do some particular courtesy or thoughtfulness to five people and see what happens. At the end of a month you will have five new friends. But you will also have a deeper capacity for friendship and a far richer personality. In addition, think how greatly the friends themselves will have been helped! Our most valuable possessions are those that can be shared without lessening. In fact, our most valuable possessions actually multiply when they are shared. We should practice the philosophy of always having a little encouragement and some helpful ideas to give to others on every occasion. The philosopher said

> All who joy would win must share it
> Happiness was born a twin.

The social side of life is one of doing things. The kind of people that Jesus liked most were the doers. We have lots of talkers, there are plenty of heads filled with knowledge, but there are not many people whose lives generate effective action.

During the Spanish-American War, Theodore Roosevelt instructed his soldiers that, "There should be more shooting and less shouting, fewer words and more work. Words alone will not win a war, nor plow a field, nor construct a home, nor build a great nation, nor develop a productive personality. There must also be discipline, industry and service. Wearing the uniform does not make a man a soldier. A soldier is one who does things." Even faith dies when works are omitted.

Then we come to favor with God, which is the base of our checker. This involves the development of our spiritual health. Man is primarily spirit. One great man told of climbing up a trail toward a mountain peak. His five-year-old grandson was struggling to keep up. "Are you tired, Jimmy?" the grandfather asked. "My legs are tired," replied the grandson, "but myself isn't." Myself was Jimmy's spirit. Climbing this trail was a great adventure for five-year-old Jimmy. Climbing the greater trail of life will be an even greater adventure for a twenty-year-old Jimmy, or a thirty-year-old Jimmy, yes, even a fifty-year-old Jimmy. As long as his spirit is in good condition, Jimmy will continue to climb. Tired? Of course, his body will get tired. But as long as Jimmy has a vigorous spirit to urge him upward,

Jimmy will continue to reach higher peaks of accomplishment and give greater blessings of service. If this side of our nature is not adequately developed, then we begin to suffer from a dreadful lopsidedness. So often we are overfed on one side of our natures, but look dismally thin and starved on the other.

We remember the lopsided man who came out of the tombs in the land of the Gardarenes to meet Jesus. He had an unclean spirit. (Mark 5:5) This man reminds us that most of us have a job of housecleaning our spirits that needs to be done. Living right can be so much more pleasant than living wrong. Doing good is a far more thrilling experience than doing evil. Physical sickness robs us of time, courage and money. But spiritual disease takes away our relish for living, destroys accomplishments, and even jeopardizes eternal life itself.

It would be a poor general who would attack the enemy on three fronts and then lose the advantage by retreating on the fourth. Just so, it is poor strategy in the battle of life to stop with three-fourths of a victory when a complete triumph is within our reach. Spiritual success is our greatest "do-it-yourself" project. In the past we have left far too much of our spiritual development to the teachers, preachers, parents and friends. It is not possible to put on the radiant side of life just once a week like a Sunday suit and hope for a four-square life. Paul said to his young friend Timothy, "Stir up the gift of God which is within thee." That is a great idea. We must keep the base of our lives solid if we would avoid lopsidedness.

It is wonderful to say our prayers every night, but they are not worth very much unless we take vigorous action on them tomorrow. We have spent billions of dollars to get a man into his orbit for a few trips around the earth. But a four-square life can get us into the orbit of God in the Celestial Kingdom forever.

The Gift of Courage

MANY YEARS ago the late Paul Speicher wrote a magnificent little book entitled *The Gift of Courage*. In it he challenges our thinking with some interesting questions. He says, "If, as a gift, you could have your heart's desire, if you could have your fondest wish fulfilled, what would it be? Would you choose a million dollars, abounding health, a solution of your business worries, or would you choose to escape from those ills of life that are common to all men. What would make it easiest for you to solve your daily problems?"

Mr. Speicher points out that there is one gift that will best enable you to enjoy because you have fought, to rest because you have labored, to reap because you have sown. This magnificent gift lies within your easy reach. It will clear the troubled roadway ahead and set your feet firmly upon the pathway of real happiness. But only *you* can give it to yourself. This gift is the gift of courage.

Mr. Speicher says that greater than intellect, experience, ability or foresight, is that fighting edge that one has when he is not afraid. Then with self-confidence and enthusiasm he answers the call to each day's struggle, and generates the drive that will carry him on to victory.

James L. Allen says that you can never do anything worthwhile without courage. Next only to honor, courage is the greatest quality of the mind.

Then Mr. Speicher says, "Give yourself the gift of courage. The courage to act now. The courage to meet the problems of life each day, to do those things that must be done. Without this gift we tend to sit and wait for fairer

days while life slips through our listless fingers and is lost.
For always when we waste life, life wastes us."

O. Henry tells the story of a New York artist, who
planned the masterpiece of his life. His picture was to be
colossal. Those who heard him tell of his plans were thrilled
by his conception. The work he expected to accomplish
would send his name echoing forever down the ageless cor-
ridors of time. It would make him the companion of the
immortal da Vinci and the magnificent Rembrandt. But he
couldn't start the picture today. Things weren't right.
A touch of rheumatism, a lack of enthusiasm, a gloomy
day, or a bad light held him back. His postponement continued from week to week until one day they found him
dead. His friends took up his lifeless body and buried it
with his masterpiece still unborn.

But you also have an unborn masterpiece. Someday
you will do great things. Someday you are going to make
a record that will surprise everyone. Someday the world
will be startled by your accomplishments. Then you will
surmount the troublesome problems that worry and dis-
courage you. Someday you will cease to stand idly outside the banquet hall of life, but you will work your way
inside where the table of good things awaits you.

However, the fabric of life is growing thinner every day,
and many die before their masterpieces have been painted.
Therefore, give yourself the gift of courage today. Take the
first step now towards those wonderful goals that you have
always talked about. Don't allow your dreams to be buried
with you. The gift of courage will enhance the glory of
your life.

Then Mr. Speicher says, "Give yourself the courage to
keep on trying." He asks when is a man a failure? Is he a
failure when his business falls off, or when he stumbles in
his effort? Is he a failure when he makes a mistake or when
his goals are not realized? Disheartening as these things may

be, they do not make any man a failure. A man is a failure only when he quits trying and contents himself to live at less than his best. We should write this truth deep into our hearts and come back to it again and again. No one belongs to himself alone, and we have no right to stamp the ugly sign of failure on our foreheads for want of the courage to try again.

If you could look into the inner life of almost any successful man, you would find long months and longer years when nothing that he did seemed to bring results. You would find him, time and again, despairing of the achievement that he sought. And yet you would find him working on in spite of his despair. He finally became a great success because he kept trying. If he had stopped trying, at that very moment he would have been a dismal failure. But thank God for the courage to try again.

Washington met the most serious adversity at Valley Forge, but he didn't stop. Lincoln fought despair and melancholia all of his life, but he kept on going. Paul the Apostle said, "I fight on lest I myself should be a castaway." And Jesus said, "He that endureth to the end shall be saved." Then give yourself that gift that makes you continue to climb the mountain of life. And when you slip back, may you have that sublime quality that keeps you from shedding a tear.

Give yourself the courage that led Henley, a hopeless cripple, to sing victoriously,

> It matters not how straight the gate,
> How charged with punishments the scroll;
> I am the master of my fate,
> I am the captain of my soul.

Give yourself the courage to build a philosophy of life by which you can live as God intended. Granted integrity and intelligence, most men need only a little added courage to rise to the stars.

Give yourself the courage to meet life's little tests. The things that batter down morale and make us feel that we can never again pick up the load, are not the big things but the little things, not the grave emergencies, but the insignificant irritations. A thousand and one petty disturbances gnaw at our patience, upset our poise, and work us into a state of nervous instability, until we feel that we can no longer stand the strain. It is these little things that stretch us on the rack until the cords of poise and patience break.

Usually we can find the courage to face life's big tests. What we need most is the courage to follow the routine of life, the courage to stick to our plans, the courage to keep petty distractions from sidetracking our efforts, the courage to keep going hour after hour and day after day. We need to give ourselves the courage that strengthened the heart of Columbus and held him steadfast while he sailed into unknown seas. And through the dark days and stormy nights, enabled him to greet his fear-stricken sailors with the cry of faith and say, "Sail on! Sail on! Sail on and on!"

Then give yourself the courage to utilize your full potential. We remember the story from the old fifth reader of the lion cub lost in a flock of sheep. As he grew up he ran and played with the sheep and behaved like a sheep, and he believed that he was a sheep. Then one day on the distant skyline there appeared the silhouette of a great lion. His head was thrown back, his tail was lashing about him. With a great roar, the lion on the hillside sent his voice across the fields of the valley below. Then the lion playing with the sheep stopped his playing. Something stirred within him. Like was calling to like. Then he knew that he was a lion and not a sheep, and with an answering roar that sent the timid sheep scattering before him, the lion with the sheep ran to join the lion on the mountainside.

Sometimes we go on and on through life while the lion sleeps within us, never realizing that our lot in life is not in the meadows with the sheep, but on the mountainside with the lions.

Some of us never really make an earnest attempt to arouse and to utilize the potential power that creation has placed within us, because we are satisfied to measure our records against the ordinary. We have far too much satisfaction in mediocrity. The man who is only average is as close to the bottom of life as he is to the top. The average man frequently lays aside creation's design for his life and accepts mediocrity in its place.

Once upon a time when a middle-aged man was clearing out the rubbish from his attic, he discovered an old notebook that he had kept as a boy. Its pages were discolored by the years, but it contained the plans that long ago he had set down for himself. It mentioned great things to be done and definite ways of doing them. It told of a life that someday would amount to something. He would make a name that would be reckoned with. The man sat down on the attic stairs and slowly read each page, without the heart to throw the book away. It was the biography of the man he meant to be. It was the specifications of the man that he might have been. The dreams of his youth had not become the accomplishments of his later years, because he had become content to measure his efforts and their rewards by those of average men. Think what it would mean to someday meet the man you might have been. The poet says:

> Across the fields of yesterday,
> He sometimes comes to me.
> A little lad just back from play,
> The lad I used to be.
>
> And yet he smiles so wistfully,
> Once he has crept within.
> I wonder if he hopes to see
> The man he might have been.

Give yourself the courage to dream of the man you may become. This God-given ability to dream great dreams was not given us to mock us. Therefore give yourself the courage to say

> Though everything looks dark and drear
> I shall succeed.
> Though failure's voice speaks in my ear,
> I shall succeed.
> I do not fear misfortune's blow.
> I tower with strength above each foe.
> I stand erect because I know
> I shall succeed.
>
> Night swoops on me with blackest wings,
> But I'll succeed.
> I see the stars that darkness brings,
> And I'll succeed.
> No force on earth shall make me cower
> Because each moment and each hour,
> I still affirm with strength and power,
> I shall succeed.

Give yourself the courage to believe with Paul that, "All things work together for the good of them that love God." The world is planned for good. Night is as necessary as day. Labor is as important as ease. Uphill is as good as downhill. Sickness and death serve us quite as well as health and strength. The test is, whether we love God, whether we think right, whether we have the courage to do the best we know. We should never let the consequences of right frighten us. We should be as brave as the little boy who used to be awakened night after night screaming because of a repeated nightmare in which he met a great tiger. He was so affected by his nightly terror that his parents counseled with a physician who said to the little boy, "The next time you dream about the tiger, say to yourself, 'This nice old tiger hasn't come to hurt me. He wants to be my friend. I am going to walk right up and pat him on the head.'"

The boy agreed, and that night the anxious parents stole into his room. There he lay tossing nervously in his sleep. Then they saw his face whiten, his breath grew shorter and through tightly closed lips the father and mother heard a desperate little voice saying, "I am not afraid. I know you want to be my friend. I am going to walk right up and pat you on the head." Then the little boy smiled in his sleep, and the parents knew that the tiger would never again send him screaming from his bed. Give yourself the courage to meet the tigers of life.

Fears, problems and discouragements are all a part of life. But they do not come to hurt us. If we love God every problem will be our blessing in disguise and we will hear the voice of the Master saying to us, "Lo, it is I, be not afraid." May God help us to live at our best by giving to ourselves the gift of courage.

Gratitude

WE HAVE a very interesting custom among us of setting aside special days on which we think about special things. For example, we set aside the second Sunday in May as Mother's Day and we let our minds reach up and try to understand the purposes for which the day was set apart. We set apart the third Sunday in June as Father's Day for the same reason. And somebody has pointed out that the human mind has some of the qualities of the tendrils of a climbing vine. It tends to attach itself and draw itself upward by what it is put in contact with.

We have some other interesting days when we put our minds in contact with other wonderful ideas. We have Easter and Memorial Day and Christmas. We set aside the fourth day of July as our nation's birthday. This is the day when we think about our freedom and try to understand what it means and what it has cost, and what our lives might be like if it were lost.

Then as one of the most interesting and beneficial of all of our special days, we set aside the fourth Thursday in November as Thanksgiving. This is a day when we count our blessings and express our thanks for the many good things of life. On this day we try to build gratitude into our lives by thinking and doing those things appropriate to this day. It is an interesting fact that as we identify and recount our blessings we increase their power to benefit us. Of all of the virtues, gratitude is one of the most beautiful as well as one of the most worthwhile. Cicero, the ancient Roman statesman, calls gratitude "the mother of virtues." For once it is established in one's life, it begets a whole line of the most worthwhile posterity.

Gratitude and goodness are almost synonymous terms. They are inseparably united in people's hearts. It would be very difficult to be grateful without being good, or to be good without being grateful. Gratitude is one of those capital virtues that should be most eagerly sought and enthusiastically practiced.

Our great country was born in gratitude as the Pilgrim Fathers knelt at Jamestown and Plymouth Rock to thank God for their lives, their freedom and each other. Then when the first harvests were gathered in their new land, a time was set apart for prayer, feasting and thanksgiving. The virtue of gratitude is not only one of the most helpful to *us*, but it is also one of the most pleasing to God.

Jesus himself is our greatest exemplar of this godly quality. Jesus was always giving thanks for even the most simple things. There was a continual daily outpouring of his spirit to God. The sacrament is a prayer of thanksgiving coupled with a promise to remember. Most of the miracles of Jesus were preceded by an expression of gratitude.

But sometimes we can understand a thing best by thinking about it on both its positive and its negative sides. That is, gratitude shines brightest when contrasted with the dismal vice of ingratitude and the blight and heartaches that go with it. And just as gratitude is the mother of virtues, so ingratitude becomes the mother of evil.

Swift said, "He who calls a man ungrateful sums up all the evil of which one can be guilty." And Shakespeare said, "I hate ingratitude in man more than lying, vainness, babbling, drunkenness or any other taint or vice whose strong corruption inhabits our frail blood."

One of our greatest literary classics is Shakespeare's masterpiece *King Lear*. Here Shakespeare shows us ingratitude at its naked worst, as ungrateful children tread upon the disappointed broken heart of their sire. As King Lear began to get old, he decided to place the affairs of the empire in younger hands, and accordingly divided the kingdom between his two daughters. Immediately after the transfer had been completed the children turned upon their father, and their ingratitude with its companion sins, drove him insane. In his despair and heartbreak the old king said: "How sharper than a serpent's tooth it is to have a thankless child." He said, "Ingratitude, thou marble hearted fiend more hideous when thou showest thee in a child than in a sea monster." Then Shakespeare wrote his famous lines saying:

> Blow, blow thou winter wind
> Thou art not so unkind
> As man's ingratitude,
> Thy tooth is not so keen
> Because thou art not seen
> Although thy breath be rude.
>
> Freeze, freeze thou bitter sky
> Thou dost not bite so nigh
> As benefits forgot.
> Thou, thou the waters warp
> Thy sting is not so sharp
> As friend remembered not.

But Shakespeare's tragedy also serves us as a kind of miniature reflection of what often takes place in the larger family of God, where we frequently see people receive gifts and then turn against the giver. The two greatest of the religious commandments are largely built upon gratitude. One has to do with our devotion to God, and the other with the love and service we render our fellow man. God is our Father. He created us. Our interests are his interests. He gives us life and vitality. He lends us breath. He enlightens our minds and quickens our understandings. Every day he sends us energy, food and vitality from the sun. More than any other thing he desires our eternal exaltation. He has a holy hunger for our success and happiness.

Then how frequently we show ourselves like the unworthy children of King Lear as we repudiate God's teaching and commit sins that are repulsive to him. We commonly take his name in vain and treat him with such ingratitude and disrespect as would break the heart of any godly Father. In King Lear, Shakespeare tried to show us how far this vice can go. Ingratitude in children can bring parental torments sufficient to unbalance their minds. But how much more intense must be the suffering of our Eternal Father when his children are unfaithful. When Jesus took upon himself our sins, the torment caused him to sweat great drops of blood at every pore. But vicarious suffering does not stop here. King Lear also suffered for the sins of his unrighteous children, and this is the burden and most serious unhappiness of many parents.

The scriptures tell of a woman whose daughter was possessed of an evil spirit. In great agony the mother came to Jesus and said, "Have mercy on me, oh Lord, . . . my daughter is grievously vexed with a devil." Jesus told the woman that his mission was only to the lost sheep of the house of Israel. But although she was not an Israelite she would not be put off. She continued to cry, "Have mercy on me." She was suffering for the affliction of her daughter. She did not say to Jesus, "Help my daughter." She said, "Help me." She didn't say, "My daughter is suffering"; she said, "I am suffering." Then in granting her the blessing she sought Jesus said to her, "Be it unto thee even as thou wilt." And her daughter was made whole from that very hour. Jesus didn't say, "Be it unto your daughter as thou wilt," but he said, "Be it unto *thee* even as thou wilt." The mother's suffering was relieved only when her child had been cured. And so it must always be with good parents, including God.

Think of the suffering we could lift from others if we cleansed ourselves of evil, for not only God and our parents but everyone else suffers for our sins. A challenging poem has been written entitled:

HOW MANY HURT

"Suppose," said I, "you chanced to see
A small boy tumble from a tree,
How would you tell that tale to me?"

"Why, Dad," said he, "I'd simply say
I saw a boy get hurt today.
And two men carried him away."

"How many injured would there be?"
I asked. "Just one, of course," said he.
"The boy who tumbled from the tree."

"No, no," I answered him, "That fall
Which hurt the lad brought pain to all
Who knew and loved that youngster small.

"His mother wept, his father sighed,
His brothers and his sisters cried,
And all his friends were hurt inside.

"Remember this your whole life through
Whatever pain may come to you
Must hurt all those who love you too.

"You cannot live your life alone,
We suffer with your slightest groan,
And make your pain and grief our own.

"If you should do one shameful thing,
You cannot bear alone the sting,
We spend our years in suffering.

"How many hurt, we cannot state,
There never falls a blow of fate,
But countless people feel its weight."

—Wisconsin Public Service Co.

And some of the worst of our sins and the most painful of our sufferings are caused by the base evil of ingratitude.

On the other hand, what a beautiful and uplifting grace is thankfulness. Gratitude and appreciation are primary parts of worship. And just as there are very few things that can make an earthly father feel better than sincere appreciation from his children, so also our Heavenly Father is pleased when we show our appreciation in our worship. And who is more entitled to our gratitude than God? We would be most grateful to a friend who gave us money, land or other wealth. Then why aren't we more thankful to him who gives us the freedom and command of the whole earth? He gives us the blessing of life and health and our families and our reason and his eternal glory. Then why should we so frequently think of ourselves as under no obligation to God? What ambition could be more worthwhile than gratitude to our Heavenly Father? Shakespeare cried out, "Oh God who lends me life, lend me a heart replete with thankfulness." The worship that is most acceptable always comes from a thankful, cheerful, loving heart. And our main Thanksgiving prayer might well include Kipling's phrase, "Lord God of hosts, be with us yet, lest we forget, lest we forget."

Seneca says, "If I only have the will to be grateful, I am so." But again eternal vigilance is the price of safety, and we can fall into this ugly sin of ingratitude almost without knowing it.

I know of a man who has a rather severe physical affliction. This affliction has aroused a sympathy in other people that has caused them to go out of their way to help him. Through a long practice of receiving favors, he has come to expect them as a right. Probably because his attention has been so centered in himself he has never learned to be grateful. Although he is now in comfortable circumstances financially, he continues to receive favors but renders none. To his mind his affliction gives him a kind of immunity from the normal calls of service required of others.

In hiding behind this shield where he is protected from the normal bumps and jars of life, he has become unduly critical. Unconsciously relying on the fact that others will not fight back, he accepts kindnesses, and then treats his friends in some measure as King Lear's daughters treated their father.

It is so easy to develop an attitude toward life similar to that of a child who demands everything of a parent, and then after the service the parent is rejected as King Lear was rejected and as God is often rejected. We frequently get as many favors as we can from life and from God, but we render as few as possible. Therefore every day in some degree we are re-enacting the tragedy of King Lear in our own lives. To accept favors and give none is ingratitude, but to accept favors and give injury is sin. Ingratitude in us even deprives God of some of his ability to help us. And John Bunyon has said, "He who forgets his friend is ungrateful to his friend; but he who forgets his Savior is unmerciful unto himself."

What a thrilling day we have in Thanksgiving, a day set apart to build the traits of gratitude and appreciation more solidly into our lives, and may God bless us in our effort so to do.

His Many Mansions

ONE OF THE most interesting of all of life's great questions is recorded in the 13th chapter of Luke. Luke says, that as Jesus went through the streets and villages teaching ". . . said one unto him, Lord, are there few that be saved?" (Luke 13:23.) In the language of our day this man might have said, "Lord of all of the billions of God's children who live upon the earth, how many will be saved in the kingdom of heaven?" This question was not only a very important one for the people of that day, but nothing could be more important to us. What are our chances for earning happiness and success for that interesting period which lies beyond this life? Apparently Jesus did not consider the question as an improper one in any way, and yet he did not give his questioner an answer. Instead he used the question as a kind of text upon which he gave to those around him a brief address on some other subjects. He may have purposely evaded the question, because his listeners were not prepared to understand the answers, or he may have given them an answer that was not recorded. We know that a very large majority of the answers of Jesus never got into the Bible. If all of the recorded sayings of Jesus were put together they could be read in about thirty minutes. Whereas, the Apostle John says, "And there are also many other things which Jesus did which if they should be written every one, I suppose that even the world itself could not contain the books that should be written." (John 21:25.)

Not only were most of the statements of Jesus left out of the Bible, but even those that were put in were not generally believed by the people who heard them. And one of the doctrines that they seemed especially confused about was how many would be saved. Like many of the people of our day, some of those who lived in the time of Jesus believed that there were only two places for people to go after the resurrection; one was called heaven and the other was called hell. Some believed that all of those who didn't qualify to live with God in heaven were consigned to dwell forever with Satan in hell. But, in the great discourse given to the Apostles immediately prior to his death, Jesus helped to set us straight when he gave a partial answer to this important question. He said, "In my Father's house are many mansions." (John 14:2.) Nothing could be more reasonable than the great Christian doctrine that in the future life there will be as many mansions or gradations of conditions, or degrees of glory, as there are degrees of merit in the lives of people. This idea is further explained by the Apostle Paul, in writing to the Corinthians about the resurrection, he said, "There are also celestial bodies and bodies terrestrial. But the glory of the celestial is one, and the glory of the terrestrial is another. There is one glory of the sun, and another glory of the moon, and another glory of the stars: for one star differeth from another star in glory. So also is the resurrection of the dead." (I Corinthians 15:40-42.)

In his second letter to the Corinthians, Paul gave the names of two of these heavens or glories as the Celestial and the Terrestrial. He mentions a third, but does not give us its name. Modern revelation supplies this missing information and tells us that this lowest glory is called the Telestial. Paul very aptly compared these three degrees of glory to the respective brilliancy of the sun, the moon, and the stars. There are also gradations within these three general subdivisions, for Paul says, "One star differeth from another star in glory. So also is the resurrection from the dead." However, Paul did not tell us very much about these various glories or who would qualify for them. What information could be more important to our salvation than this, and yet it is not given any place in the Bible? although it was plainly mentioned, indicating that it was taught as one of the doctrines of Christ.

However, in 1832 the Lord again took up this subject, this time through the Prophet Joseph Smith and Sidney Rigdon. The prophet tells us of this circumstance as follows: "For while we were doing the work of translation, which the Lord had appointed unto us, we came to the twenty-ninth verse of the fifth chapter of John, which was given unto us as follows: Speaking of the resurrection of the dead, concerning those who shall hear the voice of the Son of Man, and shall come forth—They who have done good in the resurrection of the just, and they who have done evil in the resurrection of the unjust—Now this caused us to marvel, for it was given unto us of the Spirit. And while we meditated upon these things, the Lord touched the eyes of our understandings and they were opened, and the glory of the Lord shone around about." (D&C 76:15-19.)

Then the Lord gave one of the greatest revelations ever recorded. It fully answers the old question of how many shall be saved, and it tells what the condition of each group will be. It enables us to prejudge ourselves and determine in advance to which of these kingdoms we will belong after the resurrection. Concerning the Celestial, or the one that Paul describes as the glory of the sun, the Lord said, "They are they who received the testimony of Jesus, and believed on his name and were baptized after the manner of his burial, being buried in the water in his name, and this according to the commandment which he has given." (D&C 76:51.) He says, "These shall dwell in the presence of God and his Christ forever and ever." "These are they who are just men made perfect through Jesus the mediator of the new covenant, who wrought out this perfect atonement through the shedding of his own blood." "These are they whose bodies are celestial, whose glory is that of the sun, even the glory of God, the highest of all, whose glory the sun of the firmament is written of as being typical." (D&C 76:64, 69, 70.) This group is comparatively small in number and is the group referred to by Jesus when he said, "Strait is the gate, and narrow is the way, which leadeth unto life, and few there be that find it." (Matt. 7:14.)

It is the greatest tragedy of our world that only "a few" of God's children will ever find their way to this tremendous place called the glory of the sun. The Celestial order is the one to which God himself belongs. In it will be found the highest of all possible standards of living, the greatest possible happiness and glory. But all of those who don't qualify for this extreme exaltation will not be lost. The prophet tells of the next lower order, which is represented by the moon. Of it he says, "And again we saw the terrestrial world, and behold and lo, these are they who are of the terrestrial, whose glory differs from that of the church of the Firstborn who have received the fulness of the Father, even as that of the moon differs from the sun in the firmament. Behold these are they who died without law; and also they who are the spirits of men kept in prison, whom the Son visited, and preached the gospel unto them, that they might be judged according to men in the flesh; who received *not* the testimony of Jesus in the flesh, but afterward received it. . . . These are they who receive of his glory, but not of his fulness. These are they who receive of the presence of the Son, but not the fulness of the Father. Wherefore, they are bodies terrestrial and not bodies celestial, and differ in glory as the moon differs from the sun. These are they who are not valiant in the testimony of Jesus; wherefore, they obtain not the crown over the kingdom of our God." (D&C 76:71-79.)

Here a striking contrast is drawn between those who obtain Celestial exaltation and those who receive only Terrestrial salvation. To attain the latter one does not need to be baptized into the church of Christ nor to be valiant in serving him. In this glory will be found the honorable men of the earth according to human standards. They shall inherit great glory and will have great power and wonderful opportunity,

but they will not have a *fulness*. They will be saved, yet
they must be content with something less fine and far less
glorious than those who are exalted in the Celestial kingdom. The number qualifying for the Terrestrial kingdom are
far more numerous than those in the Celestial.

Then this revelation gives a description of the conditions
of those qualifying for the lowest order of glory. They are
as far below the Terrestrial as the light of the stars is below
the luster of the bright full moon. They are they who make
their way to glory through the fires of hell, where for a time
they endure the suffering of the damned. Of this kingdom
the prophet said, "And again, we saw the glory of the Telestial, which glory is that of the lesser, even as the glory of the
stars differ from that of the glory of the moon in the firmament. These are they who receive not the gospel of Christ,
neither the testimony of Jesus. . . . These are they who are
thrust down to hell. These are they who shall not be re-
deemed from the devil until the last resurrection, until the
Lord, even Christ the Lamb, shall have finished his work."
(D&C 76:81-85) These ". . . received not the gospel neither
the testimony of Jesus, neither the prophets, neither the everlasting covenant. . . . These are they who are liars and sorcer-
ers, and adulterers, and whoremongers, and whosoever loves
and makes a lie. These are they who suffer the wrath of God
on earth. These are they who suffer the vengeance of eternal
fire. These are they who are cast down to hell and suffer
the wrath of Almighty God until the fulness of times, when
Christ shall have . . . perfected his work." (D&C 76:101-106.)

The Telestial glory is the most numerous of any of the
three orders. The Lord says that this group is "as innumerable as the stars in the firmament of heaven, or as the sand
upon the seashore." (D&C 76:109.) It may seem a little
strange to designate the Telestial order as a kingdom of glory
when within it are to be found those who have been thrust
down to hell. The answer is found in the fact that this second resurrection does not take place until after the thousand

years of the Millennium has been finished, and those qualifying for the Telestial glory will have been purified in the
fires of suffering and will have in some measure paid the
penalty for their sins.   Then, through repentance and forgiveness, their suffering will be abated.   One of the most glorious
and merciful of all the Christian doctrines is that hell has an
exit as well as an entrance, and when the sentence has been
served and retribution has been made then the prison doors
shall swing open and the repentant captive shall be brought
forth.   Not to the supreme exaltation of the Celestial Kingdom, but to the exact order to which his life entitles him.

But, even of this lowest degree of glory the prophet said,
"And thus we saw, in the heavenly vision, the glory of the
telestial, which surpasses all understanding." (D&C 76:89.)
We cannot comprehend even the glory of the lesser of God's
kingdoms of glory.   This agrees with the Apostle Paul, who
says, "Eye hath not seen, nor ear heard, neither have entered
into the heart of man, the things which God hath prepared
for them that love him."   (I Cor. 2:9.)

But in addition to the three kingdoms of glory, there is
another kingdom, which is not a kingdom of glory.   Far below the Telestial order is the place prepared for the devil
and his angels, which shall be shared with those unfortunate
few of earth's children who have sinned unto death.   These
are called sons of perdition.   These are they who have sinned
in full consciousness, they have become and remain willfully
degenerate, denying the Christ and the Holy Ghost after the
divine testimony has been given them.   The comparative few
who reach this state of extreme condemnation are doomed to
remain in hell with the devil and his angels throughout eternity.   Of these the Lord said, "Thus saith the Lord concerning all those who know my power, and have been made partakers thereof, and suffered themselves through the power of
the devil to be overcome, and to deny the truth and defy my
power—they are they who are the sons of perdition, of whom

I say that it had been better for them never to have been born."   (D&C 76:31-32)

Here then we have the Lord's own answer to the important question, "Shall many or few be saved."   The answer is that he saves all of the works of his hands except a comparatively few who will be cast out forever.   All of the rest shall be saved in one of the kingdoms of glory.

Jesus was not given the designation of "Savior" and "Redeemer" because he saves only a few.   He saves almost all of God's children, even though it requires the assistance of the fires of hell in some cases.   But by the kind of lives we live we ourselves must select the order of glory to which we will belong.   It is the law of God that we may have any blessing that we are willing to live for.   What a thrilling idea that by our faithfulness we may make our way to that wonderful place described as "the Glory of the Sun."

Honor Thy Father and Thy Mother

WHEN ONE IS able to make an important idea fully usable by his mind and personality, an exciting, uplifting improvement is bound to take place in his life. One of the most thrilling and worthwhile of these stimulating situations can be brought about by mastering the fifth commandment. From the top of Mt. Sinai, amid fire and the vapors of smoke, the Lord said, "Honor thy father and thy mother: . . ." (Exodus 20:12)

Trying to understand as nearly as possible what the Lord had in mind, I recently looked up the meaning of the word "honor." The dictionary says that honor denotes trustworthiness. In its highest sense it typifies what is right, and the course of an honorable life is always based on the highest and most worthy principles.

As an illustration of honor we might think of the life of Abraham Lincoln. Lincoln based his life on honesty, fairness and righteousness. Just before Lincoln's mother died she said to her nine-year-old. son, "Abe, go out there and amount to something." And throughout eternity Nancy Hanks Lincoln will receive honor because Abe strictly followed her direction. Forever, Lincoln's mother will receive great pride, joy and happiness that could never have come to her in any other way. But Lincoln also honored his country. He honored the people of his day and the people of all future generations will join with Nancy Hanks Lincoln to share in his glory.

If you would personally like to have a thrilling experience, just try to live what God had in mind on that memorable occasion 34 centuries ago, when out through the thunders and lightnings of Sinai came that thrilling command saying, "Honor thy father and thy mother: . . ." Or we might try to understand the feelings that God had for his own son, when on four different occasions he has said, "This is my beloved Son, in whom I am well pleased."

In giving us this ennobling commandment, God was trying to elevate us to a higher rank and inspire us to live lives of greater distinction. How can any parents experience a greater thrill of joy than that which comes from being honored by righteous children? Of course, some races and some individuals develop this trait to a greater degree than others.

Not long ago a New York judge wrote to the New York *Times* saying that in the seventeen years he had been on the bench, not one Chinese teenager had ever been brought before him on a charge of juvenile delinquency. Then P. H. Chang, Chinese Consul General in New York commented that he had heard this statement made many times before by other judges. Love of family seems to be a cardinal virtue among the Chinese. Chinese children are brought up with a great ambition to honor their fathers and mothers. Before a Chinese child does anything of consequence, he is taught to determine what the effect will be upon his parents. And what could be more ennobling to the child than this adoration of parents? How far superior is such a life to that of the young man or woman who thinks only of his or her own pleasure, and characterizes his life by disrespect and disregard for those who brought him into the world.

Of course, the home is the place where this super virtue is most readily developed. A child's disinclination toward delinquency will usually bear a direct relationship to his desire to honor his parents. If a child feels he must do something wrong in order to please ill-advised associates, he will still think the importance thus attained not worth while if it makes him ashamed in the presence of the greater love existing in his own home.

Of course, the importance of this parent-child relationship runs in both directions, and this tremendous commandment implies that the parents must merit the love and respect of their children. The children must know that their parents love truth and always stand for what is right. Then the children can always keep the compasses of their lives regulated, because the parents serve as their North Star.

What a tragedy takes place when for any reason children are cut loose from godly parental influence! There are very few good substitutes for parents, and when substitutions have been attempted all too frequently confidences have been misplaced and eternal lives have been lost.

Better than anyone else, parents are equipped by creation to perform this magnificent office of furnishing guidance for their offspring. In order to get this association off to a good start creation ordained that the first few years of this parent-child relationship should be given an enlarged importance in the eyes of both parents and children. Of course, this stimulating mutual adoration may grow weak or lapse if it is not continually merited and strengthened. For honor cannot be commanded, and love cannot be enforced. There must be mutual confidence and a stimulating example. No "do as I say, not as I do" philosophy can take the place of an actual demonstration of righteousness. We recall that stimulating line from Emerson saying, "I cannot hear what you say, for what you are is thundering in my ears."

Probably we can best develop a proper appreciation of this parent-child relationship by thinking about it on both its positive and its negative sides. That is, the opposite of honor is dishonor. Dishonor means shame, infamy, and discredit. There is probably nothing quite so tragic as children who dishonor noble parents.

Some time ago I interviewed a mother who had recently made two attempts to commit suicide, one by taking poison, and the other by slashing her wrists. She had had a very unhappy life. Her husband had been brutal and had abdicated his paternal office at a very early date, leaving her to be both father and mother.

Because of her need to make a living, her son was left alone much of the time. In the process he had fallen into undesirable company, and as he adopted the ways of sin he came to resent and blame his righteous mother. She used up her meager resources to get him out of one scrape after another. And in each transgression she was humiliated before her friends. Her spirit was demoralized and she came to feel inferior even in her own eyes. But she continued to follow her son through the filthy paths of evil until he arrived at the federal penitentiary.

His mother tried to visit him at the prison, but he would not even see her. On their occasional contacts he said bitter, unkind things causing her great anguish and a broken heart. In a desperate attempt to be a good mother she had centered her life in him, but he had responded negatively. Yet even now if she could, she would gladly take his place in the penitentiary or endure beatings, starvation or the most severe physical torture, if only for a few hours she could hold in her heart the mental picture of an honorable, godly son. Though she lives without hope in her own life she continues to pray that God will let her re-enact Gethsemane, and take his sins upon her own soul in order to leave him clean and honorable for eternity. But this mother's prayers cannot be answered by anyone except her own son, and his only desire seems to be to dishonor and torture her by his evil. Not only does his life dishonor his mother, but it dishonors God and all his fellow beings. Everyone is hurt by his evil deeds and even if the mother's next suicide attempt should be successful, how can she ever escape his sins? Or how can she forget her son, even in eternity? Her body was the mold in which he was formed. She loved him into life and has supported him with her whole soul, in return for which he will probably continue to bring her misery and torture throughout this life and eternity as well.

I have frequently tried to imagine what emotions are produced in the heart of our Heavenly Father when *his* children are dishonorable, rebellious and shameful. How could *his* suffering be less than that of a righteous earthly parent? We remember the great drops of blood shed in the pain of Gethsemane. We know that godly parents still suffer the greatest torments for the evil of their children. It is characteristic that many people still love Satan more than God. Men and women continue in their unrighteousness. God hates evil and he can never do otherwise. Therefore, our unrighteousness must always make him unhappy. In several places the scriptures refer to "the anger of the Lord." What a serious situation is involved when we go so far as to arouse God's anger! Think how sorrowful God must have felt when he decided to destroy his children by the Flood. But as regrettable as the death of their bodies must have been to him, it was less serious than to allow them to continue on in their defiling sins and thereby bring death upon their souls.

Some time ago a loving and devoted mother was bidding farewell to her son as he left home to serve two years in the army. Out of a heart overflowing with love for his fine, clean manhood and excellent spirit, she told him that she would rather have him return to her in his coffin, than to come back without his honor. Apparently the Lord also feels that physical death is far more to be desired than the spiritual death caused by sin. To this end the Lord has given us something to think about when commenting about our own future he said, "Behold, the day of the Lord cometh . . . both with wrath and fierce anger, to lay the land desolate: and he shall destroy the sinners thereof out of it." (Isaiah 13:9) "For great is the anger and the fury that the Lord hath pronounced against his people." (Jeremiah 36:7)

It is a sinful thing to grieve and dishonor godly parents. Our sins distract them in their work and we may continually torment them even though they have spent their lives in our service. But how much worse it is to distract and grieve our Heavenly Father to such an extreme that he would rather see us occupy untimely graves than to continue to live ungodly lives!

I have thought that God must feel a good deal like one couple for whom I have always had great respect. They were always very good parents. They were industrious and thrifty. They built a home that was a delight. It was the center of family devotion and love. Regular prayers were said, and blessings were asked upon all. Every possible good thing was done for the family members. The parents took real delight in helping their children to get good educations, firm convictions of faith and in every other way help them to get a good start in life.

But one of the children made it very difficult for the parents. While they were trying their best to help him he was doing the very things that displeased them most. How difficult it is to lavish praise and love and material blessings on a wicked, rebellious child who continually insists on untruth, disobedience and uncleanliness! Continuing in his evil this young man married a wife with attitudes and standards closely corresponding to his own. He broke his parents' hearts and helped to put them into premature graves. After they had passed away, he and his wife moved into the old family home. What a change in spirit they immediately brought upon it. It now reeks with the stale, unpleasant smell of tobacco and liquor. You feel the coarseness of the lives of the occupants the minute you step inside the door. Now no prayers are ever said, and no blessings are ever asked for anyone, even for themselves. The name of God goes unmentioned except in profane oaths. How could these parents be happy even in paradise with the knowledge that the family shrine they built and loved as a center of worship and family devotion has now become a den of evil, where grandchildren are being trained in wickedness to bring eternal destruction upon their own souls!

With this situation as a starting point can we imagine how God must feel when year after year, and generation after generation, the children for whom he has such great love continue to rebel against righteousness? God hates evil far more than these earthly parents and yet throughout our lives we sometimes force him to observe it day after day, night after night, and year after year.

How vigorously we should avoid sin and what tremendous privilege it should be for us to live honorably! What a great joy we should get from honoring our parents, and even more from honoring God! The scriptures are clear on the point that there is great joy in heaven over one soul that repents and turns to righteousness. And if we know the thrilling experience that we get from bringing joy and happiness to our earthly parents, how much more exciting should be the thought of pleasing God? Happiness is the purpose of life. "Men are that they might have joy." And the most exquisite joy always comes to us as we bring it to someone else. The key to one of life's most important secrets can be found in that great commandment wherein God our eternal Father has said, "Honor thy father and thy mother: that thy days may be long upon the land which the Lord thy God giveth thee."

The Hour of Decision

THE GREAT evangelist Billy Graham has a coast-to-coast religious radio program entitled, "The Hour of Decision." The central purpose of Reverend Graham's ministry is to get people to make some firm decisions about the great religious truths. One of the most destructive difficulties presently plaguing our world is our human weakness of failing to make up our minds. There can be little doubt that our indecisions in religion and in life generally are even more destructive to our best interests than are our wrong decisions. We get success by design but failure usually comes by default.

Someone once asked Billy Sunday what a person needed to do to go to hell. Mr. Sunday replied, "Not a thing." Most people go to hell only because they have never definitely decided to go some other place. Ignorance, indifference, sin, lethargy, discouragement, despair and failure are almost always mixed up with a good measure of indecision. We procrastinate, equivocate, rationalize and temporize but frequently we never quite get around to getting things settled on a definite, permanent basis.

I know of one man who almost wears himself out every morning trying to figure out whether or not he is going to shave. He feels his whiskers and thinks about where he is going, then he makes up a mental balance sheet of pros and cons and argues the point back and forth trying to get a reluctant mind to come to a conclusion. By hesitation and vacillation we sometimes so mistrain our faculties that getting a decision either for or against becomes an extremely difficult process.

The story is told of a man badly in need of employment who finally got a job sorting potatoes. He was instructed to put the big potatoes in one pile, the little potatoes in another pile, and the spoiled potatoes in a third pile. He was very grateful for the job but he soon gave it up with the explanation that he couldn't stand the constant strain of making so many decisions.

Sometimes our thinking patterns resemble those of the mental patient to whom the psychiatrist said, "Do you have trouble making up your mind?" The patient answered, "Well, yes and no."

As a contrast to indecision, Winston Churchill was once accused of being partial. He admitted the charge and said he must not be otherwise. He said he hoped the time would never come when he was impartial as between the fire brigade and the fire. But so many of us are impartial between success and failure, right and wrong, good and evil.

Because of this natural weakness in human beings, Billy Graham goes about the world asking people to "make decisions for Christ." In his large public meetings he asks people to leave their seats and come and stand before the pulpit and make a public religious commitment. He thinks that regardless of one's religious affiliations everyone should make some decisions and then make a public statement as to where they stand personally. When some of the children of Israel relapsed into their idol worship and made the golden calf, Moses said to them "Who is on the Lord's side?" (Exodus 32:26) In a similar spirit we sing a song, which says,

> Who's on the Lord's side, who?
> Now is the time to show,
> We ask it fearlessly,
> Who's on the Lord's side, who?

There are a great many people who have sung this song on numerous occasions without ever a thought of answering the question for themselves. Isn't it interesting that so many people still maintain an attitude toward the important issues of life very similar to the sports fan who continues to go to the baseball games and then cheers for both sides? This detached feeling of impartiality has a destructive influence both on our religion and on our general success in life.

Recently a university graduate student made the boast that in writing his master's thesis he had not made a single positive assertion. And there are a great many people who practice their religion largely on that basis. Their religious convictions have been neutralized. They tell themselves that all roads lead to the same place, that they are not personally responsible for what they do, and so they develop this philosophy of impartiality as between right and wrong. They frequently look on good and evil with equal favor as they cheer heartily for both sides at the same time.

It was once reported that while Pat was lying on his deathbed an advocate of deathbed repentance asked him if he had prepared himself to die by renouncing the devil. Pat replied that he thought he was in no position to start making enemies at this time of his life. Pat was cheering for both sides. But frequently we do about the same thing, and we develop that damaging kind of permanent neutrality that caused the Lord to so severely rebuke the members of the church at Laodicea. He said to them, "I know thy works, that thou art neither cold nor hot: I would thou wert cold or hot. So then because thou art lukewarm, and neither cold nor hot, I will spue thee out of my mouth. Because thou sayest, I am rich, and increased with goods, and have need of nothing; and knowest not that thou art wretched, and miserable, and poor, and blind, and naked." (Rev. 3:15-17)

Apparently the Lord was trying to get these poor folks to make up their minds as to whose team they were going to play on.

In reading some of the dialogues of Socrates I was impressed that Socrates may not have considered himself a great teacher as such. His main effort was not to get people to learn anything new as much as it was to get them to put into practice some of those things they were absolutely certain about. Twenty-five hundred years ago as now, the problem was to get people to take a firm stand on the issues that they believed in.

A few years ago Charles E. Wilson was Secretary of Defense; he once told some of his friends that he had a good job opening in the Pentagon that could be filled only by a one-handed man. When questioned a little the Secretary said that he had many people in the Defense Department who are always saying, "On the one hand this, and on the other hand that," with the result that their neutralized attitudes made them practically useless. Mr. Wilson thought that a man with only one hand might not have had that kind of difficulty.

He might have found an interesting alternative in the suggestion of Jesus when he said, "If thine hand offend thee, cut it off and cast it from thee: For it is better for thee to enter into life maimed rather than having two hands be cast into everlasting fire."

Just suppose, therefore, that we analyze our own lives and see how many important issues there are that we have personally left undecided and unsettled. For example, have we fully coordinated our deeds with our creed? If we really believe what we say we believe, then why do we do what we do? Or, how many of us have made up our minds firmly enough about honesty that we never allow an exception? Have we sufficiently made up our minds about the Ten Commandments that we are actually putting them in force? Judging from what we see on Sunday, how many have made up their minds about keeping the Sabbath Day holy? How many firm decisions have we made about self-improvement, reading the scriptures and living by what we learn?

How many of us go along year after year gathering facts and getting ideas, and then insist on maintaining the kind of neutrality enabling us to cheer with equal vigor for both sides? Many of us go to church, say our prayers and memorize the great Christian doctrines; at the same time we are reading low-grade literature, using profane language, attending immoral movies and cheering loudly for both sides. When we live the destructive philosophy of impartiality between good and evil, then the wheat and the tares are allowed to grow harmoniously together in our lives until one cannot be pulled up without dislodging the other. More than perhaps anything else, we need to make up our minds.

A famous Canadian athletic coach once said that most people in and out of athletics were hold-outs. What he meant was that we have too many reservations about things. We go into life with our fingers crossed so to speak. And when we hold out on life, life holds out on us. The Laodiceans were holding out on God. Undoubtedly many of them were fine folks. But they had too many reservations, and a substantial mental reservation makes any accomplishment impossible. A good decision with a 51% reservation is actually a negative decision. A 51% reservation means that the prize goes to the adversary by default. A decision with a 50% reservation is still no decision at all.

Mr. Aesop tells of a donkey starving to death between two piles of hay. The mule got into trouble only because his mind was equally attracted. Even a decision with a 25% reservation is at best very weak and is easily nullified by a little influence from the other side.

Mohandas K. Gandhi once said, "I hate mental reservations." So does God. The scripture says, "See that ye serve him with all your heart, mind, might and strength, that ye may stand blameless before God at the last day." There are no signs of any reservations here. We should give our minds the power of an overwhelming majority. Then we may be able to get the same dominion over our lives that we have over the members of our body. If the mind tells the fingers to

bend, they bend. However, the mind usually doesn't develop that kind of control over the emotions and the problems involved in our day-to-day living. We could get
absolute authority over our temperament and personalities
if we could just learn to get our minds thoroughly made
up and all on one side; for no one is ever defeated in the
battle of life until he allows his mind to be taken captive.
That fiery old Prophet Elijah in his contest with the wicked
King Ahab said to the wavering people, "How long halt ye
between two opinions? if the Lord be God, follow him: but
if Baal, then follow him." (I Kings 18:21) But the people
then had the same trouble that we have now. They just
couldn't decide between Ahab and Elijah, or between God
and Baal, and so the record says, "And the people answered
him not a word." Like some of the neutral nations of our
day who are looking for handouts, the people of Elijah's
time wanted to be on both sides of the fence at the same time.

Sometimes we hear an immoral person described as a
"loose" person. Psychologically, spiritually and socially that
is an accurate description. Such a person is not properly
integrated or sufficiently tightened up within himself. He
is not fused together into one piece. He is a "yes and no"
kind of person.

Abraham Lincoln once pointed out that no nation could
survive while half-slave and half-free. No real success can
survive while we are half "for" and half "against." God
provides no place for compromises with evil. There is no
half-way point between church and the movies on Sunday
evening. Satan gets easy control over the lives of people whose
neutralized minds have convictions going in both directions.
He has a fertile field among those who have made no commitments to righteousness. Billy Graham would say that
the ones who fall before the onslaughts of Satan are the ones
who have made no decision for Christ. Satan is desperately
trying to destroy success and righteousness and freedom and

truth and godliness. He is anxious that everyone should be miserable like unto himself. Satan would like to destroy America and freedom and the Church, and he knows that the easiest way to gain his purpose is to first neutralize the minds of people so that they are neither one thing nor the other. When Satan can get people cheering for both sides, then evil will have an easy win by default.

Probably the most important single influence in anyone's life is this ability to make firm decisions based on righteousness. And that includes little decisions as well as big decisions. The Reverend Mr. Graham says, "How would you like to change your life? How would you like to be forgiven of all of your sins? How would you like to be transformed into a wonderful new person?" All we need to do in bringing about any desired change in our circumstances is to firmly make up our minds to that end. The hour of decision is now. We should turn from our evil, accept the message of him who died for our sins and then be faithful doers of the word throughout our lives.

The Lord has said, "No man can be saved in ignorance." But it is also true that no man can be saved in indecision. Our eternal destiny depends upon our ability to throw off our vacillation, discontinue our procrastination and make strong, firm, righteous decisions about important things. Then our wills will not be demoralized because we are trying to hang on to righteousness and success with one hand while clinging to evil and failure with the other.

If You'll Follow the River

THERE IS A wise old Gaelic philosophy that says, "If you'll follow
the river, you'll get to the sea." This is one of those interesting metaphors drawn from the experience of travelers
and explorers to point out some of life's important relationships. To follow the rivers has always been one of the first
rules of exploration. It has saved the lives of many travelers
and guided them safely to where they wanted to go.

It would be difficult to find an illustration furnishing
a closer parallel to our success. The most important journey
that anyone ever undertakes is the journey of his own life.
And if we are to be successful in reaching the highest objectives, there are certain basic fundamental rules that must be
followed.

For one who has no tested program to guide him, life
becomes very difficult and hazardous. We should keep in
mind that not all lives have a happy ending either here or
hereafter. This fact is impressed upon us by the realism that
caused Shakespeare to make more than half of his plays into
tragedies. Shakespeare's plays were intended to portray our
lives in miniature. He said his purpose was "to hold the
mirror up to life," to show us possible goals as well as the
hazards that might challenge our success. By this process
of comparison we can also see the river highways of life in
clearer perspective.

One of the things that makes life's journey difficult and
its destination uncertain is the fact that in our daily program
as well as in our religious affairs, too many of us subscribe to
that old sectarian doctrine that all roads lead to the same
place, and that no matter what we do or which way we go,

everything will come out right in the end. Nothing could be further from the truth or more destructive to our success. *Everything* depends on which road we take and what we do along the way. If we go in the wrong direction we are bound to end up in the wrong place.

This is particularly true in the journey of life. Inasmuch as everyone is covering new ground, we need some dependable rivers to follow. We are all making our way through a region where we have never been before, yet we are permitted only one try. Because we only make this important journey of life once we must be right the first time.

Recently a 64-year-old man came in to talk about his troubles. He said, "If forty years ago I had thought as I think today, I would have done differently." Then he said, "I wish I could live my life over again." But that is ridiculous. There are no rehearsals in life. We can't rehearse birth, or life or success or death. We have only one opportunity to live. If we go in circles, lose our way, mire in the quicksands, or have to backtrack, valuable time is lost which must be deducted from our total allotment. This may mean that we will not get to our destination on time.

The early explorers, confronted with similar problems, used the rivers as their highways. They knew where each river would take them. That is a pretty good idea for us, as life also has its rivers and they are headed for different destinations. If we follow the river of industry, we will arrive at the sea of accomplishment. If we follow the river of idleness, we will come to the sea of failure. There are rivers of knowledge and right action that will lead us to the seas of wisdom and happiness. If we seek the seas of wealth, usefulness, prestige or love, we need to follow the rivers that will take us there. We should never say that it doesn't matter.

There are some rivers that lead to the exact places that we don't want to go. If one does not want to find himself in the sea of drunkenness, he should not follow the river of intemperance. If he does not want to end up in the sea of immorality, he should avoid the river of wrong thinking. It is very easy to set treacherous undercurrents in motion in our lives that will make us miss our goal. Life has its little streams, its larger creeks and its still greater rivers, and they are all headed for a particular destination. We can depend upon it that impure thoughts will awaken impure feelings. Impure feelings will arouse impure desires. Impure desires beget impure actions. Impure actions crystalize into impure habits. And impure habits make an impure life. If we follow the streamlet we will become a part of the creek and soon emerge with the river. The river of impure thoughts becomes a part of the sea of impurity, which is one of those unpleasant places that we had hoped to avoid. We have heard the interesting phrase about some people being "sold down the river." We start selling ourselves down the river the moment we begin following the wrong creek.

Recently I talked with a young man who had become involved in a great many difficulties. I asked him why he had done these things. He said that he had merely been taking a fling at life. I asked him if he didn't realize where these activities were taking him. That he was actually headed for a place that he didn't want to go had never occurred to him. He was not aware that he was moving down a forbidden river. He had not really tried even to see where he was going. He was only concerned with the immediate sensations and circumstances involved in his fling at life. I tried to point out to him that actually he was not taking a fling at life at all, he was taking a fling at death. He was headed down that broad way that leads to destruction.

Because this young man had been following the wrong course, he had already traveled far enough to separate himself from his former companions and the spirit of the life that he really desired. His fling into the field of dishonorable activities had made him an unacceptable companion to those who had previously been his friends. This had caused him to become discouraged. He now thinks that life is picking on him, and he tells himself that it is too late to change his ways. He has never learned to swim upstream, and so he drifts further and further in the direction that he does not want to go, propelled by those dominating appetites which he himself has set in motion to dominate his life. Although he is unhappy with his lot, he still does not look ahead or make any effort to visualize his final destination. He clings blindly to his unsupported hope that all roads lead to the same place, and that some miracle will give his life a happy ending, even though he follows the wrong course. He will not permit himself to realize that the river of immorality and dishonesty does not lead to the sea of honor and happiness, or that the river of irresponsibility does not lead to the sea of self-respect and prestige among his fellows. It seems impossible for him to understand that the river of idleness does not lead to the sea of power. He hasn't yet discovered that one cannot spend his energy flinging at death and still arrive at the sea of life.

Recently I talked with a young man who had just been released from serving a term in the penitentiary. He had made several inquiries about getting a job and he was very upset that his prospective employers did not always accept him with open arms. He talked a great deal about the hypocrisy and lack of charity to those who were unwilling to trust his promise to change his ways. He wasn't willing to take his medicine and by following a different course in life prove to everyone that he had learned his lesson. It didn't seem to occur to him even now, that he was the one who had brought his situation about. One of our most dependable ways of judging a man's future is by his past. After we follow the wrong rivers long enough, they begin to seem right to us. Then it is pretty difficult to get new attitudes and head for new objectives. Employers have been fooled many times by those who do not have an honorable record to back up their professions. Most people will have confidence in us if we always follow those rivers that lead to confidence.

The Prophet Joseph Smith was once asked to give the reason for his great success in the leadership of a large heterogenous group of people, gathered from all races, creeds and occupations. The Prophet said, "I teach them correct principles and they govern themselves." That is the key to every success. We need to learn to master and to follow the basic fundamental principles of righteousness and success and then every accomplishment is easy.

One of the most important of these principles is to have the right objectives and the determination to follow them. The journey of life can end in disaster when we allow too many exceptions to success or permit too many deviations from right. One prisoner at the State Penitentiary has been released and returned to prison five different times. Each time he was released he promised faithfully that his evil would never again be permitted. But he always seems to find some reason to make an exception. And when too many exceptions are made, the will is weakened and the trust of others is destroyed. Too many exceptions to honesty not only means that one is dishonest, it also means that he is a fool deceiving himself. Too many dishonorable deeds make an honorable destiny unattainable. As little streams become big streams so little sins become big sins. Appetites grow by what they feed upon just as rivers do. Little evils by themselves are important, but they are even more important for where they are leading us.

Isn't it interesting that without exception, every one of us wants good things. We want financial security, a good home, a faithful family, unquestioned honor, and a Godly spirituality. And yet how frequently we fail to follow the course that leads us in that direction. It is so easy to center our minds on good and then allow so many exceptions that we are actually going in the opposite direction without knowing it. The continual conflict that we permit between creed and deed causes confusion, frustration and discouragement in us. It gives us a split personality and makes our planned destiny unattainable. One evil soon begets another. One sin makes another necessary to cover it up. One bad habit leads on to the next. And thus we go further and further down the river of guilt until we arrive at a place which at the commencement of our career we would have died rather than to have attained.

There is a sea of eternal death, and there are many rivers that lead to it. But no one ever arrives at this unpleasant place suddenly. He merely gets started on the wrong course and before he is aware, he cannot tell evil from good. It seems to the ex-convict that it is the other people who are causing his trouble.

E. H. Chapin says that the most fearful characteristic of vice is its irresistible fascination. We are all aware of the ease with which our cherished sins can sweep away our resolution and cause us to forget our goals. Righteousness can be robbed so easily while in the embrace of indulgence. Someone has said, "Let no man trust the first false step for it hangs on a precipice, the bottom of which is lost from view, but the one who falls over it ends in perdition."

Saul of Tarsus was a man of great education and attainment. He was a member of the Sanhedrin, doing what he believed was right. But actually he was following the river running in opposition to truth. One day on his way to Damascus he was stricken down, and under the pressure of blindness he was persuaded to change his course. Then setting his sails in another direction he followed the river of righteousness and devotion. He finally arrived at the sea of peace and contentment. At the end of the journey he said, "I have fought a good fight, I have finished my course, I have kept the faith. Henceforth there is laid up for me a crown of righteousness which the righteous judge shall give me at that day." When Paul changed his course he also changed his destination. Then for our benefit he gave that great line saying, "Be not deceived; God is not mocked; for whatsoever a man soweth, that shall he also reap. For he that soweth to his flesh shall of the flesh reap corruption, but he that soweth to the Spirit shall of the Spirit reap life everlasting." (Gal. 6:7-8) In other words, Paul said, "If you'll follow the river you'll get to the sea."

Most of us may not have Paul's good fortune to be stricken down by some super-mortal means to warn us that we are off the course. We may have to make our navigational changes on our own power. But we do not need to make a mistake about our destiny or the means of getting there. The broad, basic principles of success and Godliness are clearly written out for our benefit in the Holy Scriptures and we may take a fling at eternal life by merely following the rivers that lead there. Occasionally we should check up on ourselves to make sure that we are headed in the right direction.

For at the end of the right river we will always find the appropriate sea. Judas Iscariot followed a different river than did Simon Peter and they arrived at different places. Benedict Arnold followed a different course in life than did George Washington. And whether we take a fling at life or a fling at death, it is the fundamental basic law that if we follow the river we'll get to the sea. This old Gaelic philosophy has a tremendous importance in our lives. May God grant us a vision of that sea of eternal glory and a determination to follow the river that will lead us there.

Jack the Giant Killer

Some time ago I reread that very interesting old English folk tale entitled, "Jack the Giant Killer." It recounts how, in the days of King Arthur, a giant by the name of Cormoran lived on Cornwall Island, a short distance beyond Land's End. Cormoran frequently indulged in a very bad habit of wading across the intervening bit of sea, frightening the people out of their villages, and then loading himself up with their cattle and sheep to carry back to his island.

Living in the village was a young farmer boy whose name was Jack. Jack was a very resourceful, thoughtful young man, and one day he asked his father why something wasn't done about Cormoran. Jack's father explained that Cormoran was a giant and even King Arthur's knights sought no fights with giants.

But Jack told his father that his teacher from Salsburg had explained to him that there was a solution to every problem and Jack said that he believed there was a solution to the problem of Cormoran and he intended to find it.

A few nights later Jack put an ax, a pick and a shovel into his boat and rowed out to the island where the giant lived. While Cormoran was asleep Jack dug a deep pit in front of the cave where Cormoran slept. Then just before dawn Jack sent a loud blast from his horn through the cave. The giant was very angry, and roaring with rage, and uttering threats of vengeance, he stumbled out through the darkness and fell into the hole. Jack was on hand with his ax and gave the giant a good sound thump on the head that was hard enough to solve forever the problem of Cormoran.

When the people living in the next county heard that Jack had killed the giant, they immediately ivited him to come and perform a like service for the giant that was troubling them. But when Jack got there he found that their giant had two heads, and this required a little different handling. But Jack knew that there was a solution to every problem; and all he needed to do was to find the right answer.

Jack's success at solving giant problems was soon noised around, and other requests began coming in, but every giant problem required a different answer. Some of these giants had eyes in the backs of their heads. One had a magic coat that made him invisible. One had a magic cap which enabled him to learn things no one else knew. One had a magic sword that could cut through the strongest iron. One had a pair of magic shoes that gave him extraordinary swiftness. But Jack knew that there was a solution to every problem, and when the right solution was supported with sufficient skill, courage and industry, every problem could be solved. Finally he was given the highly complimentary title of "Jack the Giant Killer."

This is far more than just a very interesting story. It is also a most worth-while philosophy of life. Our worst difficulties arise because of our inability to solve our problems properly. As one example, we see the giant nations roaring and snarling at each other and threatening to destroy the world and everyone in it because they can't solve a problem. Think what a wonderful world we could have if all of the great nations would stop creating problems and develop a little greater ability as problem-solvers. That might also serve as one of the primary objectives for our own individual accomplishment. We should, of course, keep in mind that not all of our problems come from giants. The most tiny problems are often too much for some of us to solve. We frequently fail because we spend so much time worrying about the problem, that we have no time left to work out good solutions.

We might get some helpful ideas from a famous problem-solver of the Old Testament by the name of David. David could not go into the army as his brothers did because he was too young, and so he stayed at home and looked after the family sheep. But one day Father Jesse sent David to King Saul's camp to take his brothers some food. When he arrived the camp was a scene of great confusion. A giant from Gath by the name of Goliath was challenging Saul's soldiers to choose a champion from among them to fight Goliath and decide the war by a single combat. Everyone in Saul's camp was desperately scared. In their fear no one was thinking about solutions, and it looked as though they would all soon be slaves to the Philistines.

But David had had some experience as a problem-solver. When a lion and a bear had come among his sheep, he didn't run and hide, but solved the problem by killing the lion and the bear. Seeing the confusion and the helplessness of the Israelites, David set out to help them with their problem.

He went to King Saul and said, "Let no man's heart fail because of Goliath, for I will go and fight with this Philistine." Saul pointed out the danger and called attention to the fact that David was a very young man, whereas Goliath was not only a giant, he was also the champion warrior among all of the Philistines. Goliath was clad in a coat of mail and carried a spear like a weaver's beam. But David did not abandon himself to fear as the others had done. He said to Saul, "This uncircumcised Philistine shall be to me as the lion and the bear, seeing he hath defiled the armies of the living God."

Saul tried to put his armor upon David, but David said, "I cannot go with these, for I have not proved them." Then

David picked up five stones out of the brook, and armed with his slingshot he went out to meet the giant.

Goliath was a little surprised that his challenge had been accepted by one so young, and he began to threaten and abuse the shepherd boy. But David said to the Philistine, "Thou comest to me with a sword, and with a spear, and with a shield; but I come to thee in the name of the . . . God of the armies of Israel, whom thou hast defied. This day will the Lord deliver thee into mine hand." I suppose that that is what you could call the faith that moves mountains or at least the faith that kills giants. But David also had a practical program. He put a rock in his slingshot, and as he whirled it to get up momentum, he ran to meet the Philistine. And just at the right time and in the right way, he let the rock go; and it buried itself in the forehead of Goliath. The giant fell forward on his face, and David finished the job by cutting off his head with his own sword. And the record says, "And when the Philistines saw their champion was dead, they fled." (I Sam. 17th chapter)

The problem had been solved and so David delivered his brothers' lunch and went back to the sheep. In passing it is interesting to remember that David had used his slingshot before. Unlike Saul's armor, the sling had been proven and David knew how to put enough steam behind a rock that the problem of Goliath would stay solved for a long time.

One of the great lessons of the Bible is found in this story of David, the giant killer, and this is one of those lessons that we most need to learn. In our day we are not bothered with many physical giants who steal our cattle, or threaten us with a sword like a weaver's beam; but just the same there are a lot of giants that need to be slain. Like Saul's soldiers, we have a choice between being giant killers or being their slaves, and we are also placed in servitude to every problem that we do not overcome.

Therefore, suppose that we think of ourselves as "problem-solvers" and work out some solutions to the giant fears that are giving us so much trouble and are robbing us of so much of our success and happiness. There are also some giant discouragements that are annihilating our industry and self-confidence. There are some giant doubts that are destroying our faith in God. Some of our bad habits have attained giant status and are threatening us with a life of serving evil. What we need more than perhaps any other thing is the courage and skill to be a giant killer. Too many Cormorans that should have been gotten rid of long ago are still getting fat at our expense.

An interesting thing about this situation is that everyone must kill his own giants. And certainly one of the most profitable of all undertakings is to develop our skill as problem-solvers, for we know that when we overcome the giant of discouragement, our own strength is immediately increased. But if by faith and study we destroy our doubts and settle our confusions then our strength is multiplied.

One of the best ways to improve our ability as problem-solvers is to think more about the solution, and spend less time wallowing around in the problem. A fine, middle-aged couple recently came to see me about a marital problem. To begin with they had selected each other from among all of the people in the world, and yet they couldn't get along together. They both maintained that they wanted to save their marriage. They had no other heart interests, but they seemed to dearly love to point out the problems of each other, but neither seemed to do very much about them. One of the husband's complaints was that his wife had invited her mother to live with them. He said he didn't think that was fair. I asked him how long his mother-in-law had been in their home. His wife spoke up and said that she had died more than eight years previously. I was impressed that almost anyone could figure out a solution to their problem, but that no matter how good the solution was, they would not be able to follow it because they were more interested in fixing the blame and having a fight than in making each other happy. They insisted on wading around in the mud puddle of their problem rather than in cleaning themselves up with an answer. They had created their own giant Cormoran who was robbing them of love, happiness and success.

I gave them each a couple of sheets of paper and asked them to do some homework, by writing out a clear-cut statement of their problem, and then putting down on paper as many solutions as they could think of, and bring their papers back to me in a week. It is an interesting fact that there are always several solutions to every problem. There may not be several successful solutions, but it develops one's problem-solving ability to make one's canvas of the alternatives as complete as possible, and then be able expertly and objectively to evaluate and weigh the advantages and disadvantages of each.

The trouble with Saul's soldiers was that they could only think of one way to kill a giant; and that was the impossible way of running a sword through his heavy armor. David found a spot that had no armor at all, and he also thought of a better way to do the job. David had already developed the skill with a slingshot that would enable him to put his plan into successful operation.

Many people live lives of desperation and confusion because they devote themselves to the problems instead of the answers. Because of this defect in procedure some people can't solve even the most tiny problems. For example, some intelligent people spend a lot of time worrying about occupational success, who can't get the beds off their backs in the morning. They can't kill inertia, sloth, lethargy, or indifference even in themselves. Isn't it interesting that some people spend their entire lives and never learn how to get up

on time in the morning? Try as they may they can't get rid
of the bad habits of caffeine, nicotine, alcohol, or overweight.
We consent to be the slaves of negative thinking, evil speaking, profanity and disbelief rather than develop a plan for
digging a trap in front of their caves to enable us to solve the
problems.

We read in the Bible about people who were possessed
of devils. But how much better off is one who puts himself
in the clutches of an unsolved problem, and permits himself
to be the slave of evil, being forever tormented by some
demon that he himself has created?

For many years Peter Marshall was a chaplain in the
United States Senate. He prayed "Lord, help us to be a
part of the answer, not a part of the problem." Sometimes
we make a quicksand quagmire out of a problem, and then
the more we struggle and accuse and fight, the deeper we
sink into the difficulty.

One of the worst enemies of solutions is postponement.
In the confessions of St. Augustine he pictures himself as
a flagrantly, worldly and licentious young man. He con-
fessed that the prayer of his wild, youthful days was, "Oh
God, give me chastity and self-control, but not just yet."

Referring to the Indians, Brigham Young once said, "It
is better to feed them than to fight them." That logic may
be all right for Indians, but it is no good for killing giants.
Little problems can become giants with very few feedings,
and we must either get rid of our Goliaths, or they will get
rid of us.

Keeping Up with the Joneses

DATING BACK to a time before anyone can remember, a kind of conspiracy has gone on against a particular group of people called "the Joneses." This in spite of the fact that they have probably done more good in the world than perhaps any other group that ever lived in it. Being one of the largest families, the Joneses are mixed in among us so that no one lives very far beyond their influence. Our problem arises from the fact that they sometimes upset our composure when their accomplishments challenge us to adopt a more progressive program for ourselves.

But in spite of all of our moanings and groanings about keeping up with the Joneses, yet it is still true that a good example from others is one of our most powerful success factors. The Joneses stimulate our imagination by showing us that worth-while things can be done though they may at first seem impossible to us. The pressure of a good example keeps us on our toes, for which we owe the Joneses a debt of the greatest magnitude.

A recent magazine article tells the story of a sleepy little village called Brownsville. The homes had a run-down look. The fences were falling apart and the yards were filled with unsightly weeds. But one day the Joneses moved into Brownsville. They bought, remodeled and painted one of the run-down houses. They cleared out the weeds and built an attractive, nicely painted, white picket fence around the yard. Then they covered the fence with red rambler roses. This greatly upset the status quo that had so long prevailed in Brownsville. It caused a wave of troubled consciences and inferiority complexes to sweep over this easy-going community and made most of the people feel very uncomfortable.

But important consequences soon followed. A good example frequently sets in motion a mysterious force that will not let people rest until the newly discovered virtues are luxuriously growing in their own lives. It was not very long before this uplifting force was transferred to other members of this community. A kind of self-improvement fever started to break out as people began to take a little more pride in their surroundings.

Some of the symptoms of what was taking place was the rash of white picket fences covered with red rambler roses that began brightening the face of Brownsville. Some neatly painted houses began to appear, and flower gardens greatly increased in popularity. Some of the people even began paying a little more attention to their personal situation and began to clean some of the weeds out of their own attitudes and personalities.

It was not long before the townsfolk got together, and with considerable community pride and pleasure changed the name of their village from Brownsville to Rosedale.

It has frequently been pointed out that "One man can, if he will, change the morale of a whole community." Thomas Carlyle reminds us that "we reform others when we walk uprightly." It was one of the important teachings of Jesus that "man does not live by bread alone." Everyone needs a touch of beauty in his life and an occasional dose of inspiration helps one to brighten up his outlook and make life more worth while. James T. White gave voice to an important part of this philosophy of success when he said:

> If thou of fortune art bereft
> And if thou hast but two loaves left to thee
> Sell one and with the dole
> Buy hyacinths to feed the soul.

Thomas Carlyle, Jesus and James White gave this philosophy its form, but it was left to the Joneses to put it in force in the lives of others. Getting ideas into actual operation by example goes far beyond planting flower gardens. It also reaches into the fields of developing good attitudes, a firm faith and a determined ambition which will build spiritual, social and financial success.

The story is told of a one-time complacent gentleman who owned a small-town grocery store. Its chief characteristics were the cracker barrel and the loitering place where certain idle townspeople could sit while they whittled, philosophized and chewed tobacco. But as the community grew some Joneses moved into town. They bought the property across the street, and built the most up-to-date building in town. When it opened for business the community discovered that it had a small-scale supermarket with the most modern equipment, the finest stock and the most effective marketing methods. The cracker barrel grocery man stood in his doorway and watched his former customers come out of the new store with smiles on their faces and their baskets filled with groceries. According to his own story, he was the maddest man who had ever lived. He thought that the Joneses were robbers who had invaded his territory to steal his business. He felt that they were purposely humiliating him in his own community as well as taking away his customers and friends.

After a few months he discovered that getting mad wasn't bringing his customers back, nor was it helping him with his personal problems. It wasn't legal to try to run his competitor out of town or blow up the supermarket. He didn't particularly relish the idea of starving his family or losing his business. Finally by a process of elimination he decided that the best thing to do was to imitate the vision and industry of his competitor. For the first time he realized that he did not live on the flat stationary earth that people once believed in. It seemed quite unlikely that civilization would soon slow down its pace merely to accommodate his unprogressiveness.

The stimulation he received from these new ideas caused him to take a little more honest look at himself. Then he began taking a new look at the grocery business and at life generally. He gradually became aware that the horse and buggy and the cracker barrel had gone out of style without him realizing it. He finally came to the conclusion that keeping up with the Joneses had some advantages.

His problem had been so acute and his awakening so real that the pendulum of his ambition began swinging towards the other extreme. In fact, he soon got something resembling an overdose of the spirit of progress and in the following few years he not only caught up to the Joneses, but he actually passed them. He was recently cited as the "Grocery Man of the Year" in his community. But what was even more important, he also became an industrious, successful and happy man in the process.

The power of a good example is one of the most worthwhile forces in the world. And more than most other things we need someone to actually show us the way. We need more and better real live working models of success and righteousness. It is easy to become great in the company of great men. It is easy to become good in the company of good men. It is easy to become successful when we come face to face with the principles of success in actual operation. In more ways than one, competition is the spice of life. It spurs our wills and challenges our ambitions. There are far too many people who practice the deadly philosophy of defeatism. We are frequently victimized by that terrible disease that sometimes makes failure seem more desirable than success. We need the Joneses to help us clear the cobwebs out of our brains and stir up our spirits. There is far more happiness in victory and success than in defeat and failure. And so frequently it is all in our own minds. We think, "It can't be done" until we see someone doing it. But even defeatists can't argue with actual accomplishment. Then it becomes a logical step to think that if other people can do great things, why can't we?

Without the influence of the Joneses we are sometimes left sitting around the cracker barrels of life with no one to show us more worth-while objectives or better methods of doing things. An example can sharpen our abilities and stimulate our desire to succeed. A little leaven can sometimes make the whole lump worth while if we can just get it started to work.

At first everything seems impossible. At one time no one could swim the English Channel. Then Captain Webb did it, then Gertrude Ederle did it, and since then dozens of others have done it. Until May 6, 1954 no one could run a four-minute mile. But after Roger Bannister had done it, it soon become more or less commonplace.

This great law of success applies in every field. When one studies the life of Abraham Lincoln it often starts a whole new train of the most worth-while thoughts in the mind of the student.

I once knew a young man whom I believed to be the homeliest person I had ever seen. But he had a great teacher who served him as an ideal. The fact that he wanted to be like his teacher had helped him to set his heart on getting a good education for himself. At great sacrifice he worked his way through college and then went East for further training. For a few years I lost track of him and when I saw him again I would not have believed that he was the same person. There was an interesting radiance shining in his face and there was a calm confidence in his manner. Success was manifesting itself in every part of his personality. He was no longer homely but exactly the opposite.

I thought about Socrates, who was also noted for his lack of physical beauty. But Socrates prayed, "Make me beautiful within," and then he proceeded to answer his own prayer. Socrates planted a flower garden of ideas and ideals in his mind and he became the first one to whom the term "philosopher" was applied. Philosopher means a lover of wisdom. Wisdom and beauty of spirit soon manifest themselves in the personality. The right kinds of thoughts can make the plainest body beautiful. We have all seen plain people transformed by holding beautifying thoughts in their minds and hearts. The working of a radiant personality and a Godly spirit transforms our bodies into their likeness.

The scripture tells us that even in the resurrection the degree of glory acquired by our bodies will be determined by the quality of our spirits. Only a celestial spirit will be able to resurrect a celestial body. Those who have lived well will come forth in "the resurrection of life," and those who have lived unsuccessfully will come forth in "the resurrection of damnation." It is also in the realm of the spirit where we are best served by keeping up with the Joneses, as we adopt ideals and develop virtues most readily when we see them in operation in the lives of those we love. This indicates the area of our greatest opportunity, as poverty and riches alike are largely of the spirit. The shiny new automobile in our neighbor's driveway does not stimulate our instincts to acquire, nearly as intensely as does the godliness that shines from the face and personality of an ideal. And after all, most of our worth-while abilities and virtues were transferred to us from someone else.

Jesus spoke of the power of a great example as a light upon a hill. He instructed his disciples that their lives should be such that men would see their good works and glorify their Father in heaven. This is a clear-cut case of keeping up with the Joneses. In fact, one of the primary functions of the life of Jesus was to serve as our example. When he said "Come follow me," he was challenging us to discard our sins and imitate his excellence. And just think of the effect that his life has had upon those who have followed him. A group of ordinary unlearned men were transformed by his example into something far greater than themselves. And their wisdom and philosophy is still being quoted after the passage of twenty centuries. The chief priests explained this transformation in the lives of Peter and John by saying, "They had been with Jesus." As they had tried to keep up with his example of faith and devotion they were lifted toward their own eternal exaltation.

The real worship of God is the greatest of all of our opportunities. As we keep the first and great commandment we bind ourselves to God. As we intensify our worship we immediately elevate the quality of our own lives. It's a matter of following the philosophy that says, "Hitch your wagon to a star, keep your seat and there you are." What wonderful people we could become if we would always keep our wagon hitched to the star of him who said, "I am the way, walk ye in it."

A recent newspaper article told of a group of astronomers who claimed that their life expectancy had been increased 20% because of their intense interest in such an exalted study as astronomy. But a study of God the Creator is far more important than a study of any of his creations. And by putting our lives in contact with him and properly living the gospel that he has designed for our good, we will not only increase the length of our lives but their breadth and depth as well. The greatest of all objectives is eternal life, and to help us attain it the greatest intelligence of heaven next to the Father himself was sent into the world as the standard of perfection to show us the way and light our path to eternal glory. May we devote ourselves wholeheartedly to living up to this exalted standard.

The Kingdom of God Is Within You

ON ONE occasion Jesus said to some Pharisees, "The kingdom of God is within you." A note in the King James' version indicates that he meant, "The kingdom of God is among you." And that is probably what he did mean. The term "Kingdom of God" is generally used in the scripture to indicate the church that God has established upon the earth. But in another sense we might also think of the kingdom of God as a condition, a condition embodying in us those attitudes, virtues, talents and determinations necessary to qualify us for real church membership. I suppose that even the Lord's organization upon the earth will not help us much unless we prepare ourselves to make our membership therein worth while. That is, even if we were baptized every fifteen minutes it would not solve our problems unless we made our lives acceptable to God. Many great benefits accrue to us when *we get into the church,* but the most important benefits come when *the church gets into us.*

I like to think that when Jesus said, "The kingdom of God is within you," that there may have been a second meaning reminding us that God our Father has already laid up within our souls all of those qualities necessary to bring about our own eternal success and happiness. Actually every man carries within himself the very things that he seeks. Not only did God create man in his own image but he also endowed him with a set of his attributes, the development of which is one of our greatest responsibilities. If we seek faith, we need only look within ourselves, for God has already implanted in our own hearts the seeds of faith, waiting only for us to make them grow. If we need courage, it can be found within ourselves, waiting our command.

God has stored up in the earth everything necessary for our material success and happiness. The scientists have discovered 102 different elements in nature. There are carbon, hydrogen, oxygen, nitrogen, iron, etc. These are nature's building blocks. Out of these elements in the right combinations and proportions nature fashions all of the material things of the world. Water, sugar, steel, glass or rubber can all be represented by a chemical formula.

But God *reserved* the best of the elements and stored them up in his own children. The earth is God's handiwork but man is his son, and he has endowed his children with all of the elements necessary that the offspring may become like the parent. Some of *these* elements are kindness, honor, integrity, courage, industry, ambition, diligence and faith. God has placed within us the *causes* of whatever happens to us. Brigham Young once said, "I do not feel disposed to ask God to do for me something that I can do for myself." For example, there is no need to ask God to forgive our enemies, as we can do that ourselves. Why should we ask God to make us holy, obedient, faithful and deserving? That is why he has given us the powers of reason, resolution, organization and industry. All we need to do is to learn to *use* more effectively these great powers that God has hidden within us for that purpose.

Then when we put these *personal* elements together in the right combinations and proportions, we have what someone has called "a magnificent human being." The greatest wonder of creation is a child of God at his best. The Lord said, "The kingdom of God is within you." (John 17:21) That is where we find the source of all action. Brigham Young said, "Anyone can preach, but it takes a good man to practice." It takes a good man to actually put the commandments of God in force in his own life. But we may reach any goal, either spiritual or material, by effectively using the great gifts with which we have already been endowed.

Jesus said, "Seek ye first the kingdom of God, and his righteousness; and all these *things* shall be added unto you." (Matt. 6:33) That is, we must develop the "talents" first and the "things" will follow. "Things" always follow "talents." "His righteousness" is what we get into us and then "his kingdom," "his power," "his glory," "his success," comes as a natural consequence. Both the *talents* and the *things* are all ready, awaiting appropriate action on our part.

The first atomic bomb was exploded in 1945, yet all of the necessary elements had been lying under our feet since the morning of creation. During the Dark Ages we had just as many potential wonders available to us as we have now. We had just never learned to utilize the elements of power that God had laid up in the earth for our benefit. We have recently made great progress in utilizing the potentialities of uranium. But we have not made much progress in harnessing the powers of faith or repentance, or the powers of our own wills! One of our most serious sins is that we make such an insignificant attempt to realize our God-given possibilities. Rather at the end of our days we send back to God a life with most of its potentialities undiscovered and unexplored.

The Lord expects our lives to be productive. Paul said to Timothy, "Stir up the gift of God, which is within thee." (II Tim. 1:6) He said, "For God hath not given us the spirit of fear, but of power, and of love, and of a sound mind." (II Tim. 1:7) I wonder what would happen if any one of us ever fully developed these wonderful gifts of power.

Dr. Oliver Wendell Holmes once said that a doctor who can smile, makes $5,000 per year more than the one who cannot smile. The ability to obey God, the power to love our fellow men, and the magic to exercise our own industry are also worth a great deal, though they often lie as much unused as did the uranium under the feet of our forefathers.

Paul mentioned that God had endowed us with the power of a "sound mind." But frequently that is also allowed to remain as unproductive as the fig tree that produced no fruit mentioned by Jesus. Woodrow Wilson once said, "The greatest ability of the American people is their ability to resist instruction." This would certainly apply to us particularly in the way we usually seek God's "righteousness." Our forefathers killed the prophets. But we may accomplish about the same general end by ignoring them. The world would not listen to the Son of God when he came to the earth in person, but how much better are some of us doing? We just don't seem to be able to learn the great lessons of life. We want the "things" but we are not interested in developing the talents. In general we make about the same mistake that Pilate did when he said to Jesus, "What is truth?" and then, apparently without waiting for an answer, he turned and walked out of the room.

Mr. Khrushchev, Mr. Mao and Mr. Castro are also very concerned with getting "things" even if they have to take them by force or blow up the world in the process. If Jesus had a "condition" in mind when he said "The kingdom of God is within you," we might also remember that that is also the place where the kingdom of hell is.

When we develop "his righteousness" in the right combinations in our lives, the greatest power in the world is born. Then we "stir up" this power within us, which like a slumbering giant awaits only to be aroused. God has planted the potentiality for godhood within us. All we need to do is to learn to command the shaft by which we draw out the gold.

Claude Bristol says, "The minds of most of us are allowed to become like junk-strewn attics with obsolete attitudes, rusty ideas, broken-down beliefs about ourselves and the world we live in. These self-imposed handicaps prevent our accomplishment." It is so easy to become slaves to confusion and frustration, to burden our minds with a lot of mental rubbish. We fall easy victims to fears, worries, tensions, nerves, timidities and other ills that keep us chained to mediocrity. We need to houseclean our minds and emotions, and remove every barrier that blocks off our goals. The great truths of life become known only to those who are prepared to accept them.

God does not want us to be dull, negative, unattractive or unlearned. He has said, "No man can be saved in ignorance." Ignorance is probably the most potent factor by which we set up our own limitations. God is not pleased when we live little, dwarfed and stunted lives. Jesus wants us to produce. He said, "Give, and it shall be given unto you; good measure, pressed down, and shaken together; and running over. . . . For with the same measure that ye mete withal it shall be measured to you again." (Luke 6:38) Certainly there are no limitations on our possibilities mentioned here.

Everything that has ever been accomplished has had its origin in the mind. Every building, every statue, every painting, all wealth, both spiritual and material, began with someone as a thought. Talents attract success. Every thought that we think has a literal value. The mind has a great power upon the body. For example, when someone brings you some sudden bad news you may go pale or tremble, you may even fall in a faint. Bad news can be severe enough to kill. We sometimes see one who is feeble-minded dragging his feet, stumbling over the slightest obstructions that may lie in his path. That is the natural consequence of a weak mind. A falling state of mind is always productive of a falling state of the body because every thought tends to reproduce itself in an act. Thoughts of sin, sensuality and vice reproduce themselves in acts and even change the physical appearance of the body.   On the other hand, a great faith, a great courage or a great industry in us, reproduce themselves in our circumstances as well as in our faces.   Benjamin Franklin said, "Keep up your spirits and they will keep up your body."   One man said to his son, "I know that you have it in you."   We can actually see success in some people.   God knows that there is something important in us because he put it there.   Therefore we should not pass too lightly over this second meaning of the saying, "The kingdom of God is within you."   For that is where all worth-while things are.

You may travel the world over to find wealth, success or peace, but unless you find that which God has hidden within yourself, nothing else will amount to very much, whereas if we make full use of what we already have nothing will be withheld from us.   Jesus said, "According to your faith be it unto you."   He said, "All things are possible to them that believe."   That is, he says to us, "You have it in you."   The fears and the forebodings that have dominated us in the past must be cleared away to make room for those wonderful transforming powers of faith and works.   For the moment that one really understands the fact that he can rise, then he will rise.   As someone has said, "Whether we think failure or success we will be right."

Recently in the process of a stake reorganization it was my privilege to sit in on personal interviews with 59 men, none of whom I had ever seen before.   There did not seem to be much difference between them physically, but looking into their faces and listening to their speech, and feeling of their spirit, it was very easy to realize what a great difference there was between them on the inside.   I thought of Peter at the trial of Jesus when in the palace of Caiaphas, even the servant girl knew him for what he was.   She said, "Thy speech betrayeth thee," and so it is.

We all develop identifying personality marks as characteristic as our fingerprints.   And the great difference between men is the extent to which we have developed the powers that God has already implanted in our souls. They become our most important possessions.

The kingdom of God is within you. The secret of success is within you. The power of great faith is within you. The ability for great leadership is within you. The key of great beauty is within you. These divine gifts light up and adorn the personality and make it magnetic. Whatever you become on the inside gets in your speech, takes possession of your handshake, lights up your eyes, and shines in your face in letters of light that everyone may read. It is an index to your character and a price tag indicating your value in this world and in the next. Someone has said, "You can't take it with you." But that is ridiculous. *Everything* of real value you can take with you. Our purpose on earth is to lay up treasures in heaven. We sow in this world, we reap in the next, whereas those who accumulate *things* outside of themselves lose it all at death, as there is no real wealth outside of people. "The kingdom of God is within you," and may you make the most of it.

The Lamplighter

THE tremendous book called the Holy Bible begins its history of the world in the following words, "In the beginning God created the heaven and the earth. And the earth was without form, and void; and darkness was upon the face of the deep. And the Spirit of God moved upon the face of the waters. And God said, Let there be light: and there was light. And God saw the light, that it was good: and God divided the light from the darkness. And God called the light Day and the darkness he called Night. And the evening and morning were the first day." (Genesis 1:1-5)

It is an interesting speculation as to what it must have been like before that first morning of creation. Suppose we had been present to feel the brooding, unbroken darkness that covered creation, and then imagine our feelings when in the march of progress God first said, "Let there be light."

What an exciting experience it can be just to watch the sun rise! We glory in the daily repetition of this miracle of creation as darkness is again pushed back by the rays of God's great sun, sending its beams of light across the earth. Each twenty-four hours we experience the alternating periods of light and darkness, and sense therein the eternal conflict raging between the two. The mysterious blackness of physical night periodically shuts us up within ourselves and in some degree blots out the beauty and wonder of the universe.

But darkness manifests itself among us in more than just its physical form. There is also a mental and a spiritual darkness. There is the mental darkness that we call ignorance, and the moral blackness that we call sin. Paul refers to the wicked people of his day as the "children of darkness." To be enveloped by a brooding, oppressive physical night is one thing, but our most vexing problems arise when darkness gets into our minds or lays its withering hands upon our souls.

Isaiah foresaw the approach of the apostasy from God that brought the Dark Ages upon the world, and he said, "Darkness shall cover the earth, and gross darkness the people." (Isaiah 60:2) Hopelessness and despair always possess us when this sinister condition separates us from God. All kinds of evil flourish most in the dark. When the physical light fades from the world, the dens of evil open their doors a little wider. This is only one of the reasons that from the very beginning of time people have been afraid of the dark. Darkness in one form or another is always present when degradation and unhappiness takes hold of people's lives. It seems unfortunately appropriate therefore that the final place of punishment should be characterized by a blackness, gloom and despair to match those lives that suffer there. The scripture speaks of "everlasting punishment" and describes the place where it is suffered as "outer darkness." The scriptures also tell of "weeping, wailing and gnashing of teeth." (Matt. 8:12; 22:13)

In all of its aspects the word "darkness" literally means the absence of light. (Matt. 27:45) God himself uses this term as the symbol of sin denoting the lack of righteousness. This word has also been used to stand for that dreadful condition called the second death, when the powers of evil will gain complete control of some lives so that in them only sin will flourish and decency and godliness shall die. From this final judgment there shall be no remedy, but then as the prophet says, "he that is filthy shall be filthy still."

From any possible point of view, one of the most important parts of creation took place when God said, "Let there be light," and our greatest responsibility is to more firmly establish it in our own lives in all of its forms. As the death of William Sidney Porter (O. Henry) approached he said to those surrounding his deathbed, "Lift up the shades, I don't want to go home in the dark." It is tragic for anyone to go home in the dark, and it is tragic for anyone to live in the dark. Only in the presence of light can we fill the purposes of our lives and find real satisfaction and happiness. For just as physical life cannot long flourish in the absence of sunshine, so our eternal life and happiness cannot live very long in spiritual, mental and moral darkness. Progress is brought about when we use the sunlight of truth to roll back the boundaries of ignorance, kill the germs of evil, and light the lamps of intelligence, righteousness, and happiness. Great ideas and ambitions catch fire in the presence of God's light, they light up other minds and become purifying torches to bring about eternal glory for man.

The Apostle John speaks of this greater spiritual light in about the same terms used in Genesis to describe that first morning of creation. He says, "In the beginning was the Word, and the Word was with God, and the Word was God. The same was in the beginning with God. All things were made by him; and without him was not anything made that was made. In him was life; and the life was the light of men." The record says, "There was a man sent from God, whose name was John. The same came for a witness, to bear witness of the Light, that all men through him might believe. He was not that Light, but was sent to bear witness of that Light. That was the true Light, which lighteth every man that cometh into the world. . . . But as many as received him, to them gave he power to become the sons of God." (John 1:1-12)

Jesus made announcement of his own mission by saying, "I am the light of the world: he that followeth me shall not walk in darkness, but shall have the light of life." (John 8:12) Then he gave us another important reason for being afraid of the dark when he said, "If thine eye be evil, thy whole body shall be filled with darkness. If therefore the light that is in thee be darkness, how great is that darkness."

God himself lives in light and that is where every one of us should live also. The light of God can quickly kill the germs of sin, and for this reason God has appointed light-bearers to assist in pushing back the darkness and bring happiness into the lives of his children. With this in mind the writer of Proverbs has given us a helpful figure of speech, saying, "The spirit of man is the candle of the Lord." (Prov. 20:27) And Jesus used this same idea when in instructing his disciples he said, "Ye are the light of the world. A city that is set on an hill cannot be hid. Neither do men light a candle, and put it under a bushel, but on a candlestick; and it giveth light unto all that are in the house. Let your light so shine before men, that they may see your good works, and glorify your Father which is in heaven." (Matt. 6:14-16)

The primary function of every child of God is to become an effective candle of the Lord, and assist in spreading the light of intelligence, righteousness, and understanding. Then just as the sun's rays reach out across the world, the light of Christ can banish darkness and destroy evil from among men.

Jesus is the light of the world, ordained to provide the source from which our candles may be lighted. It can help us to be more effective when we live the philosophy of the song that says:

> The Lord is my light; then why should I fear?
> By day and by night his presence is near.
> He is my salvation from sorrow and sin;
> This blessed assurance the spirit doth bring.
>
> The Lord is my light, though clouds may arise,
> Faith, stronger than sight, looks up through the skies
> Where Jesus forever in glory doth reign.
> Then how can I ever in darkness remain?
>
> The Lord is my light, the Lord is my strength.
> I know in his might I'll conquer at length.
> My weakness in mercy he covers with power,
> And, walking by faith, I am blest every hour

The Lord is my light, my all and in all.
There is in his sight no darkness at all.
He is my Redeemer, my Savior, and king.
With Saints and with angels his praises I'll sing.

Where could we ever find a more constructive employment than to function effectively as candles of the Lord?

Sir Harry Lauder used to love to tell the story of the old lamplighter in the small community where he lived as a boy. Each evening as dusk came on, the old man would make his rounds with his ladder and his light. He would put the ladder up against the light post, climb up and light the lamp, step back down, pick up the ladder and proceed on to the next lamp. "After a while," said Sir Harry, "the lamplighter would be out of sight down the street. But I could always tell which way he had gone because of the lamps he had lighted."

But in one way or another, lighting lamps has been the chief employment of all great men. Louis Pasteur was a lamplighter. He helped to dispel the clouds of ignorance and superstition in the field of medicine. He devoted his life to killing disease and giving people a longer life lighted with greater health and happiness.

George Washington was a lamplighter. He pushed back the darkness of political bondage and lighted our entire land with liberty and independence.

Abraham Lincoln was a lamplighter. In his heart he also heard the divine command saying, "Let there be light," and he devoted his life to that end. Under his stimulating endeavor, human slavery was abolished in our country, and he opened the way for equality, opportunity and human dignity among men. The light that he lighted still shines forth in a free America. Lincoln adopted the philosophy of the psalmist saying, "Thy word is a lamp unto my feet, and a light unto my path." (Psalms 119:105)

One of the greatest of the lamplighters was a contemporary of Lincoln. He was an American Prophet by the name of Joseph Smith, who was the instrument through which the Gospel of Jesus Christ was restored to the earth in this dispensation. Jesus said, "Behold, I sent you out to testify and warn the people, and it becometh every man who hath been warned to warn his neighbor." (D&C 88:81) That makes us all lamplighters. If we are to adequately prepare the way before the glorious second coming of Christ the lamps of intelligence, righteousness, and universal understanding must be lighted for all men. The place of God's presence is a city of light, there is no darkness, sin, ignorance or misunderstanding in his presence. What a thrilling opportunity to light our individual candles at this great source of supply, and then carry it to every corner of the land to help prepare the children of God to live in the "city of light."

An idea came out of India many years ago that around every individual there is an aura or a kind of spiritual atmosphere formed by his individual thoughts, attitudes, ambitions and personality traits. Our greatest opportunity is to light our lives at the eternal source of light, and then use this influence or radioactivity in us to light the lives of others.

Dr. Edward Rosenow, formerly of the Mayo clinic in Rochester, Minnesota, once told of the experience that caused him to choose the field of medicine as his life's work. When Edward was a small boy living in Minnesota, his brother became acutely ill. The family suffered severe distress until the doctor arrived. As the physician worked over his sick brother, Edward stood behind the doctor with his eyes riveted on the anxious and anguished faces of his parents. Finally the doctor turned to the parents with a smile and said, "You can stop worrying now, for your boy is going to be all right." Young Edward was profoundly impressed with the change that the announcement made in the faces of his parents. In relating the incident years later he said, "I resolved right then and there that I was going to be a doctor so that I could also go around putting light in people's faces." As a physician Dr. Edward Rosenow became a lamplighter.

One of the reasons that Jesus was called the great physician was because he was able to put the light of eternal life into the faces of people. And by following him we may also banish darkness and sin from the lives of others and make celestial glory shine in their faces.

What a thrilling opportunity that in our basic assignment as candles of the Lord we may re-enact the glory of creation as with our lives we say, "Let there be light." We may thereby fulfill the words of the prophetic hymn saying,

> The morning breaks, the shadows flee;
> Lo, Zion's standard is unfurled!
> The dawning of a brighter day,
> Majestic rises on the world.

Life's Arithmetic

THE STORY is told of a little boy who went to church with his grandmother on Easter Sunday. Up behind the pulpit, a large cross had been erected for the occasion. The little boy was very interested in the things around him, and with some of his recent arithmetic experience fresh in his mind, he said to his grandmother, "Why do they have the big plus sign up in the front of the church?"

And that is a pretty good church question. It is a pretty good business question. It also has some important applications for life itself. The little boy had been impressed with what a great difference a plus sign could make in his arithmetic answers. It could make two fours into an eight, whereas a minus sign made the same two fours into a zero. But as this little boy learns the important lessons of success, he will discover that other plus and minus signs will make as much difference in life's answers as they do in the problems of his arithmetic class. If he uses enough pluses in life he will discover that doing right is a far more thrilling experience than doing wrong. Positive thinking and living are much more rewarding than their negative counterparts. What a great difference in the result when we put some plus signs by honesty, courage, faith, industry and spirituality!

Jesus put the plus sign on good works as he kept calling for doers of the word rather than hearers only. Emerson said, "The world belongs to the energetic." That means a plus sign. A well-developed energy quickens every faculty in life.

There is far too much talk among us about the danger of wearing ourselves out by work. Dr. H. O. Thompson says that too many people are being counseled to take life easier when they should be counseled to take their responsibilities more seriously and discharge them with an increased vigor. The best way to get rested, is to speed up. For when we get ahead of our work we love it and it is easy. When it gets ahead of us we hate it and it becomes difficult. Someone has said that the tired businessman is the one whose business is not successful. We might make a similar application to our efforts in that great enterprise that Jesus characterized as "my Father's business." In either undertaking no one gets tired while he is ahead. Whether our work is physical, mental, social or spiritual, it is still true that "the pace that kills is the crawl."

It is one of the interesting truisms of life that the Lord fits the back to the burden. That calls for a plus sign. We can get a stronger back by undertaking a heavier load. We can develop greater energy and more ability by increasing our effort. Dr. Thompson believes that most people who suffer from spasms or fatigue are not really tired at all. They are merely bored or discouraged or lack of an absorbing purpose in life. These traits all carry minus signs. More rest and inactivity usually increases the problem rather than producing an answer. Good, hard, meaningful work is one of the best all-purpose medicines ever discovered.

Abraham Lincoln was once told that his eyes looked tired and that he should rest. The President replied that it was his heart that was tired, and in order to rest his heart he must go on. That is still the best procedure. Not many people ever get sick because of worth-while work. We can live long, interesting, useful lives if we have erected enough plus signs, whereas the minus signs signify evil and evil shortens our lives.

A heavy user of alcoholic beverages recently said that he did not like the taste of liquor. He said he drank it because he liked the effect it produced. When this man's affairs don't go well, or when life gets him into a corner, he just takes off and gets drunk. This banishes the feeling of reality and he loses that disturbing sense of responsibility. When liquor takes him over he acquires a feeling of importance and worthwhileness that he doesn't have when his sober intelligence is in command. But intoxication always hoists the minus sign and then we start losing things. Liquor doesn't really solve anything, but it subtracts from our dependability, impairs our health and reduces our bank balances. It destroys family happiness and the confidence and trust of friends.

This reminds us of the occasion when the old legend says that some of Satan's imps got into the display window of life's department store and mixed up the labels. They put cheap price tags on expensive articles, and expensive price tags on things of little value. They thought it great sport to see people paying the highest prices for worthless things. These Satanic imps have also been at work in the arithmetic book of life and have mixed up the pluses and minuses.

Recently a man in a state of some confusion was trying to explain his many business failures. He said, "I guess I am just too honest to be successful." Satan's imps had gotten into this man's mind and hung a minus sign on that priceless gem called honesty. And my friend had accepted the devil's evaluation at its face value. When our minuses and pluses get mixed up, then we sometimes believe that it is smart to cheat and clever to deceive, and popular to be immoral. It makes us feel important to be drunk.

Looking down to our own day Jesus said that even some of the very elect would be deceived by this confusion. (Matt. 24:24) We ourselves see this prophecy's fulfillment. Satan's imps, with a little assistance from us, have mixed up the labels, some of which say that religion is only for weaklings, that to believe in God is a sign of ignorance, and that anyone is a sissy who follows righteous principles. Actually the most courageous thing in the world is honor and honesty. The most manly of activities is unwavering obedience to God. And the most profitable business procedure is to live the gospel.

We need to unmix the labels and see that the right price tags are on the right articles. We need to go through life's arithmetic book and make sure that we understand which activities carry pluses and which carry minuses.

Irreligion carries one of life's most severe minus signs. Negative thinking has a minus sign. Profanity has a minus sign. Disobedience to God has a minus sign. All minus signs indicate that a process of subtraction is going on within us. That is how we lose our desire for good and our determination to succeed. The minus sign robs us of our strength and leaves weakness, wickedness and failure in its place. Minus signs bring deficits and require the use of red ink in our life's accounting. Any variety of poor health is written with red ink. Sickness robs us of our time, courage, money and ability. So does sin. There is far too much red ink in the accounting procedures of our lives. There are too many misunderstandings and too many refusals to look the facts in the face. The minus signs start to appear when first the negative idea gets into our thoughts.

The successful life is the one that turns the minus signs into pluses before too much red ink has been used. Good mental, spiritual and physical health places enormous plus signs up in the front of our lives. Good health is one of the most profitable and enjoyable of all of life's experiences and keeping mentally, spiritually and physically fit should never be allowed to become tedious. We should at least treat our bodies, our minds and our spirits with as much consideration as we would give to our automobiles or our animals. We should never contaminate our minds or our bodies with harmful things.

One of the most sinister inventions of our time is the coffee break. This is a period when coffee addicts guzzle down barrels of a habit-forming liquid evil. Some people can almost live on caffeine. There are others who can't do without it. The beggar's plea, "Can you spare a dime for a cup of coffee?" indicates the pressure this minus sign can exert. There are many ways in which we could more profitably spend our lives than using them up in coffee breaks. We could stand a few more prayer breaks and some repentance breaks. We might profitably use a little of this time out to stimulate our ambitions and repair our mistrained appetites.

I know a man who has been told by the doctor that he must give up smoking. He is very disturbed about it. He feels sorry for himself even at the thought of parting with his favorite bad habit. He is not at all disturbed that he never prays to God, and is ignorant of the thrilling literature of the world or the holy scriptures. He feels no regrets about violating the Sabbath Day. The principle part of his religion is to do limitlessly whatever his badly trained appetites urge him into. He has little thought for personal improvement or self-discipline. He has small concern for doing what is right. He says, "I hate the idea of standing over myself like a policeman, always telling myself I must do this or I must do that." He says, "How could it do me any good to quit smoking if I have to threaten myself with a club to get myself to do it?"

Isn't it strange that we sometimes have to stand over ourselves with a club even to get ourselves to save our own souls or bring about our own happiness? This strange attraction for evil can become almost irresistible if early in our lives we erect too many minus signs in our spiritual mental and physical tastes. When our labels are pluses we learn to love the successful, the beautiful and the godly. It is a great compliment to one when goodness is pleasant and he doesn't have to stand over himself with a club to get each righteous act in force. When it becomes difficult for us to be decent, we had better find out what is wrong with our arithmetic.

Try to imagine God on a coffee break or threatening himself with a club to keep away from a cigarette. It is impossible to think of God with a negative attitude or having a personality covered with minus signs. God loves everything that is right, and it is easy for him to be godly. On the other hand, who can imagine Satan receiving great pleasure and satisfaction in doing good and making others happy? Satan's main job is to mix up the labels, to subtract all of the possible good from our lives. What a dreadfully uncomplimentary thing it would be to have it said of us as it was of Cain, that he loved Satan more than God. (Moses 5:18) When we begin feeling a natural affinity for evil and the necessity for clubbing ourselves into doing right, then is the time that we should be giving a little more thought to our plus signs.

In St. Paul's cathedral there is a tablet erected to the memory of General Charles Gordon from which we read these stimulating words:

> At all times and in all places
> He gave — His strength to the weak
> His substance to the poor
> His sympathy to the suffering, and
> His heart to God.

What wonderful sources of strength these plus signs can be. We were all created for pluses. It was intended that we should be honorable and grateful and faithful. Our most outstanding ability should be that of addition. The life of Jesus is best represented by a plus sign. In trying to stimulate our positive arithmetic he gave us the parable of the talents. Three servants were given resources according to their abilities. Two of the servants doubled their talents. But the other was an unprofitable servant. His life bore a minus sign. He sought to justify his failure by saying, "I was afraid so I hid my talent in the ground."

This kind of fear is a minus sign. As Shakespeare says, "It makes us lose the good we oft might win by fearing to attempt." The unprofitable servant hid his talent in the ground, then he had his only talent subtracted from him by his own minus sign.

One of the thrilling parts of life's arithmetic is this wonder of addition. Our success in life will be determined by our ability to take down the minus signs of life and erect pluses in their places. Even if we don't like this program at first we will surely like the effect it produces. No limitation has been placed on the number or the quality of our pluses. A fervent belief in God is a plus. To love good is a plus. To effectively serve our fellow men is a plus. To understand the great doctrines of christianity is a plus. The truths that these doctrines stand for are all pluses, like the great cross at the head of the church. The atonement is a plus. The literal resurrection of a celestial body is a plus. Eternal life is a plus. The development of our own God-given abilities is a plus. To live the gospel of Jesus Christ is a plus.

The most effective expenditure of any life is realized in the saving of it, and we may help that process by understanding and utilizing the significance of the Easter cross, as it symbolizes the thrilling pluses of our daily lives.

The Lost Chord

SOMETIME ago a friend of mine was telling his banker about his large income. He was justifiably proud of the fact that the quality of his service had made him one of the highest paid members of his firm. The banker recognized the character, intelligence and industry, required to bring about this favorable situation. However, he pointed out that it is not what one earns but what he saves that has the dominating influence upon his financial standing.

One of our biggest money problems comes from the fact that there are so many ways of losing it. Even good investments sometimes turn sour. Errors in judgment frequently cause us serious losses. And our spending habits sometimes mean that even a large income doesn't always reach very far. This common financial experience supplies us with a very interesting analogy for some of the other departments of our lives. And one of the greatest of our tragedies in every field comes in our losses. If we are not careful we can lose our friends, our faith, our ideals, our ambitions and even our hard-won knowledge. Someone has pointed out that it's easy to become a captain, but it's hard to stay one. That applies in every field. There are many wonderful people who look like champions in their early years, but, their later life does not always fulfill the promises of their youth.

For example, in his last sad hours on lonely St. Helena, Napoleon the Great said, "What a pitiful creature I have become."

General Benedict Arnold and Apostle Judas Iscariot once basked in the promise of a wonderful future only to be victimized by a serious shortage in their own conduct. Along life's way they lost some of the traits and attitudes which if retained would have written success in big letters across their lives.

Adelaide Proctor gives us an interesting illustration of this possibility of loss in her classical music entitled "The Lost Chord." Of this experience she says:

> Seated one day at the organ,
> I was weary and ill at ease,
> And my fingers wandered idly
> Over the noisy keys.

Then by some inspiration the organist struck a beautiful, wonderful chord which Mrs. Proctor said:

> . . . Flooded the crimson twilight
> Like the close of an angel's psalm.

Like this organist, we sometimes have the experience of doing some commendable, ennobling, inspiring thing. There are certain periods in our lives when we are at our best. Then it seems that we have clear sailing, with nothing to stop us. But our total success does not depend on mere flashes of excellence. In our personal and cultural lives as well as in our finances, total success depends upon our permanent "accumulations." The big question is, how well can we hang on to what we acquire.

Jesus gave this thought meaning when he said, "He that endureth unto the end shall be saved." Judas, Napoleon and Benedict Arnold got into their difficulty because their good qualities didn't stick it out to the end. If we can just hang on to our virtues, then we can reproduce excellence over and over again. The organist in Mrs. Proctor's verse lost the chord and the inspiring music forever vanished from her life. She says:

> I have sought, but I seek it vainly,
> That one lost chord divine,
> Which came from the soul of the organ
> And entered into mine.

How frequently we have the frustrating and costly experience of losing some wonderful idea, or some great enthusiasm, or some soul-satisfying conviction. Then we are left cold and unresponsive where every effort at recovery or recall seems in vain and then the spirit of accomplishment dies.

What a tragedy is the loss of a great virtue! God can resurrect a dead body, but who can resurrect a dead faith, or a lost ambition, or a lifeless desire? Mrs. Proctor concludes her classic by saying:

> It may be that death's bright angel
> Will speak in that chord again,
> Yet it may be that only in heaven
> I shall hear that grand amen.

It may be that even in heaven we will not be able to recover those priceless riches of mind and spirit that we lose here. Our lives must be made up as we go along, and when we slip back a step, that must be deducted from our gross gain. But, we can lift ourselves to any happiness or success if we acquire and retain the right kind of ideals and emotions. The reason that some lives never rise above mediocrity is not because they have no impulse to rise, more often it is because there are too many leaks in their success.

Some of us are always getting, but never growing; we are going forward, but we are also slipping backward. The investment department of our lives is very active, but it shows too many losses and bad investments. Inspiration, information, ideas, and attitudes never come as permanent gifts, and when, like the lost chord, they once get away from us, they are sometimes pretty difficult to recover. Shakespeare gives us an interesting line in which he says, "There is a tide in the affairs of men which taken at its flood leads on to fortune—omitted all the voyages of their lives are bound in shallows and in miseries. On such a full sea are we now afloat, and we must take the current when it serves or lose our ventures."

Every day our tide goes out often carrying these inspiring flashes of faith and ambition with it. This is sometimes because these elements were not harnessed and put to work soon enough. We always intend doing a lot of things later on, but neither ideas nor faith wait on the proscrastinator. As soon as faith is isolated from its appropriate task it dies. There can be no such thing as preserved faith. Ideas or ideals never live very long in a vacuum, neither does righteousness grow strong by disuse. Many of us spend our lives in the shallows and the miseries because we let the tide slip out of our minds and take our ambition along.

Then we lose contact with the emotions and ambitions which previously impelled us to the hilltop of accomplishment. This constant devasting loss that so many of us continually suffer is further illustrated by a story in the life of Samuel Taylor Coleridge. He tells of an experience that happened in the summer of 1797. He had retired to a secluded cottage between Porlock and Linton in Devon, England, so that he could be undisturbed while doing some important writing and thinking. He had had some slight physical indisposition and had taken some medicine which had caused him to fall asleep in his chair while he was working on his ideas. He continued in a profound sleep for about three hours, at least his external senses slept, but his subconscious mind was not asleep and during those three hours it effectively put the ideas together to fulfill the very purpose of his being there.

On waking with these inspiring ideas clearly in his conscious mind he took his pen in hand and feverishly began putting them down on paper, but just as he began to write he was called out of his room by a "visitor from Porlock," on urgent business. The visitor detained Mr. Coleridge for about an hour. When the visitor had gone and Mr. Coleridge had returned to his room, to his great dismay he found that some of these valuable ideas had completely passed out of his mind and the rest had become so blurred and indistinct that they retained little meaning. They were now like images in a stream after a stone had been thrown in causing a ripple to blur the picture. Because of this interruption the impression had gone from his mind and his enthusiasm had gone with them.

This reminds us of King Nebuchadnezzar, who had a similar experience. The king dreamed a great dream but in the morning the vision had gone from him. He knew that he had received some great message, but he didn't know what it was or what it meant. The king was disturbed and offered great rewards if his astrologers and magicians would tell him what he had dreamed and what it meant.

Whether we have ever thought about it or not, this is also one of our biggest problems. All of us sometimes have great dreams and wonderful visions that we allow to get away from us, then, like Nebuchadnezzar, we don't remember the vision or why we had it. Nothing is more costly or damaging to our success.

Mr. Coleridge had been well on his way toward accomplishing something worth-while, but when he was interrupted, the spirit had been broken, the ideas had vanished, and the accomplishment was lost forever. Sometimes we allow our material interests or an indulgence in evil to serve as our visitor from Porlock to rob us of our greatest treasures of both mind and spirit. What a tragedy when a lost idea or a lost ideal, or a lost ambition, or a lost art, or a lost spirituality, takes from us our greatest blessings, including even eternal life itself! This is especially unfortunate when the loss is brought about by a distraction that we ourselves cause. So frequently we permit some little thing to spoil the spirit of what we are doing and then the charm of our success is broken. These most precious of life's investments have values only when we keep them safe and in usable form. In this, as in everything else eternal vigilance is the price of safety.

In our striving for success we often let our minds and hearts wander too far from the main business of life. Or we break the spell by entertaining too many conflicting interests.

Emerson once said that he always lost the spirit of writing when he divided his attention. He said that it was difficult to write with a pen in one hand and a peat knife in the other. The final difference between success and failure is often very small and even the greatest success sometimes hangs by a thread. If the thread is broken, the spirit is lost. When our pursuit of success is interrupted even for a short time, excellence often gets away from us, the scent is lost, the water is muddied, the tracks are obliterated, and further pursuit is made impossible. Success must be prepared for in advance. It is often born unexpectedly, and it usually comes with a sudden insistence that brooks no delay. While success is being born everything else should be put aside. Then a visitor from Porlock or a mind centered on the wrong things may cause a major disaster. A very large percentage of plans miscarry when some distraction breaks the cord of their lives. Then interruption or negligence may bring death to our most prized accomplishment.

Like Nebuchadnezzar, we sometimes get a great vision, and inasmuch as we may not always be able to get hold of a Daniel to recall it for us, we had better learn to hang onto it while we have it. When we write it down, memorize it, and take immediate action, we increase the probability that it will remain with us.

The most pathetic tragedy in our world is our losses. We lose our faith or allow our manhood to disintegrate. This is made more hazardous because the moment of forgetting, like the moment of death, is an unconscious moment. We merely say, "I am not the man I used to be." Such losses have little salvage value. And the greatest virtues can completely disappear. Like the lost river, they just sink into the sand and we see them no more. The inspiration of the Lost Chord reminds us that we should keep the investment department of our lives operating effectively, and only those virtues that we keep in good condition can make our lives profitable and happy.

The Love of Liberty

URING THIS coming week we will commemorate the birthday of American independence. During this period of the year we re-live those thrilling days of '76, and we think about our freedom and what it means and what it has cost and what it would be like if it were lost. We should always remember that one of our most important responsibilities is to keep this God-given love of liberty always burning brightly in our hearts. We are aware of the fierce struggle that free men have always been willing to make against the most overwhelming odds in order to remain free. Sometimes we place the value of this tremendous gift even ahead of life itself. During our revolutionary period Patrick Henry said, "Is life so dear or peace so sweet as to be purchased at the price of chains or slavery? Forbid it, Almighty God. I know not what course others may take but as for me, give me liberty or give me death."

Freedom and free agency was the cause for which the war in heaven was fought, and in one way or another it has been the cause of all the wars since that time. God himself is committed to our freedom above almost everything else, yet some of the strongest forces in the world are set in opposition against it. Isn't it interesting that of the estimated forty billion people who have lived upon the earth in the last two thousand years, only one billion have been free. All the rest have lived in some kind of bondage.

In our present celebrations of freedom we remember the plight of our unfortunate neighbors in Hungary, East Germany, Cuba and Poland. We sympathize with the vast hordes in China and Russia whose masters hold over them the tyrant's power of life and death. In many instances they are told where they can work, what they can believe and what they can do. The only possible employer is often the communist party. The people are forbidden to own property and in many cases they give up their children to the care of the state, and their own lives are placed in the hands of godless dictators. We often make comparisons between these two great ideologies. It seems to me that one of the most striking for this season of the year is between America where we have to make laws to keep foreigners from flocking here to over-run our country, and East Berlin where they make laws supplemented by Russian walls constantly patrolled by armed guards to keep people from getting away from communist rule.

The powers of evil seem just as anxious for all men to be enslaved as God is for them to be free. But America's mission is not only to maintain her own liberty. America is the world citadel of freedom established by God himself with the divinely appointed mission to keep liberty alive for all of the people of the world. America has some 185 million people, all of whom are free politically, and yet even here we have a tendency to bind ourselves in some kind of personal slavery. For example, five million of our people have become alcoholics. Others have bound themselves with the chains of immorality, lawlessness and every other kind of evil. And as Epictetus says "No man is free who is not master of himself."

Charles Kingsley has pointed out that, "There are two freedoms. The false where one is free to do what he likes, and the true where he is free to do what he ought." And Edmund Burke reminds us that, "There is no liberty in wrongdoing. It chains and fetters its victim as surely as any other effect follows its cause." It has been pointed out that everyone is free even to go to hell and as Kingsley says, "The freedom of some is the freedom of the herd of swine that ran violently down the steep place into the sea and were drowned." The real liberty that we seek is the liberty of order and virtue. It is the freedom that gives enlargement to our energies, intellects and virtues, and finally gives eternal life to our souls.

One of the most important enterprises in the world is man's struggle to be free. When I was in the seventh grade I was greatly impressed by Elijah Kellogg's account of the inspiring speech about freedom made by Spartacus the old Grecian gladiator, which seems to have a message for our day, as it forms an interesting chapter in the history of man's struggle for liberty. In those days great training schools for gladiators were established in Rome, Capua, Ravenna, and other cities. These gladiators were mostly slaves, captured enemies or condemned criminals. They were forced to fight each other to the death in the arena in order to amuse the Roman populace so frenzied with the blood of their own conquests and civil strife. Spartacus, a Thracian by birth, was captured during the conquest of Northern Greece, sold as a slave, and sent to the training school at Capua. Here he was trained to be a skillful fighter, and for twelve years was hired out to fight at public and at private entertainments. Spartacus was an educated Greek with all the Greek love of liberty he naturally resented such cruel and bloody slavery, yet in every combat he fought as became a valiant soldier.

After having proven his prowess and skill in many a combat, Spartacus incited the gladiatorial slaves at Capua to insurrection, and finally escaped with seventy comrades to the crater of Mt. Vesuvius. Here he issued a general emancipation proclamation to all the slaves of Italy. For three years he defied the Roman power. Four Roman armies met disaster at the hands of his freedom-loving band. With a large force, he marched past Rome, entered the Po Valley, and planned to cross the Alps, disband his army, and send his warriors as free men back to their homes. But his men refused to leave Italy, and demanded that they be led against the power of Rome itself. During the campaign against Rome, the slave army met many reverses, it was finally defeated, and Spartacus was slain.

Mr. Kellogg gives a memorable account of this historic freedom attempt made by Spartacus after twelve years of bloody combat on the arena sands. Determined to be free he also stirred up his fellow captives in an inspiring though unsuccessful strike for liberty. Of this event Mr. Kellogg says,

It had been a day of triumph at Capua. Lentulus, returning with his victorious eagles, had amused the populace with the sports of the amphitheatre to an extent hitherto unknown even in that luxurious city. The shouts of revelry had died away; the roar of the lion had ceased; the last loiterer had retired from the banquet; and the lights in the palace of the victor were extinguished. The moon, piercing the tissue of fleecy clouds, silvered the dewdrop on the corselet of the Roman sentinel, and tipped the dark waters of Volturnus with a wavy, tremulous light. It was a night of holy calm, when the zephyr sways the young spring leaves, and whispers among the hollow reeds its dreamy music. No sound was heard save the last sob of some retiring wave, telling its story to the smooth pebbles of the beach; and then all was silent as the breast when the spirit has departed.

In the deep recesses of the amphitheatre, a band of gladiators were assembled, their muscles still knotted with the agony of conflict, the foam upon their lips, the scowl of battle yet lingering on their brows, when Spartacus, rising in the midst of that grim assemblage, thus addressed them:

"Ye call me chief; and ye do well to call him chief who for twelve long years has met upon the arena every shape of man or beast that the broad Empire of Rome could furnish, and who never yet lowered his arm. If there be one among you who can say that ever, in public fight or private brawl, my actions did belie my tongue let him stand forth

and say it. Or if there be three in all your company dare
face me on the bloody sands, let them come on. And yet I
was not always thus,—a hired butcher, a savage chief of still
more savage men! My ancestors came from old Sparta, and
settled among the vine-clad rocks and citron groves of
Syrasella. My early life ran as quiet as the brooks by which
I sported; and when, at noon, I gathered the sheep beneath
the shade, and played upon the shepherd's flute, there was
a friend, the son of a neighbor, to join me in the pastime.
We led our flocks to the same pasture, and partook our
rustic meal together. One evening, after the sheep were
folded, and we were all seated beneath the myrtle which
shaded our cottage, my grandsire, an old man was telling of
Marathon and Leuctra; and how, in ancient times, a little
band of Spartans, in a defile of the mountains, had with-
stood a whole army. I did not then know what war was;
but my cheeks burned, I knew not why, and I clasped the
knees of that venerable man, until my mother, parting the
hair from off my forehead, kissed my throbbing temples, and
bade me go to rest, and think no more of those old tales and
savage wars. That very night, the Romans landed on our
coast. I saw the breast that had nourished me trampled by
the hoof of the warhorse; the bleeding body of my father
flung amidst the blazing rafters of our dwelling!

"Today I killed a man in the arena; and when I broke
his helmet-clasps behold! he was my friend. He knew me,
smiled faintly, gasped and died;—the same sweet smile upon
his lips that I had marked in adventurous boyhood when
we scaled the lofty cliffs to pluck the first ripe grapes, and
bear them home in childish triumph! I told the praetor
that the dead man was my friend, generous and brave; and
I begged that I might bear away the body, burn it on a
funeral pile and mourn over its ashes. Ay! upon my knees,
amid the dust and blood of the arena, I begged that poor
boon, while the assembled maids and matrons, and the holy
virgins they call Vestals, and the rabble, shouted in derision,

deeming it rare sport, forsooth, to see Rome's fiercest gladiator turn pale and tremble at the sight of that piece of bleeding clay! The praetor drew back as if I were pollution, and sternly said, 'Let the carrion rot; there are no noble men but Romans!' And so, fellow gladiators, must you, and so must I, die like dogs. O Rome, Rome! thou hast been a tender nurse to me. Thou hast given to that poor, gentle, timid shepherd lad, who never knew a harsher tone than a flute-note, muscles of iron and a heart of flint; taught him to drive the sword through plaited mail and links of rugged brass, and warm it in the marrow of his foe; to gaze into the glaring eyeballs of the fierce Numidian lion even as a boy upon a laughing girl! And he shall pay thee back, until the yellow Tiber is red as flowing wine, and in its deepest ooze thy life-blood lies curdled!"

Then Spartacus said to his fellow gladiators, "Ye stand here now like giants, as ye are! The strength of brass is in your toughened sinews; but tomorrow some Roman Adonis, breathing sweet perfume from his curly locks, shall with his lily fingers pat your red brawn, and bet his sesterces upon your blood. Hark, hear ye yon lion roaring in his den? 'Tis three days since he's tasted flesh; but to-morrow he will break his fast upon yours, and a dainty meal for him ye will be. If ye are beasts, then stand here like fat oxen, waiting for the butcher's knife! But if ye are men—follow me! Strike down yon guard, gain the mountain passes, and there do bloody work as did your sires at old Thermopylae! Is Sparta dead? Is the old Grecian spirit frozen in your veins, that you do crouch and cower like a belabored hound beneath his master's lash? O comrades, warriors, Thracians! if we must fight, let us fight for ourselves. If we must slaughter, let us slaughter our oppressors! If we must die, let it be under the clear sky, by the bright waters in noble, honorable battle!"

Suppose that from this old Grecian spirit we take a little tighter hold on our own love of liberty. Circumstances change, but liberty is as dear to us as ever. Present day powerful forces of men and devils boast of their design to enslave every human being upon the earth and will attempt to do so without a moment's hesitation as soon as they think they can. We should also strike down all of the forces of evil that would enslave us in any way. God has told us that freedom can only be preserved in righteousness. "Bad men cannot make good citizens." "It is impossible that a nation of infidels or idolaters should be a nation of free men. It is when the people forget God that tyrants forge their chains and corruption flourishes in men's lives." Therefore as individuals we must also free ourselves from every evil influence.

Edmund Burke says, "Men are qualified for . . . liberty in exact proportion to their disposition to put chains upon their own evil appetites . . . it is ordained in the eternal constitution of things that men of intemperate habits cannot be free, their passions forge fetters by which they bind themselves."

The Gospel of Jesus Christ is the perfect way to freedom and happiness. Apostle Paul says, "Where the spirit of the Lord is, there is liberty." (II Cor. 3:17) And to the Galatians he said, "Stand fast therefore in the liberty wherein Christ hath made us free, and be not entangled again with the yoke of bondage." (Gal. 5:1) What a tremendous philosophy for our own time. We have the most wonderful things to fight for, and one of the greatest is to keep alive in our individual hearts this God-given love of liberty with which we were endowed in the council in heaven, and which we must further increase so that we may help our nation and ourselves carry out our divine destiny. For this we should devote our prayers, supported by the full industry and courage of our lives.

The Marred Vessel

RECENTLY I talked with a man who had so many problems that he seemed to represent a miniature composite of our troubled world. He seemed to have an uncanny ability for making all of the mistakes personally. His home had been broken up. His children were in trouble. He had lost his job, his self-respect and his faith. His life had been pitted and pocked with evil, and he was now going from one psychiatrist to another in a frantic attempt to find someone who would accept the responsibility of salvaging something from his miserable misspent life.

Thinking that it might help his situation, I told him about the Lord sending Jeremiah down to the potter's house to see the potter make a vessel on his pottery wheels. When the clay became marred the potter made it over, eliminating the original blemishes and carefully preventing any new ones from occurring.

Then with this experience as a kind of visual aid, the Lord sent Jeremiah out to show the people how the ugly blotches of sin were making marred vessels of their lives. The Lord was suggesting that the people imitate the potter in starting over and making something worth-while out of themselves. The Lord is always grieved when we corrupt ourselves and make our lives destructive and repulsive with evil. Through Jeremiah he said to the people, "Return ye now every one from his evil way, and make your ways and your doings good." But the Israelites did not seem to be interested. They said, "There is no hope; but we will walk after our own devices, and we will every one do the imagination of his evil heart." (Jeremiah 18:1-12)

This seemed to closely match the attitude of my friend. He had brought so much ugliness and discouragement upon himself that reform seemed not only impossible but almost undesirable so far as his effort was concerned. He had been psychoanalyzed, threatened and begged to change his ways. But he had given evil such a stranglehold on his wishy-washy will that he seemed powerless to erase the repulsive scars or straighten out the confusion of his mixed-up, disobedient, unhappy existence. He seemed completely unskilled in righteousness and his evil bungling had produced a marred, unsightly vessel at its worst.

It is understandable that God, who created us in his own image and above everything else desires our happiness, should want to be proud of his work, just as any good potter would like to turn out beautiful, flawless, valuable china. What a thrilling idea, and yet what a tremendous responsibility, that in agreement with the divine law of free agency, God has placed in our own hands the controls of the pottery wheels that fashion our lives. That is, the creation of man was not something that was finished and done with in the garden of Eden. The creation of man is still going on and we are the creators. We ourselves are shaping the attitudes, ideals, ambitions, desires, enthusiasms, and skills that will determine what we will be throughout all of eternity. The soft clay of our lives may be turned by us into vessels of beauty, or with faithless, sinful hands we may cause damaging cracks and ugly scars to mar our work forever. In any event, we are confronted with the challenging truth that what we will become is up to us.

What a pity that anyone should take so little interest in himself, that by his own hand he should produce the ugly marks upon his soul to represent tragedy at its naked worst.

My friend caused me to think of a man who carries a large, rough, purple birthmark covering almost his entire face. His lips protrude grotesquely and his face is distorted to give it an almost inhuman appearance. This sickening blotch makes people shudder with pity, and after only a few seconds they turn away their faces. Of course, this unpleasantly marked man is extremely self-conscious and unhappy in spite of the fact that his face was marred through no fault of his own, and there is no reason for him to feel condemned or unworthy.

The physical imperfections of faithful people will be corrected in the resurrection. But what about those who bring ugliness upon themselves by their own disobedience? Imagine standing in the presence of God with the filthy blotches of our own sins disfiguring our minds and souls.

It is difficult to understand why the Israelites or anyone else should reject God when he is only trying to cleanse our lives and help us to qualify for celestial glory. But like the Israelites, in one way or another most of us say, "We will walk after our own devices, and each will follow the imaginations of his evil heart." How ridiculous can we be? We know that sin is the most disfiguring disease in the world and it always stamps its loathsomeness upon us and thereafter shows itself in everything we do. Yet our actions seem to indicate that we are frequently more interested in *acquiring* blemishes than in removing them. At least the subject we most dislike to talk about is repentance or reform or any other program calculated to turn us from evil. Only when it is too late will some of us discover that repentance is the most thrilling, exciting, constructive idea that there is in the world. It is through repentance that we remove the ugly blemishes so that we can possess and live beautiful, useful, happy lives.

At one time Mary Magdalene, doubting Thomas and impetuous Peter were marred vessels. But they took advantage of this remodeling process to remove the ugly scars and make *another* kind of a vessel which would please both themselves and God.

The early life of Mohandas K. Gandhi also bore many glaring imperfections. He was a coward. He possessed a bad temper. He had some very serious sex problems. Then realizing the disadvantages that these unfavorable traits imposed upon him, he deliberately started out to remake himself, and later he called himself "a self-remade man." If you would like to have a good phrase backed up by a powerful idea, here it is. Every really successful man is "a self-remade man." And many more of us *could* be successful if we could be converted to a good program of remodeling. But many people won't even talk about redoing themselves on the pottery wheels. They would rather continue to cover themselves with the leprous blotches of sin and the unsightly scars of thoughtlessness. And while reworking our own clay is one of our greatest opportunities, yet the privilege is not everlasting. The living clay in our hands, like that worked by the potter, sometimes becomes unpliable. The poet made an interesting comparison for us, when he said:

> I took a piece of plastic clay
> And idly fashioned it one day
> And as my fingers pressed it still
> It moved and yielded to my will.
>
> I came again when days were past,
> The bit of clay was hard at last,
> The form I gave it still it bore,
> But I could change it now no more.
>
> I took a piece of living clay
> And gently formed it day by day.
> I worked it with my power and art
> A young child's soft and yielding heart.
>
> I came again when days were gone.
> He was a man I looked upon,
> He still the early impress bore
> But I could change him nevermore.

What a dreadful thing it might some time be to find that we were so hardened in our sins that we were no longer subject to change! What an unpleasant experience it would someday be to suffer eternal damnation while those with whom we previously associated were in full possession of a happy exaltation! Then *their* lives may be sparkling like perfectly formed, beautiful china, whereas our own must forever remain marred, ugly and unacceptable. What could be more heartbreaking than to spend eternity with our lives permanently blotched, dirty, miserable, guilty and unwanted, and to know that we come so far short of the blessings that we could have received? What could make less sense *then*, than the statement made to God by the Israelites saying, "We will walk after our own devices, and we will every one do the imagination of his evil heart"? What could be more bitter then than our own regret, or harder to bear than to know that we had missed the glory that others enjoy and that we could have had? The most devasting of all human emotions is the sense of being alone of being unworthy and unwanted. I wonder what repentance would mean if offered to a damned soul, and if that soul happened to be one of us, how much would we then be willing to pay in toil, tears, suffering, or blood, if we could just turn back the calendar and have another chance to get our hands on our own pottery wheels?

It is unpleasant enough to have a broken disfigured body or an unbalanced twisted mind, even through no fault of our own. But what will be our torment if by our own hands we turn out a defective soul and bring eternal suffering upon ourselves and others. Sin is the most destructive of all influences. It destroys friendships, breaks family ties and leaves our lives eternally blotched and unsightly. Through sin we bring loneliness, failure and unhappiness upon ourselves by our own choice.

Sin caused "the fall of man," and it also caused the fallen condition of the earth itself. God said to Adam, "Cursed is the ground for thy sake. In sorrow shalt thou eat of it all the days of thy life. Thorns also and thistles shall it bring forth unto thee." Because of Adam's transgression he was driven out of Eden. It was through his own sin that he turned his back on the fertile fields of paradise with its fruit-laden gardens, its abounding rivers, its indescribable beauty, and its unspeakable fellowship with God. With every possibility for happiness and success in Eden, and with unlimited access to all but one of the trees in the garden, man initiated a characteristic human action. After God had withdrawn his presence they partook of the forbidden fruit. As a consequence, instead of being able to bask in the glorious light of Paradise, Adam and Eve cast themselves out into a lone and dreary world. And because of subsequent disobedience, the world of men has lived largely as aliens from God.

Even now while enjoying a most advantageous position, where we are so freely offered God's choicest blessings, we re-enact some of those ancient scenes as we turn our backs on righteousness and make a bee-line for the things that are forbidden. Strewn all along the shores of time we see the broken and discarded fragments of once beautiful vessels, marred beyond all usefulness by their own action. In the light of history we see the faithless people of Noah's generation perishing in the flood. We know of the judgment and suffering in Egypt, because the wicked Pharaoh wantonly defied God's commands. We see Samson who had once known great strength and the presence of God's spirit, enslaved by the Philistine to blindly and remorsefully turn the mill wheels of his enemies. We see King Saul consumed with envy, falling on the point of his own sword. We remember Jezebel, defiant and unbelieving cast from the window of her palace for the dogs to eat. We see King

David broken and shattered, with blood on his hands and sin in his heart, being cast into hell.

Then we take a look at ourselves and our own day, where humanity is again running headlong toward destruction as we say with the Israelites, "We will walk after our own devices, and we will every one do the imagination of his evil heart." And as a consequence, gloom, despair and loneliness settles over us in this life and casts their dismal shadows across the next.

What happened in Eden was a kind of preview of what is happening every day in our own drama of human life. Many Edenic scenes are presently being re-enacted, and we are trading our divine right as heirs to the Celestial Kingdom, for the tawdry things of this world. Each day thousands of people turn their backs on their own best interests to become marred vessels on their own pottery wheels.

The one redeeming feature of this situation is that the same power of choice, that leads us away from God, can lead us back. The same hands and the same potter's wheel that marred the vessel, can also mend it. We can turn away from sin and put ourselves in the hands of God, who above everything else desires that our lives may be clean and beautiful.

In spite of our historic perverseness, God will guide our hands in this all-important responsibility if we will turn to him as we proceed to work at the pottery wheels of our own lives.

No Room in the Inn

Each year at Christmas time our minds go on a pilgrimage back to the little town of Bethlehem that has nestled among the Judean hills for so many centuries. The name Bethlehem means the house of bread, which might lend itself to more than one interpretation. Certainly it is wonderfully rich in its long and interesting history. It was here that Jacob buried his wife, Rachael. Bethlehem is where Ruth gleaned in the wheat fields of Boaz. It was also here that Ruth's great-grandson David was born and where he tended the sheep of his father Jesse. It was here that he was anointed by Samuel to be the king of Israel. This little town finally called itself by the name of its most famous son and was thereafter known as the City of David.

But the Old Testament Prophet Micah had foretold that one greater than David should also be born in Bethlehem and that the most important event in the history of the world should here take place to distinguish little Bethlehem above all of the great cities of the world. Since the meridian of time, Bethlehem has been remembered primarily as the birthplace of the Savior of men.

For that first Christmas, Mary and Joseph had come some 65 miles from Nazareth in Galilee to Bethlehem in Judea in response to the decree of Caesar Augustus that all the world should be taxed each in his own city. They arrived in Bethlehem at about the time that Jesus was to be born. And Luke says of Mary, "And she brought forth her first-born son and wrapped him in swaddling clothes and laid him in a manger, because there was no room for them in the inn."

As we think back to the birth of Jesus we feel a certain sense of shame and regret that there was no room in the inn for the Savior of the world to be born. It is also a very interesting thought that the King of Kings and Lord of Lords should be born in a stable. With his Heavenly Father he had created the earth in the first place, and yet there was no room in it for him to be born. But this fact is something more than an isolated event of interesting significance, it indicates what almost amounts to a theme song for his life. "No room" was one of the chief characteristics of his entire mortal existence. He himself summed up his experiences by saying, "The foxes have holes, and the birds of the air have nests; but the Son of man hath not where to lay his head." (Matt. 8:20)

He was not very old before the fierce opposition of Herod was directed against him. As soon as Herod learned of his birth from the wise men he sent soldiers to Bethlehem to kill the children. Judea was not big enough for a peaceful co-existence of both Herod and Jesus, so while Herod remained in power, Joseph and Mary took Jesus into far away Egypt because there was "no room" for him in the domain of Herod. But after Herod's death others kept the antagonism going as they continued the cry of "no room," "no room." There was "no room" for his teaching, "no room" for his doctrine, "no room" for his miracles. The chief priests and religious leaders wanted him put to death because they saw in him the downfall of their religious system and there was "no room" for both. Some argued that he was a threat to the Roman government and there was no room for him in the Roman world. Even in his death there was no place for his final rest, and so Joseph of Arimathea took his body down from the cross and laid it in his own tomb.

But the birth and death of Jesus are now both ancient history. Since those historic events, some nineteen wide centuries have come and gone. The great Roman Empire has long since become little more than a memory. The problems of the religious leaders who brought about his death have long been buried with their dust. But Jesus did not give his life for his contemporaries alone, his mission applied with equal significance to us. It was our sins as well as theirs that made him volunteer his own death. What is our attitude about his life? We now delight to identify ourselves with the great name of Christian, and well we might. We have everything that others have had to convince us of his divinity. But in addition we have the judgment of time shining upon the life of Christ. We have the solemn assurance of the ancient apostles who sealed their testimony with their blood, bearing witness to us that he was divine. But on top of that, we have a great flood of testimony from many new witnesses. The question now before us is, what have we done about it? We have greatly increased our standard of living. There are very few Americans who would not now account it an unendurable hardship to have to live as Solomon lived in all of his glory. We have lengthened our own life expectancy from approximately 19 years as it was in Jerusalem in the days of Jesus to 70 years in the America of our day. We have vastly expanded our educational opportunities and our material accomplishments. We have cut in half the number of work hours required to earn our living. We have multiplied our luxury and increased our leisure time, but what spiritual advantage have we received from our superior education and the extra time placed at our disposal?

Certainly the peace that the angels sang about has never seemed farther away than now. The great nations are crouching ready to spring at each other with their hands filled with weapons too horrible to think about. The sin and evil that Jesus came to free us from is in many places now running unchecked through the world. Crime is at its awful height. Jesus came as our example. He lived a sinless life and furnished us with a working model of righteousness. His message was "Follow me." He asked us to follow him in his doctrine to follow him in his righteousness, to follow him in his love for others. But we have not followed Jesus, rather we have followed those who could find "no room." "No room" is still the significant cry of our world. We have made room for his gifts but we have found no room for the giver. We have made room for the extra leisure time, we have made room for our physical comforts, we have made room for horse races and baseball games we have made room for many violations of the Sabbath day, but we have no room for worship, no room for service, no room for the Savior of the world. Instead every day we reproduce in our lives that ancient scene at Bethlehem.

The fact that there was no room for him to be born in the inn is not nearly so significant as that there is no room for his way of life. We have not taken seriously the prayer of the angels singing "glory to God in the highest." We plan to put peace in force with atomic bombs, while we continue to re-enact that historic drama of Bethlehem over and over again, not just in the pageants that we present at Christmas time, but this is what is also presented upon the greater stages of our individual lives. It has been said that souls are not saved in bundles or bunches. Salvation is an individual matter and Jesus approaches each of us with the offer of personal exaltation. His most important message has always been strictly individual, and today as of old, Jesus is saying to us, "Behold, I stand at the door and knock: if any man hear my voice and open the door, I will come in to him, and will sup with him, and he with me. To him that over-cometh will I grant to sit with me in my throne, even as I also overcame, and am set down with my Father in his throne." (Rev. 3:20-21)

Many of the doors with which Jesus was familiar had the latch only on the inside and could not be opened from without. The door to the heart is still opened from within.

The invitation for Jesus to enter our lives must still come from the inside. The door of the heart is not easily broken down by anyone beating upon it from without, the release must be operated from within.

At Christmas time it is wonderful to sing:

> Oh Holy Child of Bethlehem,
> Descend to us we pray,
> Cast out our sin and enter in,
> Be born in us today.
>
> We hear the Christmas angels
> The great glad tidings tell,
> Oh, come to us, abide with us,
> Our Lord Emmanuel.

But even though we sing the most beautiful songs and even though he stands at the door of our lives and knocks, not many doors are being opened. Too frequently we merely send back the ancient reply, "no room," "no room."

There was no room in Bethlehem because all of the available space was occupied. That still remains one of our most vexing situations. There are thousands of people who presently can find no room for Jesus because their lives are so completely filled with the pursuit of material things that they have little time for anything else. Making money so occupies our thoughts that we sometimes don't even recognize our needs. Then like the Laodiceans we think "I am rich and increased with goods and have need of nothing." The Laodiceans did not even know that they were "wretched and miserable and poor and blind and naked." Some of us have no room because our lives are so filled with ignorance that understanding can find no place to set its foot. Others have no room for Jesus because their lives are so heavily loaded with sin. Some have hearts filled with sloth and have no room for the efforts required by salvation. You can't pour more water into a vessel that is already overflowing.

Some have no time, no time to worship, no time for meditation, no time to get acquainted with his teachings, no time to feed our hearts on the things of the spirit, no time to devote to our own souls and to the God who created us. Our time is all taken up, and our activities are already fully allotted. Soneone has said:

No time for God, what fools we are,
To clutter up our lives with common things
And leave without the Lord of life and life itself.

No time for God, as well to say,
No time to eat, to sleep, to live, to die
Take time for God or a poor misshapen thing you'll be
To step into eternity and say to him,
I had no time for thee.

Today Jesus stands at the citadel of our souls pleading for entrance. He pleads through the spoken word. He pleads through the scriptures. He pleads through the Spirit. He pleads through the voice of reason. He pleads through the witness of faithful parents and friends. But because we have no space left we reply "no room, no room." We have no room for Jesus because most of us are looking for a religion convenience, one that takes no time, costs no money, requires no effort and will fit our lives without any changes on our part.

As the spirit of Christmas fills our lives and as we are haunted by our embarrassment from nineteen centuries past, we should consider the advisability of making room for him in our own present. If we are too busy to serve God, we are much too busy. If our lives are so filled as to crowd him out, then we should empty our lives and relieve the congestion which threatens to overthrow us. If the bucket of our lives is overloaded with dross, how are we going to be able to find some way to make room for some pure gold?

In readjusting his life, one man once made up a long list of those things that he could get along without. That is a pretty good idea for our eternal success. Some of our lives are too full of sin. Some of us could get along with a little less ignorance and a little less indifference. Maybe we should pour out some of our interest in non-constructive things to make room for the things of God.

There is a famous painting entitled, "Christ Before Pilate." Some day we may see another picture entitled, "Pilate Before Christ." There may also be some future picture of some of us being turned away from celestial glory because there is no room there for lives overflowing with the wrong things. It is interesting to remember that all of these things that monopolize our interest and keeps us from God will also keep God from us. And all of these we had better learn to get along without.

There is a sacred song that says, "I Walked Today Where Jesus Walked." And wouldn't it be a thrilling thing if we could go and stand on that very spot of ground where Jesus stood and try to absorb the spirit of his life. Or suppose that we go into Gethsemane and kneel at that place where under the burden of our sins he sweat great drops of blood at every pore while we try to recapture the spirit of his life. Or suppose that we go in imagination and stand before the final judgment. Then we might be able to more easily make up that interesting list of things that our lives could profitably get along without.

It may not be practical for us to walk today where Jesus walked. But it *is* practical and a lot more important to think today what Jesus thought. We can live today as Jesus lived. We can unload our hearts of evil and clear the lethargy out of our ambition. Then we can fill our minds with our Father's purpose and our hearts with an understanding of his ways. We can loosen the latch and open the door of our souls and make room for the king of glory to come in. To make room for our Redeemer is the greatest opportunity of our lives, "For there is none other name under heaven given among men whereby we must be saved." And Jesus is still saying as in olden times, "Behold I stand at the door and knock: if any man hear my voice, and open the door, I will come in to him, and will sup with him, and he with me. To him that overcometh will I grant to sit with me in my throne, even as I also overcame, and am set down with my Father in his throne."

My Christmas wish is that we may change that ancient Christmas pageant of Bethlehem so that we may really hear the angels' song and make room for the Redeemer of the world in our personal lives.

The Odyssey

ONE OF OUR greatest writers was the blind Greek poet Homer, who lived in the ninth century B.C. His primary works consisted of two great book-length epic poems. The first is known as the "Iliad." It is the story of the famous Trojan War. Paris, a Trojan prince, eloped with Helen, the wife of Menelaus, king of Sparta. Menelaus enlisted the aid of his fellow kings of the little Greek states, including his brother Agamemnon, the great Greek fighter who was the king of Mycenae. This aggregation of fighting men sailed a thousand ships across the Aegean Sea and laid siege to Troy, a large and strongly fortified walled city near the Hellespont. The war lasted for ten long years. By a trick the Greeks finally got inside the walls of Troy. They destroyed its fighting power, sacked the city and burned it to the ground. Then they loaded their ships and sailed for home.

Homer's second book is called the "Odyssey." It is taken from the name of Odysseus, sometimes called Ulysses, who was king of Ithaca and one of the greatest of the Greek heroes. The "Odyssey" is an account of the experiences of Odysseus as he made his way across the three hundred miles of island-dotted sea lying between the battleground of Troy and his island home of Ithaca off the west coast of Greece.

Odysseus was very happy as he started for home at the head of his fleet of ships. His men were all glad that the war was over and that they would soon be at their own firesides with their families. But in this they were doomed to disappointment, for along the way they met with one

difficulty after another, many of which were far more destructive than the war had been. By the time Odysseus
finally reached Ithaca, every ship had been destroyed and
the life of every man had been lost except only that of
Odysseus himself.

This great story of the Odyssey is the grandfather of
all adventure stories. Homer knew every trick of storytelling.
The Odyssey tells of man-eating giants, bewitching sirens,
terrible monsters, frightening ghosts, roaring whirlpools,
hair-raising adventures and romantic interludes, not to mention the interest added by Odysseus himself, who was one of
the most courageous and ingratiating heroes in all of our
literature.

The "Odyssey" has lived in such fine repute through
the ages that the word itself has become a part of our language. "Odyssey" has come to mean any long wandering
difficult journey. Of course the greatest of all odysseys is
the journey of life itself. We also speak of our strivings for
success as an odyssey. But Homer was not just a great
storyteller, he also looked with keen insight into human
lives and in a very interesting way described the courage,
strategy, and superstrength with which these famous heroes
tried to solve their problems. Their errors in judgment are
made plain to us, and we are made aware of their moral
weaknesses that were so frequently fatal. Homer's skill
makes his heroes a mirror by which we can adjust our own
lives as we relive their experiences.

As Homer describes their problems, longings, and disappointments and he tells of the suffering that they
so frequently brought upon themselves, we are stimulated
to try to plan our own lives more profitably. This account
of what these Greek heroes did and thought thirty centuries
ago impresses us that human problems and frailties haven't
changed very much in that time. In fact, we might go even
further back and read from that interesting stone tablet dug

up some time ago which was supposed to have been written fifteen centuries before Troy. It says in part: "Bribery and corruption are common, children no longer obey their parents, the end of the world is at our doors and every man wants to write a book." That tablet might just as well have been written in our own day. But in any event we can learn a great deal from the people of other ages, not only from the challenge of their greatness, but their weaknesses and sins help us, as they point out some of the pitfalls that we should avoid.

Odysseus and his men had scarcely started for home when they were blown off their course by a raging wind which drove them to the island of the Lotus-Eaters. An old legend says that when men ate the magic fruit of the lotus tree they forgot about their families and responsibility and lived in dreamy forgetfulness and indolent enjoyment. Only when Odysseus dragged his sailors back aboard their ships were they able to recover enough of their ambition to continue their journey homeward.

But their troubles were not confined to the winds and the lotus fruit. They had many problems, and every one different. At one time they landed on the island of the one-eyed Cyclops and were captured and held prisoners by the giant Polyphemus. They were only able to escape by blinding the monster with a pole, the end of which had been burned in the fire. Maddened with pain and rage, Polyphemus cried out to his father Poseidon, god of the sea, and enlisted his help to avenge the wrong. Their ships stopped at an island inhabited by man-eating giants, who destroyed most of the fleet with huge boulders and speared the men like fish. This was a devastating ordeal and only the men on the ship of Captain Odysseus survived to sail wretchedly onward.

One of their greatest adventures came when they landed on the island of Circe, the enchantress. There some of the men fell into her hands and were turned into swine. But Odysseus obtained the use of a magic power by which he forced her to release her spell and set his men free. But this experience kept Odysseus and his men a full year on the island of Circe.

In the course of their journey they were required to pass an island where some bewitching sirens lived. It was known that in times past the song of the sirens had lured many sailors to their deaths. Odysseus had been warned about the hazard of listening to the music of these fascinating, dangerous creatures. When he came near to these islands, fearing that his men would not be able to withstand the temptation, he had all of the members of his crew fill their ears with wax so that they would not be able to hear the siren's song. Odysseus himself was overcome by curiosity and did not put wax in his own ears. But not quite trusting his own strength, he protected himself against weakness by having his men bind him to the mast. He gave them strict orders that no matter what might happen, they must not release him until they were past the island and out of range of the temptation. When they came within the hypnotic sound of the siren's song, Odysseus weakened and ordered his men to pull their ship onto the shore. But the ears of his men were full of wax and they could not hear his orders. The caution of Odysseus saved the day and they rowed on past the temptation.

This ten-year odyssey involved many other great dangers. After passing the sirens they were required to run the gauntlet down the narrow strait passing between the vast whirlpool of Charybdis, on the one side, and the death-dealing monster Scylla on the other. If the ship went just a little too far to the right, it would be drawn into the deadly whirlpool; if it went to far to the left, it would be within reach of the treacherous Scylla. Even though they barely missed the whirlpool and they rowed with great skill, yet six of his men were snatched from the deck as their ship passed the rock of this six-headed female monster.

Odysseus had hoped to avoid the sun god's island, but because of an unfavorable gale they were marooned there for weeks. Despite their leader's warning, his men butchered some of the sacred cattle. In revenge their ship was shattered with lightning and every single man was killed except Odysseus. And he was blown, clinging to some of the wreckage, back to the whirlpool, where an overhanging fig tree saved his life, and when the timbers again floated up to the surface and out of the whirlpool, Odysseus clung to them and struggled on alone to the island home of the nymph Calypso.

For the next seven years Calypso held Odysseus a prisoner while he longed for his home and his wife Penelope. At last, on orders from Zeus, Calypso let Odysseus sail on. But watchful Poseidon wrecked his home-made boat and Odysseus, a victim of amnesia, was flung upon the island of the Phaeacians. The king's daughter took him to her father's court. The friendly king entertained Odysseus royally and finally sent him home in one of his ships, so that at last, after ten years of wandering, Odysseus, the sole survivor of the voyage, reached the shores of Ithaca. At home after twenty years of absence, he found about as many troubles as he had encountered along the way.

In this great story, Homer intended to remind us of the odyssey of our lives. We also have problems along life's way. Very frequently we also win the great wars of our lives and then lose out while doing some comparatively easy, simple thing. There are times when, to protect ourselves, we should fill our ears with wax and put blinders over our eyes, or have ourselves bound to the mast as a protection against ourselves. If we look and listen intently enough either the sirens or their songs can sometimes be-

witch our greatest powers. Almost daily we are required to
sail that straight course between Charybdis and Scylla. Jesus
talked a great deal about this same kind of a situation, but
used a different figure of speech. Jesus called this hazardous
course "the strait and narrow way." But it is made clear
that in either case there isn't much room for meandering
or carelessness. Sometimes just one wrong step and we are
in serious trouble, sometimes disaster awaits us on both
sides. Someone gave expression to this idea by saying that
the devil was on one side and the cliff and the deep blue sea
on the other. A misstep either way and we are in trouble.

But isn't it interesting that all of these men survived
the fierce ten-year Trojan War, but only one survived what
was supposed to be a peaceful trip home? They had survived the onslaught of the strongest enemy soldiers and
then went down in defeat before the bewitching enchantment of Circe or the languorous appeal of the lotus fruit.
They could handle the hard tasks, but failed to stand up
against the easy, pleasant, beguiling, sweet-smelling sins. As
a consequence their loss which had been small during the
ten-year war was nearly 100 percent during the ten-year
odyssey. This reminds us of the statement of Jesus about
the broad road that leads to destruction. It is traveled by so
many people even though it leads everyone who follows it
to a place they don't want to go. Our odyssey is often more
difficult than that of the Greeks, inasmuch as it usually lasts
longer than ten years. But the things that usually bother
us most are not the hard, tough battles or the difficult
problems, it is the lethargy, the sloth, the little evils, the bad
habits, and wrong attitudes. And instead of putting wax
in our ears and blinders on our eyes at the right time, we
put on our magnifying glasses and turn up our hearing
aids as we pay too much attention to the wrong things.
Because we don't want to miss anything, we hold too many
"foot in the door" conversations with temptation.

Then, like Ulysses, we most often stumble and fall over the trivialities. Plutarch once said, "It is not in the lists that the victors are made, but after the contests are over." The graveyard of success in life is filled with the bones of men who killed all the dragons of the battlefield and then went to their doom during times of peace, because they could not withstand the little pleasant temptations that beckoned them.

Like the problems of Odysseus, all our problems are different, making it more difficult to be prepared against them. We get some wrong ideas and attitudes into our minds and then we allow them either to befog, befoul, belittle, belie, bewitch, benight, becalm, benumb, or betray us until we are lost. Sometimes even the extra courage and self-confidence of the hero lulls him into a false sense of security and makes him careless enough to take unnecessary chances that anyone of lesser ability would avoid. There are also experiences along life's way that, like the enchantress Circe, can cast strange spells over us to make us do strange things, sometimes even turning us into swine. Sometimes we are frightened into discouragement or paralyzed by the soft warm enchantments that get possession of our imagination.

Ulysses saved himself because he was more wise in devising his strategy and overcoming the hazards that he met along the way. But even he wasted ten years of his life fighting these beguiling enchanting sins. May God help us to win the great battles but may we also be successful in solving life's little problems in this all important odyssey of our own lives.

The Other End of the Telescope

O NE OF THE influences that reacts most detrimentally upon our success is a common distortion that frequently gets into our outlook. We often develop a kind of unreliability of viewpoint that makes our senses themselves undependable. We are all familiar with that peculiar kind of color blindness, that makes the grass look greener on the other side of the fence.

We know that a man suffering from thirst on the desert frequently sees mirages. But mirages are not limited to the desert. Most of us have some optical illusions about our hopes, our fears, and the things that we don't understand. We often have personal blind spots that prevent us from seeing ourselves in our true prespective. Consequently we frequently assume a point of view that does not square with either reason, fact or reality.

A recent survey conducted by *Look* magazine indicated that 75% of all workers hate their jobs. At first thought it would seem easy to solve such a problem. The dissatisfied workers could merely quit the jobs that they didn't like, and accept those which held for them the greatest possible appeal. This procedure runs into a snag, however, for the second job usually loses its charm more rapidly than the first. Some people never like any job. To them all jobs for which they have responsibility looks deformed and uninteresting. This defect causes many people to be continually jumping from one job to another, with real job satisfaction always eluding them.

To begin with, job satisfaction is not so much in the work, as in the worker. Job appeal like all other kinds of

appeal is primarily in people. The reason that everybody
doesn't laugh at the same jokes is because the jest is more
in the ear of the hearer, than on the tongue of the teller.
A distortion is easily possible that makes some people laugh
only at off-color jokes, or jokes causing pain to someone
else. To a very large extent beauty, truth, and appreciation
is also in the eye of the beholder. Those people who are
always getting married and divorced are usually suffering
from an unstable viewpoint.

We are all aware of how our point of view can change
as we get closer to a situation. For example we are greatly
attracted by the beauty and fragrance of the roses that belong to someone else. It is only when we clutch the stems in
our own hands that we discover the thorns. It is a dangerous
truth that "distance lends enchantment." It can cause us to
make unhappy unfavorable comparisons between ourselves
and others. This distortion in our viewpoint made it necessary
for the Lord to give the tenth commandment wherein he said,
"Thou shalt not covet." He was trying to get us to focus our
attention on the things we have, rather than on those we lack.
When covetous eyes reach across the neighbor's fence, they
see a greater opportunity, a better wife and a greener lawn.

Because most people are so unhappy with their own
circumstances someone once designed a scheme to make
everyone happy by a more agreeable distribution of their
total problems. Accordingly everyone was asked to lay his
burdens and defects in a great pile. People put down their
glass eyes, their wooden legs, their hard jobs, and their
unsatisfactory opportunities. These were to be exchanged
for problems that would be more agreeable to them. Then
they marched by the pile again to pick up a more pleasant
set of difficulties. But while no one was very pleased with
his own lot, he couldn't find anyone elses problems that
were any more satisfactory. So everyone ended up by taking
back the same defects and problems that he had laid down.

It is not a new set of troubles that we need most but a more accurate perspective for viewing those that we already have.

I had an interesting experience sometime ago at a football game when a friend allowed me to look through his field glasses at the players. With these telescopic lenses on my eyes the players were greatly enlarged and brought up close to my eyes. But when I turned the glasses around and looked at the players through the other end of the telescope the illusion was exactly reversed. The new perspective made the players seem small and a long way away. The difference was not in the players but in the lenses through which I looked.

In 1609 Galileo invented the telescope to enlarge the stars and bring them close enough for him to study. About this time the microscope was invented to enlarge invisible microbes. However it is very interesting to remember that long before Galileo, men and women were being equipped with telescopic minds capable of enlarging or belittling anything they focused upon. Our problems arise only because we don't always know how to look at things.

Someone once wrote:

> I looked at my brother through the telescope of
> scorn and said, "How small my brother is."
> I looked at my brother through the microscope of
> hate, and said, "How coarse my brother is."
> Then I looked at my brother in the mirror of truth
> and said, "How like me my brother is."

However, this interesting ability to increase size and shorten distance, can be used to help compensate for this distortion in our perspective. For example, if you look down a long row of telephone poles, the one by which you are standing seems very large and impressive, whereas the one on the distant horizon seems very small and insignificant. But if you look at the distant telephone pole with a telescope on your eye, you may restore some of its lost size and importance and accordingly avoid the deception to your senses.

This error of viewpoint applies not only to distance but also to time. If you ask your six-year-old son, which he would rather have, a quarter today or a dollar next month, unless he is very unusual boy, the quarter that will solve one of his present problems looks bigger to him than a dollar placed thirty days in the future. If you would like to perform this interesting experiment on a little larger scale, say to your wife, which would you rather have a new gown today, or a new refrigerator today, or mansions in heaven twenty-five years from now? I don't know how your wife will respond to that kind of situation, but it is a very interesting experiment. Once when a colored boy was about to steal a watermelon a friend said to him, "Rufus, if you take that watermelon now, you will have to pay for it in eternity." Rufus said, "If I can have that much time I'll take two!"

When you set the repayment date far enough into the future, any debt or any penalty or any suffering, can be reduced to insignificance in our minds. This deception tricks us into irresponsibility and procrastination. Any responsibility looks easier the more the time for its performance is postponed. This defect quickly destroys our judgment, unless we develop the ability to compensate. We remember that this was the principle that got Esau into trouble. One day Esau came home hungry and Jacob said to him, "Esau, if you will assign over to me your birthright, if you will give me all of your property your barns, cattle, houses, and lands, I will give you a mess of pottage." To one who has just eaten a good dinner that kind of proposition would sound a little bit ridiculous, but Esau was hungry now and that changed his viewpoint. I suppose he thought what difference does it make what happens tomorrow, I am hungry right now.

It is this defect of point of view that makes today loom so very large while tomorrow is either completely blotted out, or so reduced in importance that it doesn't matter much one way or another. All of us are victimized by this deception that made a poor man out of potentially wealthy Esau. A mess of pottage doesn't sound very appetizing to me, but it must have sounded differently to Esau, as he traded of everything he had to get it. Yet this same illusion is still one of our most common hazards. Very few days go by that we ourselves don't trade off some future birthright for some present pottage. Even Esau made a good deal as compared to some of us. Lowell said,

> "For a cap of bells our lives we pay,
> Bubbles we buy with a whole soul's tasking."

This defect also makes us poor traders. The people of Noah's day traded off their future right to live forever in the Celestial Kingdom for a few present years of wicked indulgence. They were drowned in the flood because they held todays sins so close to their eyes that God and their eternal happiness were almost completely blotted out. They looked at righteousness through the belittling end of the telescope whereas they magnified the importance of their sinful activities all out of proportion to the facts. Of course, the things that determine our conduct isn't so much what the facts are, it's what we think about the facts that is important.

Before we can see and judge accurately, we must be able to compensate for this natural deception. That is, the stars that Galileo wanted to study were actually not mere specks as they seemed to be. Actually they were giant bodies of tremendous importance and even the greatest magnifying glass could only restore to Galileo's eye a fraction of reality. Esau magnified the pottage, whereas if he had looked at his birthright through the big end of the telescope he never would have made such a foolish error. Of course there are some places where we *need* to reverse this process. Instead of magnifying the thorns of life we can increase our satisfaction by looking at them through the belittling end of the telescope.

A usual procedure during courtship is to look at the intended spouse through the magnifying end of the telescope. Then when the toast gets burned a few times after marriage we switch the telescope around. An exact reversal of this procedure will get far better results. An old proverb says, "that love is blind." And someone has said that we should keep our eyes open to faults before marriage and partly closed afterward. We should be at least as generous with a wife as we are with a picture, which we always give the advantage of the best possible light.

A little girl once told of an interesting technique used by her grandfather. She said that when he ate cherries, he always put on his red glasses because they made the cherries look so much bigger and redder. This procedure also makes the difference between an optimist and a pessimist. One looks at his opportunities through the big end of the telescope, while the other uses that end to look at his obstacles. Discouraged, downhearted people are often those who look at their wives, their duties and their opportunities through the belittling end of the telescope. All they need to do is turn the telescope around and get a new point of view.

Someone once wrote an interesting song about "looking at the world through rose colored glasses." Jesus meant about the same thing when he said something about loving our enemies. It all depends on which end of the telescope we look through. This idea has some other interesting possibilities, for example, suppose that all sinners should look at their evil through the magnifying end of the telescope so that they could understand the full seriousness of what they are doing. Or suppose that all failures would use a similar procedure in regard to their weaknesses and mistakes. This procedure would have saved the world in Noah's day, whereas, by belittling their sins and making them seem unimportant, Noah's contemporaries brought the flood upon themselves. Suppose that we look at our sins through the telescope that God uses. God cannot look upon sin with the least degree of allowance. What wonderful people we would be if we would develop that same kind of perspective.

What kind of a telescope do we use when we look at God and eternal life and the Celestial Kingdom. What would happen in our lives if we had a telescope to bring heaven up into the present. Someone has said that heaven is all right, it's just too far away. When heaven seems distant it also seems unimportant.

Like Galileo we need a telescope powerful enough to bring the things of the future up close enough to restore their importance to our minds. One reason why deathbed repentance is often so intense is because death brings us close to the consequences of our evil. That is we now see a gigantic telephone pole that once seemed like only a pinpoint on the horizon. If we can get a little closer to God and righteousness, new ambitions and new determinations will be incited in our minds and hearts. One with perfect vision is the one who can presently see heaven and the future in the proportions that they will have for those who actually get there. The things of overwhelming importance in the future will be the eternal things. Unfortunately for most of us our situation then will already have been determined by the way we are looking at our situation now. Therefore a wise man will frequently ask himself now if he knows how to use his mental and emotional telescope in the most effective way.

Which end of the telescope do we use when we look at sin, from what perspective do we regard the use of alcohol, tobacco, profanity, dishonesty, and immorality? There are some who say that what we think or do doesn't matter, that we are all going to the same place anyway. By this process of reasoning the great sins can be shrunk in importance so that like the antediluvians we can commit them without even blinking.

The Bible points at the fool who said in his heart, "there is no God," but someone has pointed at a far greater fool who *says* there is a God, but then *lives* as though there was none. More than perhaps anything else, we need to develop a more godly perspective about truth, and righteousness, and the word of the Lord. God knows more about heaven than we do, as he has been there. He knows more about values and happiness than we do. We can bring God and heaven closer to us by accepting God's enlarged perspective, by turning up the volume of the still small voice, by increasing in our minds the importance of the Holy Scriptures, and then actually living by our enlarged viewpoint.

Pandora's Box

THERE is a very important part of the literature of the world that comes under the heading of "useful fiction." That is, some of our literature deals in events that have never actually taken place and yet they may serve a very useful purpose. For example, in the fables, animals are given the power of speech and serve more or less as stand-ins for human beings on the stage of life. This kind of synthetic experience can often help us to develop ourselves and teach us to see our errors and weaknesses more clearly.

Soldiers can learn a great deal about war by fighting a few sham battles. Law students increase their skill in make-believe trials. And human beings generally can learn many of life's important lessons as they are presented to the imagination by animal actors. Of course, the great fables are built upon a foundation of truth with just enough fiction added to give them color and interest. For example, everyone has profited from the experience of the Tortoise and the Hare, the Fox and the Grapes, the Magician and the Mouse, and the Spider and the Fly. Under the stimulation of fictional characters the lessons of life may be given any desired degree of enlargement to make sure that the moral will not be missed.

With nothing but personal experience to learn from, we might be compared to soldiers taking their basic training with live ammunition, thereby greatly increasing the danger involved in learning. Through fiction we may accomplish what they used to attempt in ancient plays, when they put masks on the players indicating the parts they were to play, so that everyone could identify the villain and the hero as soon as the play began. Either in fiction or non-fiction, however, the events themselves may be relatively unimportant. The value comes from the fact that we are learning true principles.

There is another interesting part of this useful literature called mythology. The ancient Greeks were masters at making up stories and putting experiences together synthetically to influence conduct and motivate acomplishment. But instead of using animals, the Greeks set their stage on a much grander scale with a race of super mortals playing the principal parts. The increased importance of the actors gave more power and greater influence to the ideas presented. The Grecian mythology created an attitude and provided a motivation not possible when human imagination is left unaided. The myths, like the fables, contained a strata of truth with enough fantasy and color to give the idea glamour and appeal. The heroic outlook and the dynamic atmosphere thus created among the Greeks helped to bring about their Golden Age.

There is a very interesting Grecian story about the creation. It tells of a gigantic race of Titans, supposed to have inhabited the earth before men. They created the animals and divided the available faculties and abilities among them. They gave some of the animals courage, some cunning, some strength, some size and some swiftness. Wings, feathers, furs, claws, shells and tusks were all appropriately distributed. But the most wonderful abilities were reserved for man. Man alone was given the magnificent gifts of reason, foresight, insight, judgment, speech, will power, love, a knowledge of good and evil and an upright posture. He was also given an exclusive right to personality and is the only part of creation with the ability to smile.

Then Prometheus, one of the Titans, went to heaven where he lighted a torch from the sun and brought fire back to the earth for the use of men. Fire enabled man to make weapons to subdue the wild beasts, and to make tools to cultivate the ground. He could then cook his food, warm his dwelling, and be comparatively independent of the elements.

Then at the high point of creation a woman was brought into being to be the companion of man. But inasmuch as this event had a little extra special significance, it was done in heaven under the direction of Zeus himself.

Zeus invited all of his associates among the gods to give some special gift to the woman. Aphrodite gave her beauty, Hermes gave her eloquence, Apollo gave her music, and others made special contributions running into a long list of the most magnificent gifts. The woman was named Pandora which means a "gift from all." Thus nobly equipped and endowed, she was conveyed to the earth and presented to man by whom she was gladly accepted.

But there was another side of creation involving the important law of opposites. There is a natural duality in the universe made up of both good and evil. And while the gods were picking out these wonderful gifts for Pandora, they were locking up the evils in a great box. This was also sent to the earth along with Pandora, with instructions that it should never be opened.

Up to this point everything had been going along beautifully. But Pandora had an interesting weakness called curiosity. She was not an evil person but she was subject to a severe and continual temptation to find out what was in the box. Finally when she could resist no longer, she very cautiously opened the lid for a peek inside. But then to her horror, out came all of the plagues, the sorrows and the miseries that had provided creation's balance between good and evil. All human ills had been placed in the box, there was gout, rheumatism and the other diseases to plague the body. There was envy, spite and revenge to trouble the mind, and sin, error and evil to condemn the spirit. All of these evils have continued to plague mankind ever since.

One picture showing this horrible release, details in visual form the most hideous evil shapes taking their flight and scattering themselves far and wide over the earth. Terrified Pandora tried to replace the lid, but before this could be done all of the occupants had escaped except only one. Only *hope* remained in the box. In some way this wonderful quality of hope had been included among the evils. It alone failed to get away and fortunately for us, for no matter what ills may beset us, we always have hope to cling to. And no one is ever completely wretched as long as he has hope.

Of course, we do not need to think about this myth very long before we find a number of interesting parallels for our lives. To begin with, how could we be unappreciative of the magnificent gifts of body, mind, personality and spirit that we have in our possession? The usefulness of these divine gifts are also capable of the greatest possible enlargement by us. We have also been impressed with the important fact that the law of opposites is still with us. It is a basic part of life's program that our world is made up of good and evil, right and wrong, happiness and misery, and our purpose is to learn to choose effectively between them. Each of us may enjoy the good and we must also be on guard against the evil. In fact, in a very real way, each one of us have been presented with a Pandora Box of his own, with enough potential troubles to match our blessings. Our box has also been filled and closed and locked with instructions that all of the evils should be kept inside. And whenever we have problems, it is usually because we have opened the box and turned the evils loose upon ourselves.

To cite an historic example, Cain took the lid off his Pandora Box when he slew his brother Abel. Before this unfortunate act, Cain had everything designed to make him happy. He had been created in God's image and he had been endowed with God's possibilities. He had land, wealth, health, dominion, opportunity, peace, family, security, freedom, religion and the inestimable companionship of God himself. Pandora's problem was curiosity, but Cain's was covetousness. And like Pandora, Cain was also disobedient. Both did exactly what they had been told not to do. It probably didn't take Cain any longer to kill Abel than it did for Pandora to open her box. And both released undreamed of troubles upon themselves.

And after Cain had committed his evil the Lord said to him, "And now art thou cursed . . . When thou tillest the ground, it shall not henceforth yield unto thee her strength; a fugitive and a vagabond shalt thou be in the earth."

Then with feelings of what must have been the greatest regret for his sins, Cain said to the Lord, "My punishment is greater than I can bear." But after the deed had been done, there wasn't very much that Cain could do about it. He could no more bring back Abel's life than Pandora could get her ills back into the box.

If we could get a good clear mental picture of all of these offensive, ugly, evil shapes that are packed into each Pandora Box, it might help us to understand what a terrible thing it is to tamper with the lid that may release them. Pandora was extremely sorry once these plagues were set at large, and Cain felt that his troubles were so great that he couldn't bear them, but once released what else could he do?

It is a challenging thought that every day in some degree we open our own Pandora Box and turn loose enough troubles to vex us the rest of our lives. I know of a young woman who recently made some serious mistakes. In trying to cover them up she made some more mistakes. When an attempt was made to help her that required her cooperation and a change of attitude, she turned against her helpers and her family. She quit school, rejected her friends, and even turned against God. And as she began taking off the lid of her Pandora Box, the most hideous kinds of evil shapes began swarming around her.   In her inexperience and lack of understanding, they are not only making her unhappy but they are threatening to destroy her eternal life itself.   Her sins are not only plaguing her but they are embarrassing her brothers and sisters and breaking her parents' hearts.   But just as long as she maintains her ill-advised course and fights righteousness her troubles will continue to torment her, multiplying as they do so.

One man recently did something wrong and the troubles that overwhelmed him as a consequence prompted him to say that he thought "all hell had broken loose."   And that is a fairly accurate description of about what sometimes happens.   We remember that the poet said something about heaven lying about us in our infancy.   But I suppose it could also be truthfully said that hell also stays pretty close to us, not only in our infancy but throughout our lives.   And each of us has the terrible power at any hour of the day or night to take off the lid and turn all hell loose upon himself.

Certainly Pandora's story should greatly stimulate our determination not only to keep the lid on but also to keep it tightly locked. These potential troubles can't get out unless we ourselves remove the lid.   But even if the lid has already been removed we still have hope to cling to.   As this situation applies to us it seems that there is an amendment that can be made to this story.   Even though *some* evils have been let loose, we might still be able to get them back into the box.   For example, I know that if the young woman mentioned above would think her problems through a little more logically, then acknowledge her mistakes to herself, and go before her Father in heaven with a heart full of repentance, she could put an end to what appears to her to be a persecution from evil.   If she would lend her cooperation, her parents could help her work out some good solutions to her problems and although she already has been severely stung and badly hurt, yet she could probably even now get every one of these sinister shapes back into the box and lock down the lid. This might leave her even better off than she was before, because with the lessons she has now learned she would never want to take off the lid again. Then she would have all of her time to develop and use these wonderful heaven-made qualities with which she was originally endowed in such wonderful abundance.

A Psalm of Life

ONE OF THE very interesting and important books of the Bible is the Book of Psalms. This book contains a collection of 150 sacred poems and songs that were sung in the religious services of ancient times. They were also used in bringing comfort and encouragement to the worshipers. The fundamental character of the psalms still help us to give expression to our deepest religious feelings, and they have struck a responsive chord in the heart of men and women in every age. The strength and universality of their appeal still gives them great value in our personal lives as they promote in us the spirit of brotherhood and worship.

The version of the Psalms, as contained in the Book of Common Prayer is called the Psalter. That is also a term that an order of nuns sometimes apply to the 150 beads that makes up their rosary. The psalms themselves are sometimes memorized and used as a kind of rosary in developing the right attitudes in us.

But the same purpose is often served by the valuable ideas and inspirational poems that are not included in the Bible. For example, in 1838 Henry Wadsworth Longfellow wrote in verse an uplifting philosophy called "A Psalm of Life," in which he stimulates our thinking with a collection of great ideas urging our personal improvement. Poetry has been described as "language dressed up in its best clothes," and the poets stand next to the prophets in their ability to elevate our ideals, stimulate our hopes and charge our ambitions with power.

Each of the 150 psalms in the Bible serves some different purpose, and Mr. Longfellow's "Psalm of Life" is also

capable of making an important contribution. It may also
be memorized and added to the rosary of ideas that we store
up in our hearts to be recalled and rerun as occasion requires.
In Mr. Longfellow's "Psalm of Life" he says:

A PSALM OF LIFE

Tell me not, in mournful numbers,
   Life is but an empty dream!—
For the soul is dead that slumbers,
   And things are not what they seem.

Life is real! Life is earnest!
   And the grave is not its goal;
Dust thou art, to dust returnest,
   Was not spoken of the soul.

Not enjoyment, and not sorrow
   Is our destined end or way;
But to act, that each tomorrow
   Find us farther than today.

Art is long, and Time is fleeting,
   And our hearts, though stout and brave,
Still, like muffled drums, are beating
   Funeral marches to the grave.

In the world's broad field of battle,
   In the bivouac of life,
But not like dumb, driven cattle!
   Be a hero in the strife!

Trust no Future, howe'er pleasant!
   Let the dead Past bury its dead!
Act, — act in the living Present!
   Heart within, and God o'erhead!

Lives of great men all remind us
   We can make our lives sublime,
And, departing, leave behind us
   Footprints on the sands of time.

Footprints, that perhaps another,
   Sailing o'er life's solemn main,
A forlorn and shipwrecked brother,
   Seeing, shall take heart again.

> Let us then be up and doing,
>   With a heart for any fate;
> Still achieving, still pursuing,
>   Learn to labor and to wait.

One of our most profitable abilities is to be able to use great ideas to stimulate our lives to righteous accomplishment. In one way we are all psalmists, and the psalms that have the greatest influence upon our lives are those that we compose ourselves. Some psalmists write their psalms in the flesh and blood of human life. In fact, life itself is a kind of sacred poem. Like the psalms, each life is different and comes in a different spirit with a different message.

One of the interesting facts about the life of Henry Wadsworth Longfellow was that he lived when the blacksmith shop was one of the most important community institutions. Those of us who are a little older remember with what fascination we watched the blacksmith swing his great hammer as he shaped the hot iron upon the anvil. At every blow the sparks flew out in a fiery shower. We delighted to watch the flaming forge, and hear the clear ring of the hammer beating out its rhythm upon the anvil.

Mr. Longfellow's chief interest as a poet and a lecturer was in helping to fashion the lives of men and women to more useful service. And because of the similarity of the work of the lecturer and the smithy, Longfellow developed an unusual interest in the particular village blacksmith shop that stood in Brattle Street under the great chestnut tree. He used to watch the blacksmith changing the shape and usefulness of the iron upon the anvil. Then he made his interesting comparisons to human life. Our habits and actions are also molded by the sledge hammer of our effort. The good ideas and high examples of our experiences are turned into great accomplishment in the blacksmith shop of our lives.

Under date of October 5, 1839, Mr. Longfellow recorded in his diary that that day he had just written a new psalm of life and had called it "The Village Blacksmith." When I went to school this great poem was not only required reading but it also had to be memorized, and that still seems a pretty good idea to me. Suppose that we make Mr. Longfellow's poem a part of our rosary of great thoughts. He said:

THE VILLAGE BLACKSMITH

Under a spreading chestnut-tree
  The village smithy stands;
The smith, a mighty man is he,
  With large and sinewy hands;
And the muscles of his brawny arms
  Are strong as iron bands.

His hair is crisp, and black, and long,
  His face is like the tan;
His brow is wet with honest sweat,
  He earns whate'er he can,
And looks the whole world in the face,
  For he owes not any man.

Week in, week out, from morn till night,
  You can hear his bellows blow;
You can hear him swing his heavy sledge,
  With measured beat and slow,
Like a sexton ringing the village bells.
  When the evening sun is low.

The children coming home from school
  Look in at the open door;
They love to see the flaming forge,
  And hear the bellows roar,
And catch the burning sparks that fly
  Like chaff from a threshing-floor.

He goes on Sunday to the church,
  And sits among his boys;
He hears the parson pray and preach;
  He hears his daughter's voice,
Singing in the village choir,
  And it makes his heart rejoice.

> It sounds to him like her mother's voice,
>   Singing in paradise!
> He needs must think of her once more,
>   How in the grave she lies;
> And with his hard, rough hands, he wipes
>   A tear out of his eyes.
>
> Toiling, — rejoicing, — sorrowing,
>   Onward through life he goes;
> Each morning sees some task begin,
>   Each evening sees it close;
> Something attempted, something done,
>   Has earned a night's repose.
>
> Thanks, thanks to thee, my worthy friend.
>   For the lesson thou hast taught!
> Thus at the flaming forge of life
>   Our fortunes must be wrought;
> Thus on its sounding anvil shaped
>   Each burning deed and thought.

At the end of this poem, as it appeared in the old Fifth Grade Reader, the students were asked to center their picturing power upon the kind of man the village blacksmith was, the kind of work he did, and the kind of life he lived. The first two stanzas of the poem picture a man of great physical strength. Usually weaklings do not stand all day before an anvil swinging a heavy sledgehammer. But the blacksmith also had moral strength. In our day of forced receiverships and mounting debts we might well look with envy upon the blacksmith's life of honest toil living within his income and looking the whole world in the face, for he owed not any man. There are other qualities represented in the life of the blacksmith that are not notably characteristic of our present age. And occasionally we might turn back the calendar and absorb some of these old-fashioned virtues practiced by Longfellow's village blacksmith.

Toil and labor are a very important part of life. But there should also be a generous mixture of honor and love. Certainly into every life a measure of pathos and trouble is likely to find its way. We are inspired by the fact that the blacksmith effectively shaped his own character as well as those of his children. I like to hear Mr. Longfellow say of the blacksmith:

> He goes on Sunday to the Church
>   And sits among his boys;
> He hears the parson pray and preach;
>   He hears his daughter's voice,
> Singing in the village choir,
>   And it makes his heart rejoice.
>
> It sounds to him like her mother's voice,
>   Singing in paradise!
> He needs must think of her once more,
>   How in the grave she lies;
> And with a hard, rough hand, he wipes
>   A tear out of his eyes.

What a joy must have come to the father of these motherless children to be able to sit with them as a family in the house of the Lord on the Sabbath Day. His sons were learning the lessons of the spirit, and his daughter was worshiping God as she sang the songs of her heart in the village choir. Naturally then the blacksmith was reminded of her mother and the vacancy her death had caused in the family circle. How different our psalms of life become when our children are not properly taught or do not respond to the teachings of righteousness. But regardless of the pathos and heartache that comes into our lives, yet the world must go on. And we must go on with it. Each day we start afresh on some new task that must be done, and in our hearts there lies the hope that evening will find us a little closer to the accomplishment of one of life's objectives.

Then in this last great stanza, Mr. Longfellow expresses his gratitude to his friend the blacksmith for the lesson of his life. He says:

> Thanks, thanks to thee, my worthy friend.
>   For the lesson thou hast taught!
> Thus at the flaming forge of life
>   Our fortunes must be wrought;
> Thus on its sounding anvil shaped
>   Each burning deed and thought.

And so is life. Each of us is given a forge, an anvil and a hammer to fashion his life for good or ill. We are all psalmists and everyone is his own blacksmith.

Of course, Jesus always serves as our most inspiring example of every good. His parables are psalms in which he pictures the possibilities of our lives in miniature. In the story of the prodigal son we see a psalm of life being written by an erring prodigal, a forgiving father, and an offended older brother. It then becomes our privilege to appraise the good points that we may want to include in our own lives. We are also alerted to possibilities of wrong that must be avoided. And just as Longfellow shows us life being lived by the blacksmith, so the Master shows us life being lived by the good Samaritan, the sower, and the rich man with bulging barns who was poor toward God. Through our psalms of life we may borrow the ready-made lessons from many lives and then, in the light of these examples of good and bad, we are better able to stand before our own forge and shape our own lives to their greatest usefulness. And just as the blacksmith fashioned the iron to serve the implements of his day, so we write out our psalms, gather the raw materials of life and then with the forge of our faith, the bellows of enthusiasm, and the hammer of our ambition, we beat out upon the anvil of existence to create the desired pattern of the most precious of all commodities—human life.

Python Eggs

THERE IS an interesting story coming out of India to the effect that in that country 50,000 natives are killed annually by pythons. These deadly reptiles first coil themselves about their victims and then crush out their lives. In the spring of the year, as the pythons lay their eggs in the sand and grass, the natives search out and destroy as many eggs as possible in order to reduce the risk that they themselves may later be destroyed by the pythons.

But the people of India are not the only ones who have to worry about pythons. In our own country there are many times 50,000 people who are constantly engaged in a similar life and death struggle. At this very moment we have five million alcoholics in the U. S. whose lives are being broken by the python coils of their own appetites. Yet no one ever deliberately starts out to be a drunkard, just as no one ever knowingly puts himself within the reach of a full-grown deadly python. This powerful serpent of alcoholism begins its career as an egg, laid in the mind of its victim. The first indulgence is just one little harmless, friendly, sociable drink, often received from the hand of a good friend. There is no more reason to fear this innocent little indulgence than there is to fear the harmless-looking python egg as it lies there so inoffensively warming itself in the sand.

But whenever we make friends with a wrong idea, whether it is large or small, we had better watch our step. A seed doesn't need to be large in order to produce a poison fruit. Alcohol contains deadly germs that have the ability to bring upon the drinker a more painful destruction than the tightening coils of the most loathsome python.

But this is not the extent of our problem; we also expose ourselves to the python eggs of ignorance, wrong attitudes, and a hundred other sins that are constantly being laid in our minds and hearts. Goethe said, "I have in me the germs of every crime." That is our natural inheritance; but our trouble begins when consciously or unconsciously we begin warming these evils into activity. It is not long after we offer our friendship to a python egg before we may expect to feel the strangling embrace of a loathsome coiling python.

John Richard Moreland has said:

It was such a little, little sin
And such a great big day,
That I thought the hours would swallow it,
Or the winds blow it away.

But the moments passed so swiftly,
And the wind died out somehow,
And the sin that was a weakling once
Is a hungry giant now.

Appetites, desires, habits and ambitions, like the harmless eggs of the python, should always be judged in terms of their future possibilities. Evil gets much of its treachery and destructiveness from the fact that its danger is not fully discernible to us in the beginning. No one has ever actually seen a python *grow*, and the increasing strength of even the most vicious evil is imperceptible to its host. But even though the growth of sin is invisible, inaudible and indiscernible, yet we should never put ourselves on a buddy-buddy basis with even the smallest evil unless we are ready to be taken captive by it. Anyone who trusts a python to release him unharmed, once its deadly coils are set, is a little more optimistic than past experience seems to justify. Yet there are thousands of wonderful people who at this moment are warming into life the very sins that will destroy their success and happiness for both here and hereafter.

Many years ago I had a friend to whom life had promised every blessing.   After a substantial promotion in his
business and some other evidences of real success, he made
his life into a kind of incubator for pythons.   He began
going with the wrong crowd.   He started an association
with nicotine.   He began taking some liberties with honor
and permitting some negative spiritual attitudes to take
root in his heart.   When once the bars were down a few
python eggs more or less seemed to make little difference
to him.   But soon his bad habits had him on the defensive.
It became more and more difficult to control or to cover-up
these writhing, squirming little creatures to whom he was
giving a free ride.   Soon these ugly little traitors had a
strangle hold on his dependability and were breaking the
bones of his own self-respect.   The marks of the python
are now plainly visible in his person.   His shabby appearance indicates that he has lost his job.   His bloated face,
bleary eyes and unsteady hand testifies that he is an alcoholic.   The death of his spirituality foretells the loss of his
soul.   His life is now largely under the control of his reptile
masters, and he is still feeding the very indulgences that
have caused his ruin.   The dilapidated remains of his former
manhood shows a continued deterioration, and he is still
being mauled in that awful snake pit of sin from which he
is now unable to release himself.

The brief agony of having one's life crushed out by
the pythons of India might be considered as a picnic compared to some of the everlasting torments that we bring upon
ourselves.   But in addition the pythons of India are responsible for only 50,000 dead per year.   One of the most meaningful lines of the holy scriptures says that, "God cannot
look upon sin with the least degree of allowance."   Not
even the smallest sins are ever permitted in God's presence.
How much heartache, regret and pain we could save ourselves if we personally exercised that much foresight and
good judgment.

Present-day delinquency and crime owes its flourishing condition to the tolerant attitude of those in whose lives it is allowed to run rampant. We would be almost scared out of our wits to be confronted by a coiling killer python, but we are not in the slightest concerned about the few harmless eggs of dishonesty and immorality that are laid in the warm sands of our everyday lives.

Frequently we actually seem anxious to promote a few of the little personal popular sins, under the disguise of being sociable we warm up the little serpents of nicotine in the fires of burning tobacco leaves. Or we ask ourselves what harm it does to take a few liberties with appetite or fair play as long as the stakes are small. We are not particularly careful at all times about the kind of friends with whom we associate. And, like the chameleon, we develop a different color for each environment we enter. Anyway, we don't believe in sin or evil in the egg stage. But what we don't always realize is that evil can creep up on us without our knowing it, and before we are aware these charming little pythons of destruction are flexing their muscles to break the bones of our better selves, or give us lung cancer or place a curse upon our souls.

It is interesting that inspite of the fact that evil is the basic problem in the world, yet almost no one believes in it, or can even recognize it in any dangerous proportions in himself. Even if we do recognize the evil in ourselves it is often pretty difficult to do much about it. Mohandas K. Gandhi once said, "There are 999 people who believe in honesty for every honest man." Everyone believes in honesty and yet we remember poor old Diogenes going around Athens with a lighted lantern in the middle of the day, trying to find just one honest man. We would not believe in tolerating the pythons of dishonor except in the egg stage. But as the eggs hatch out and the pythons begin to grow, our tolerance grows with them and before we are aware, we are entertain-

ing the full-grown pythons. As Alexander Pope has pointed
out.

> Vice is a monster of so frightful mein,
> As to be hated needs but to be seen;
> Yet seen too oft, familiar with her face,
> We first endure, then pity, then embrace.

In the same way, the little sins of ignorance, indecision,
inconsistency, disobedience, carelessness and indifference
soon grow up and become strong enough to take over and
control our future.

When someone is a little careless in attending to his
church responsibilities, he thinks, "What difference does a
little irregularity make, or what is so bad about being a
little spasmodic in one's spiritual affairs?" Frequently we
see no particular reason why we should read good books
or study the scriptures, or develop strong religious convictions
in our hearts. But the eggs of vice, spiritual neutrality and
ignorance are always undergoing a process of incubation and
growth, and before we are aware these tiny eggs of evil have
us in serious trouble.

Upon the cross Jesus said, "Father, forgive them, for
they know not what they do." Even this sin, which was
history's greatest, was committed without the offenders
themselves being aware of what was really happening. They
had merely let the wrong attitudes grow unchecked for so
long that they no longer could distinguish between truth
and falsehood. But in the final analysis, almost all of the
sins of the world are the sins of ignorance. Those who take
little liberties with their conscience don't know that they
are developing an evil power in their lives that can carry
them beyond the point of no return.

We frequently miss the mark set for us by the Creator
because we become forgetful of our prayers and unmindful
of the purpose of our lives. We allow the eggs of spiritual
inertia, lethargy and sloth to hatch and grow until they

smother out our devotion to God. Of course, all good is
not destroyed in the same way. One person relaxes his
mental discipline and takes the bridle off of his self-control.
Another insists on his right to be negative or to criticize others.
One falls in love with his own faults and by a series of
rationalizations he tries to defend his own wrongs. Without
knowing what they are doing, many people are poisoning
their own drinking water. It requires only a drop of typhoid
in the barrel to make the whole neighborhood sick. The
germs of evil are also small enough that frequently those
affected can neither taste, see, smell, hear or feel them. Some
never discover their presence until wrong has its deadly coils
about them. Only then do they find that the eggs of sin
and apostasy have become powerful pythons which are now
beyond control.

We should take a leaf out of the book of the natives of
India and destroy the eggs while we can. We have the awful
alternative that either we get rid of the eggs, or the pythons
will get rid of us. We should stamp out our bad habits while
they are in their infancy. It is easier to dispose of alcoholism
before the taste is developed or at least while it is in the egg
stage, than it is to fight the deadly python when it holds us
in its vice-like grip. Everyone has seen the pitiful struggles
of some poor alcoholic trying to free himself from the mon-
strous thing that has fastened itself upon him. Similarly it
is easier to destroy cynicism, apostasy, ignorance and sloth
before these ugly traits get their growth. It is also true that
the helpful seeds of faith and devotion will grow more vigorously if planted before the fertility has all been sucked
out of the soil by the weeds of evil.

But how ridiculous it is for us to operate an incubator
filled with python eggs, and then spend the rest of our lives
fighting the loathsome coiling, hissing, deadly serpents which
we have helped to produce. It is a fact that selfishness, greed,
alcohol, nicotine, caffeine, profanity, dishonesty, immorality
and irreverence only become real temptations after we our-

selves have developed a taste for them. In the same way, vacillation, discouragement, procrastination, lethargy, and sloth can be given their destructiveness only by the victim that they have marked for elimination. Once our pythons have been given strength we must then fight them for every inch of our future progress. They then strike us at every turn, and attack us from every ambush.

A drunkard sometimes gets a case of delirium tremens. Then snakes get into his imagination and play havoc with his success. Real snakes are seldom as dangerous as these imaginary snakes that set hostile influences in motion to destroy our success.

Idleness or the lack of a purposeful design in life provides excellent breeding sands for pythons, and it is pretty difficult to clean out the reptiles from our minds as long as those minds are lying idle and unused. And where we allow ourselves to vacillate between distractions, we no sooner get one problem out of the way than another takes its place. Some people are always upset or disturbed about something. The negative opinions expressed by others tend to destroy our convictions. And we can easily become carriers of sins and weakness when we allow ourselves to pick up the germs of indecision, confusion, doubt and discouragement that are being spread by others.

Our eyes must not be too tolerant of sin or our ears too untrained in rejecting evil or our hearts too unable to distinguish right from wrong.

How unprofitable it is to become breeders of our own failure and unhappiness by offering a nesting place to the eggs of indifference, sloth, confusion, doubt, discouragement and sin, for as the pythons gather strength they will break the bones of our character and crush out our eternal life. Our most profitable opportunity is to search out and destroy the eggs of every evil and then house clean our lives of those little wriggling treacherous pythons that hold such indisputable promise of being big snakes some day.

Quo Vadis

THE extreme persecution to which the early Christians were subjected often made their lives very difficult. We might well imagine that some severe pressures occasionally weakened their determination to do their duty. There is an interesting illustration of this idea in an old legend concerning the Apostle Peter. After he had labored for a time in Rome, his enemies there decreed his death. In order to save his life, Peter decided to flee from Rome and find some other field of labor involving less hazard. The legend has it that as he fled from his threatened martyrdom, the resurrected Christ appeared to him on the Appian Way. Peter said to Jesus, "Quo Vadis," which means, "Where goest thou?" Then Christ replied, "I am going to Rome to be crucified again." Peter felt the Lord's rebuke and it stirred his soul with new courage. Peter turned around and resolutely returned to Rome fully determined to do his duty no matter what the consequences might be. Later, when he was finally sentenced to death by crucifixion it is said that he asked only one favor of his executioners and that was that he might be crucified with his head downward, inasmuch as he considered himself unworthy to end his mortal life in the same manner as his Master.

This is an interesting example of how one person's great qualities may be reinforced and strengthened as they respond to those same qualities felt in someone else. Jesus had previously set Peter a good example in courage when years before he had met his death with extreme heroism. Jesus had made no attempt to run away. There had been no evasion or excuses. He did not take a single backward step or recant a single doctrine or contradict a single word. And one of his most thrilling qualities was that never once did he waver in doing his duty. That unwavering determination was the kind of strength that Peter needed most. That day on the Appian Way, Peter must have entertained some contrasts as his mind went back to the trial of Jesus. In the palace of Caiaphas the High Priest, Peter had lacked the courage to admit to the servant girl that he was even a friend of Jesus. And during the Master's most severe afflictions Peter had denied him three times. Jesus had sadly quoted the scripture saying, "I will smite the shepherd and the sheep will be scattered." Jesus had gone to his death comparatively alone because of a lack of courage in his followers. Peter had been strengthened by this experience but not enough, and even now, years later, as he stood facing Jesus on the Appian Way, he still found himself in the act of fearfully running away because his own safety was threatened.

Peter had accepted a prominent place in a cause that was far bigger than he was, and he knew that the great issues involved should come ahead of mere personal considerations. Peter knew of the divine birth of Jesus. He knew of his literal bodily resurrection. He knew the facts surrounding his ascension into heaven. Early in their association, Peter had borne testimony of the divinity of Jesus, saying, "Thou art the Christ, the Son of the living God." In the light of this testimony, why was he now running away? This was not the first time he had received strength from his contact with Jesus, but a great power now possessed his soul as he thought of the words of the Master. And while it was Peter who had asked the question, "Where goest thou?" it was also Peter who must give the answer as to what his future course would be. That answer was not long in coming, and once his mind was set, nothing could thwart its purpose. It was for this firmness of soul that we remember this great apostle as Cephas the Rock, the Stalwart, the chief mortal support of the Savior of the world.

This simple question which Peter asked and answered had a determining influence upon his life. What a happy circumstance it would be if all of us could use Peter's question as effectively in our own interests. For example, suppose that as *Judas* left his associates in the upper room contemplating the Lord's betrayal, he had stopped long enough to say to himself, "Judas, where goest thou? Where will this course lead you? If your evil succeeds, what will be the effect upon the Church, your family, your friends, and upon the Master himself?" Judas must have thought about the fact that *he* had also been chosen as an Apostle of the Lord. A little mature thought would have reminded him that thirty pieces of silver was a very inadequate reward for the deed he contemplated. It is possible that a thoughtful consideration of Peter's question would have turned him back from his evil. It is interesting to remember that as soon as the consciousness of what he had done broke in upon Judas, he was seized by a remorse so severe that he went out and hanged himself. The tragedy was that this thoughtfulness came *after* his evil rather than before it. Because of this error in timing, the once proud name of Judas is now mentioned only to denote the most extreme unfaithfulness, disloyalty and betrayal. But most of our *timers* are also a little off. Certainly this habitual lack of advance consideration for important problems is one of the most common causes of our own difficulties.

We have a common expression where someone asks, "Where are you headed?" And while that is not quite as high-sounding as the Latin words "Quo Vadis," yet in any form it is an important question, and we should use it more often with specific reference to ourselves, and we should be sure that we get the right answer before we let the question go. Most thoughts or acts or ambitions are not as important for themselves alone as for where they will lead us.

Certainly the prospective alcoholic would never take that first little friendly sociable drink if he knew where it would take him or what the effect would be upon himself, his job, his family and his friends. Before anyone takes a drink he should ask himself, "Where will it take me?" It is thought that this interesting question might be a pretty good one for everyone to keep on hand, and always have available for immediate use.

Some time ago I talked with a fine young girl who had just turned eighteen. She had decided that she was old enough to run her own life without counsel from anyone. She thought that if she wanted to go with questionable friends and do wrong things, that was pretty much her own business. She could see no real need for her parents at her time of life. What she did not understand was that it is pretty easy for both old and young to make mistakes. The adventure of life is very complicated, primarily because we don't see in advance where events are leading us. We need the counsel of experience that can see through our blind spots and identify our personal hazards with clearer perspective. Because of the love this girl's parents had for her, and because of the touch of perverseness in her attitude they were afraid of driving her farther away from them by too much opposition to her plans. But the freedom and love that can exist between parents and children can sometimes be lost.

This young woman has many personal blind spots, but so did Peter and so did Judas, and so do we all. If these blind spots are given too much freedom of action, difficulties result. And it is not an easy thing to untangle the webs of sin and mistakes once they have been woven. Even after *Judas* was fully aware of what he had done, he was not strong enough to go back and try to undo his wrong. That is also one of our problems. It is very difficult for an alcoholic or a willful child or a thoughtless adult to turn back.

The decision of Judas to commit suicide probably seemed a more simple solution to him than to start over. The evil of Judas may have taken no longer than an hour to commit, yet forever more his life will carry the dreadful marks of a betrayer. But we can also brand ourselves just as quickly and just as definitely. In addition, when we get into unfavorable situations it is so easy for our thinking to be distorted. We sometimes forget who our real friends are, and we stamp our souls with the marks of sin before we fully realize what we are doing. The evil that gets power over us is so small to begin with that it incites no fear in us, and consequently we take no measures to protect ourselves until we have passed what we think is the point of no return. All of these unpleasant possibilities make these two little Latin words very important.

At the height of her career the fiance of Lillian Roth died, and a deep sorrow overwhelmed the life of this famous actress. For weeks she was so distraught mentally and emotionally that she got very little rest or peace of mind. Then one night her nurse suggested that she drink a glass of brandy before going to bed. That night she got her first good night's rest in weeks. Because of its pleasant effect she drank more brandy the next night and the next and the next. It was finally suggested that maybe she was going too far, but she felt perfectly capable of handling herself under any and all circumstances. But in the next few years she was married and divorced several times. She lost her large fortune, her reputation, her friends, and almost every other worth-while thing in life, and finally she was confined in an institution for alcoholics against her will. All of this trouble came about because she couldn't see where one little glass of brandy would take her.

Every bad habit and every good habit and every idea and every ambition has a destination stamped upon it, and it is very important that we should know where we are going to end up before we get started. Charles F. Kettering said, "My interest is in the future because I am going to spend the rest of my life there." That is where the primary interest of everyone should be. We are all going to spend the overwhelming part of our lives in the future, and before we get too chummy with anything, we should make every effort to learn as much as possible about its future or lack of it. The chief factor about anything, is its destination. Jesus said we should live by every word that proceedeth out of the mouth of God. That is so because the word of the Lord has the greatest future, and like everything else, the most important thing about the gospel of Christ is where it leads us to. This is what most people do not understand. When Peter decided to run away from his duty, he was headed in the same general direction as the betrayer or the alcoholic or the disobedient, and the ultimate end of such a journey is always unhappiness. The thing that saved the day for Peter was that he discovered his error in time and turned back.

Suppose that when things began to get difficult that the Master himself had run away. Is it any wiser for us to follow a wrong program, or to start on a course which has no future or where our possibilities of success are drastically reduced? More than about anything else we need to get a strong focus on a goal with a future and then never take our eyes away from it. The successful mariner strives toward his destiny with his eyes on the North Star. God our Eternal Father has set up the Celestial Kingdom as the North Star of our accomplishment. Celestial glory is the glory in which God himself dwells. That is where the highest of all standards of living is found. That is also the place of the highest standards of thinking and the highest standards of love, and the highest standards of happiness. The greatest of all the gifts of God is eternal life. Because eternity lies beyond our known experience, and we cannot fully comprehend it, we frequently occupy our minds with the wrong things and often find ourselves on the broad way that leads to destruction, or we run away from our duty and lose our greatest opportunities. The safest program for keeping ourselves on the right course is to keep our lives in harmony with our Redeemer. Every time Peter came in contact with Jesus he was made stronger. The same contact will have the same effect upon us. I like to think of Peter as he stood undecided on the Appian Way vitalizing his life by the use of those two interesting Latin words, "Quo Vadis." They can also be valuable to us if we frequently ask ourselves, "Whither goest thou?" and then make sure that we require ourselves to give a thoughtful, logical, inspired answer.

The Rebel

SOMETIME ago a psychiatrist wrote a book entitled, *A Rebel Without a Cause*. In it he points out that while trying to get along with ourselves and the universe in which we live, we separate ourselves into groups. That is, a natural sorting process is always taking place, branding and tagging us according to how we respond to life. Then life place us in the particular pigeonhole occupied by those whose characteristics correspond to our kind of behavior.

One of these general classifications is made up of people having serious mental and emotional difficulties. The number of those afflicted with this particular malady has been rapidly increasing in recent years, as indicated by the tremendous upswing in the number of calls made for psychiatric help. There is no one name that adequately describes these problems, but the author refers to the general defect as psychopathic personality. Of course, psychopathy is much more than a mere pigeonhole. It more resembles a kind of Pandora's Box filled to the brim with the makings of all kinds of malignant, social, political, and religious scourges.

The author compares a psychopath to Johnstone's rogue elephant which was fittingly described as a rebel. He says that a rebel is a religious disobeyer of prevailing codes and standards. And the author says that his own clinical experience indicates that one with a psychopathic personality can best be described as a "rebel without a cause." He is an agitator without a slogan, a revolutionary without a program. He is a fighter with nothing to fight for and no victory to look forward to. Rebelliousness is usually aimed at achieving goals that are primarily satisfactory only to oneself. The author says that this group of people are incapable of exertion for the sake of others. While their efforts are usually hidden under some protecting guise, yet in spite of the camouflage their investment is designed only to satisfy their own immediate desires.

This urge for immediate personal satisfaction is distinctly an infantile characteristic. Unlike properly matured adults, the child cannot wait upon suitable circumstances for the fulfillment of his needs. The adult is able to postpone his luncheon for a few hours if occasion requires, but the infant cries and takes other aggressive measures to get immediate satisfaction for his need. Those who are psychopathic also make their wants known by various types of immature agitation designed to bring about an immediate fulfillment of their wants. For example, the psychopath is usually unwilling to delay the gratification of his sex impulses or other bodily urges. As these urges make themselves felt, a morally immature person both ignores reason and violates convention and morality. From this group of rebels come the sex deviates who rape, murder and corrupt.

Of course, rebelliousness may manifest itself in one of many forms. When a mature person wants property, prestige, or social acceptance, he uses education, planning, industry, time and proper conduct to fulfill his needs in an acceptable way. But the socially immature cannot wait. They try to gratify their needs by deception, theft, and other unapproved means. Because the immature are generally not willing to spend the time required in preparation and industry to achieve their goals, they drop their education and other means of permanent self-improvement so that they can concentrate on their immediate desires. They begin to smoke, drink, etc., to give themselves the feeling of being adult before their time. The great burden placed upon our society by the scourge of teenage marriages is because those involved can't wait until they are properly qualified for marriage. Everything must give way before their impulses.

When fettered with this damaging personality defect some people seem completely unable to avail themselves of the restraining safeguards of normal living, and they soon find themselves in the pigeonhole labeled "rebellion." In this spirit children frequently think of running away from home or in other ways stage a revolt against their parents. The reform schools and the jails are filled with people who rebel against the various kinds of legal authority and civil restraint. This trait has helped our great free land of America to become world-renowned as the theatre of crime, vice, outlawry, drunkenness and other forms of psychopathy.

The dictionary says that psychopathy is a mental disorder, that while it doesn't quite reach the proportions of outright insanity, yet it causes serious personality defects. We help to develop this emotional instability in ourselves by permitting ourselves too much of the luxury of immaturity, disobedience, and just plain perversity. These wrongs then bring upon us all kinds of complexes, feelings of inadequacy and a warped and undependable mentality. We strengthen this near-insanity when we tolerate an undue amount of conceit, lack of common sense, a disinclination for self-analysis, a low grade of self-control, a lack of truthfulness, or too great a measure of spiritual irresponsibility. Of course, all psychopathic individuals have these bothersome traits in different combinations, and no one remedy covers them all.

A psychiatrist was recently discussing this "rebel without a cause" concept, illustrating his points with the experiences of his patients. He was asked how anyone not actually insane could be allowed by his reason to do these things. The doctor replied that the reason of the patient was not involved. He pointed out that if we would use our reason or if we had a properly trained sense of right and wrong, there would be very few problems. So many people react merely to themselves or to their immediate circumstances, with no attempt to be logical or to follow sound principles, or even to be aware of consequences. But one cannot ignore reason and right and long retain a proper mental balance. When one regards only his own selfish interests and becomes too much of a rebel, he turns back his maturity to a point where these psychopathic tendencies begin to show up. We pity the backward nations that waste their property and their lives in continual political rebellions. But there are even more destructive kinds of rebellion going on in individuals. I know of a young man who rebelled against his father and mother because they are poor, this in spite of their unquestioned devotion and their success in putting him through school, etc.

On the other hand, I know of a young woman who rebelled against her prominent well-to-do parents for exactly the opposite reasons. Her parents have worked hard and finally overcame their unfavorable financial situation. In the process they have won many honors and have tried to get their children to follow in their footsteps. The advantages won by the parents have been lavished upon the daughter, but she balks at every step. She resents being identified with the success of her parents. She feels that she can have no real personal recognition as long as anyone else is in the picture, and yet she is presently incapable of bringing about the success she seeks. Instead of cooperation and a willingness to take the time necessary to show people her worth and superiority, she has rebelled against her parents and everything connected with their success, including their religious faith. With too much thinking about herself, she has become a rebel without a cause.

This is a part of an attitude expressed by the man who said, "I am for the underdog." His friend said, "I am also for the underdog, providing the underdog is right—but suppose the underdog is wrong?" His friend said, "I am for the underdog whether he is right or wrong." This is the kind of rebellion that sets some people against the law in favor of criminals. It sets others against good in favor of evil.

It is said that a son of Abraham Lincoln rebelled against the homespun appearance of his father, while he himself became something of a fashion plate. Some also rebel against the old-fashioned honesty and virtue for which their fathers are noted, and they bring upon themselves a great many problems as a consequence.

For no good reason rebellion often turns people against righteousness to a life of sin. This was one of the problems of King Saul, and the Lord said to him: "For rebellion is as the sin of witchcraft, and stubbornness is as iniquity and idolatry. Because thou hast rejected the word of the Lord, he hath also rejected thee from being king." (I Samuel 15:23) Rebellion turns others against truth in favor of error. Sometimes when someone that we dislike is connected with a worthy cause, we turn against the cause to avoid being identified with the one we dislike.

This dangerous personality defect sometimes even sets us against God himself. We never deny God because *he* is wrong, but always because *we* are wrong. We never rebel against the work of the Lord in favor of something better; we rebel against the work of the Lord because we are rebels. When righteousness is against a rebel, the rebel always turns against righteousness. Jesus probably has had more enemies than anyone who ever lived, and yet he lived a perfect life. He took upon himself our sins and suffered for our transgressions, and gave up his life to bring about our happiness. I recently heard one poor unfortunate giving his reasons why he thought God was "unfair." It was pathetic in its tragedy, yet it is so common to become a "rebel" against God without a cause. Sin, disobedience, sloth, or a wasted life are all forms of rebellion. Certainly these traits are not noteworthy objectives to build into the only life that we will ever have upon this earth.

Lucifer was the original and most destructive rebel. In the council of heaven he turned against everything good, including God, free agency, and even the righteous principles ordained by the Father for his own good. He not only opposed God, but he also opposed two-thirds of the hosts of heaven, and through his rebellion he led away one-third of all of that congregation to their eternal damnation. Even yet, Satan continues in his rebellion and he will continue until his final banishment.

But on a smaller scale many of us live lives of rebellion, and rebellion so often ends eventually with the destruction of the rebel. The right kind of loyalty in the heart of Lincoln's son would have made him love the unquestioned honesty and homespun virtues of his great father. Then he would have built these wonderful qualities into himself. What could be worse than to rebel against God and to love evil rather than good? When we feel even a little rebellion getting into our hearts, we should take warning that we are treading on dangerous ground. A turn toward repentance is the adult and godly way to solve most of our problems, including those of rebellion. We should free ourselves from the immaturity, disobedience, indifference, perversity and other sins that lead us to do great wrong and make us transgressors before God. The word *transgression* itself means to go contrary to, or to violate, or to rebel.

No one is perfect, but instead of rebelling against honorable parents, we should try to correct any mistakes they may have made so far as our lives are concerned. Nothing would please them more than to have us excel them in honor, as with the Roman matron, Cornelia, who frequently upbraided her son that men still referred to her as the daughter of Scipio rather than the mother of Tiberius. And rather than rebelling against God we should honor him with our devotion. For any way we look at it, "the way of the transgressor is hard" and one of the transgressions that makes our lives hardest is the sin of rebellion. We make it easy to rebel against honor and righteous principles when we are not manifesting these principles wholeheartedly in our lives. Lucifer would not have debauched one-third of the hosts of heaven if he had been on his knees worshiping God.

So many of us are rebels in one thing or another, and when one of the objects of our rebellion is removed, another can be easily found. When once this dread defect is developed, it is difficult to control. The rebellion developed by the young woman against her parent's will probably be redirected at a later date against her husband. The rebellion that we develop against our work is often redirected against life generally. The rebellion we feel against our simple duty may soon be transferred to rebellion against God himself. We must not rebel merely because life tries to discipline us. When God tries to lead us to eternal glory, we should not condemn ourselves to hell by a rebellion out of spite.

What a thrill it ought to be for us to be loyal to our Father in heaven! What a privilege it ought to be for us to be loyal to truth and righteousness! What a tremendous opportunity to close up our Pandora's Box of rebellion by the simple process of growing up spiritually, mentally, emotionally, all of which can be done by the development of our reason and strict obedience to the word of the Lord! We can avoid untold misery in this life and eternal damnation in the next by destroying the awful seeds of rebellion that may be growing in our hearts and establishing therein an absolute loyalty to the God who created us.

Regulus, the Roman

ONE OF the important purposes of life is to develop our God-given abilities. We can learn many things from many sources. Books have much to teach us. The school and the church can make a great contribution to our success. Our own thought processes and the periods given to meditation greatly enlarge our outlook on life. Jesus became the greatest of all teachers by applying the truths he learned from the lilies of the field, the sower, the prodigal son, and the good Samaritan.

But probably one of the most productive sources of learning is other people. When Charles Kingsley was asked the secret of his radiant, useful life, he replied, "I had a friend." But we can also learn from our enemies. We can learn something from everyone and everything. Today marks the anniversary of the end of a devastating world war, but even the most hard and cruel experiences may be made to add to our strength. Warriors have a particularly important contribution to make to our success. We may borrow their great determination, their unyielding courage and their heroic devotion. When once developed, these traits can serve any part of our success.

For example, think how much we owe Nathan Hale, when prior to forfeiting his life before an enemy firing squad he said, "I regret that I have but one life to give for my country." Joan of Arc made an immeasurable contribution to thousands of people by choosing to be burned alive rather than deny what she believed.

And one of the qualities that we need most in order to solve our present-day problems is the unwavering courage of our convictions. We see this type of courage most highly developed on the battlefield. Sometimes it takes extreme

situations to build within us that magnificent ability to stand
for what we believe against all odds. It is more difficult
to develop this trait when surrounded by the soft living and
careless effort of unimportant situations. Our biggest problem may come in developing sufficient courage to meet our
ordinary situations. Without courage we sometimes cringe
and crawl and vacillate before every opposition or go down
in defeat before even minor contrary influences. Some people
are perfectly loyal to their country when all conditions are
favorable, but they can be easily brainwashed to become the
tools of evil in the hands of an enemy.

This want for moral strength is sometimes even more
obvious in our personal and religious lives. Many individuals have become profane, immoral, alcoholic, or dishonest
merely because they could not withstand the pressure of
opposing influences. A little ridicule, a few uncomplimentary remarks, the offer of a personal advantage, or a threat
of danger, has caused many people to lose their convictions
or renounce their faith, or betray their country, or even to
deny God. There are among us many small-scale Benedict
Arnolds, many unknown Judas Iscariots, political quislings
and personal cowards who have been turned to wrong by
a little unfavorable pressure. Unfortunately all of us do not
have the courage of Nathan Hale or Joan of Arc. But fortunately everyone can develop sufficient strength to solve his
every problem. And one of the best ways to do this is to
always keep courage in our minds by re-living the heroic
deeds of others.

Many years ago I was greatly impressed with a reading
lesson by Elijah Kellogg in an old eighth grade text. This
stimulating material was entitled, "The Return of Regulus."
The story of Regulus, as told by Roman writers and poets,
is familiar to all who have read the history of the long, fierce
struggles between the ancient cities of Rome and Carthage.
For nine years a bitter war had been waged between these
two rivals for world power. Then the Roman consuls, Regu-

lus and Manlius, were sent with a large fleet, and a land army of a hundred forty thousand men against the hated Carthaginians. The new Roman fleet was at once victorious against the larger fleet of the enemy. Under Regulus, the land forces gained many victories. Finally Xanthippus, a Spartan general, taught the Carthaginians to fight with elephants and bands of cavalry in the open plain. The result was, the Roman army was destroyed and Regulus was taken prisoner.

After five years imprisonment, a decided Roman victory forced Carthage to sue for peace, and the Carthaginians sent Regulus to Rome with their envoys to arrange the terms. Regulus at first refused to enter Rome, since he was no longer free. After this conscientious scruple was overcome, he refused to give his opinion in the senate until commanded by Rome to do so. Then Professor Botsford, in his "History of the Ancient World," tells us that—

"When Regulus was finally persuaded to address the senate, he advised that body *not* to make peace nor to ransom the captives, but to let them die in the land where they had disgraced themselves by surrender. Thus they would serve as an example to others; he himself would return and share their fate. In vain the senators remonstrated against this decision. While departing from Rome he kept his eyes fixed on the ground that he might not see his wife and children. Then, returning to Carthage in accordance with his oath, he is said to have suffered death by torture."

The common story is that he was put into a cask pierced with nails, the points of which projected inward, and that he was rolled down a hill inside the cask until he expired.

The story of Regulus gives a stimulating interpretation of the sentiments that can dominate the heart of a great soldier and patriot. Professor Botsford says:

"Here is presented the picture of a man who was absolutely faithful to his plighted word, of a stern patriot ready to sacrifice himself and his fellow captives for what he believed to be his country's good, of a strong-willed man who knew his fate and walked resolutely to meet it."

Then Mr. Kellogg tells his story as follows:

"The beams of the rising sun had gilded the lofty domes of Carthage, and given, with its rich and mellow light, a tinge of beauty even to the frowning ramparts of the outer harbor. Sheltered by the verdant shores, a hundred triremes were riding proudly at their anchors, their brazen beaks glittering in the sun, their streamers dancing in the morning breeze, while many a shattered plank and timber gave evidence of the desperate conflict with the fleets of Rome.

"No murmur of business or of revelry arose from the city. The artisan had forsaken his shop, the judge his tribunal, the priest his sanctuary, and even the stern stoic had come forth from his retirement to mingle with the crowd that, anxious and agitated, were rushing toward the senate house, startled by the report that Regulus had returned to Carthage.

"Onward, still onward, trampling each other under foot, they rushed, furious with anger, and eager for revenge. Fathers were there, whose sons were groaning in fetters; maidens, whose lovers, weak and wounded, were dying in the dungeons of Rome, and there were other thousands of gray-haired men and matrons, whom the Roman sword had left childless.

"But when the stern features of Regulus were seen, and his colossal form towering above the ambassadors who had returned with him from Rome; when the news passed from lip to lip that the dreaded warrior, so far from advising the Roman senate to consent to an exchange of prisoners, had urged them to pursue, with exterminating vengeance, Carthage and Carthaginians,—the multitude swayed to and fro like a forest beneath a tempest, and the rage and hate of that tumultuous throng vented itself in groans, and curses, and yells of vengeance.

"But calm, cold and immovable as the marble walls around him stood the Roman; and he stretched forth his hand over that frenzied crowd, with gesture as proudly commanding as though he still stood at the head of the gleaming cohorts of Rome. The tumult ceased; the curse, half-muttered, died upon the lip; and so intense was the silence, that the clanking of the brazen manacles upon the wrists of the captive fell sharp and full upon every ear in that vast assembly, as he thus addressed them:—

" 'Ye doubtless thought—for ye judge of Roman virtue by your own—that I would break my plighted oath, rather than, returning, brook your vengeance. I might give reasons for this, in Punic comprehension, most foolish act of mine. I might speak of those eternal principles which make death for one's country a pleasure, not a pain. But, by great Jupiter! methinks I should debase myself to talk of such high things to you; to you, expert in womanly inventions; to you, well skilled to drive a treacherous trade with simple Africans for ivory and gold.

" 'If the bright red blood that courses through my veins, transmitted free from godlike ancestry, were like that slimy ooze which stagnates in your arteries, I had remained at home, broken my plighted oath to save my life. I am a Roman citizen; therefore have I returned, that ye might work your will upon this mass of flesh and bones, that I esteem no higher than the rags that cover them.

" 'Here, in your capital, do I defy you. Have I not conquered your armies, fired your towns, and dragged your generals at my chariot wheels, since first my youthful arm could wield a spear? And do you think to see me crouch and cower before a tamed and shattered senate? The tearing of flesh and the rending of sinews is but pastime compared to the *mental* agony that heaves my frame.

" 'The moon has scarce yet waned since the proudest of Rome's proud matrons, the mother upon whose breast I slept, and whose fair brow so oft had bent over me before the noise of battle had stirred my blood, or the fierce toil of war nerved my sinews, did, with fondest memory of bygone hours, entreat me to remain. I have seen her, who, when my country called me to the field, did buckle on my harness with trembling hands, while the tears fell thick and fast down the hard corselet scales—I have seen her tear her gray locks and beat her aged breast, as on her knees she begged me not to return to Carthage! and all the assembled senate of Rome, grave and reverend men, proffered the same request. The puny torments which ye have in store to welcome me withal, shall be, to what I have endured, even as the murmur of a summer's brook to the fierce roar of angry surges on a rocky beach.

"'Last night, as I lay fettered in my dungeon, I heard a strange, ominous sound; it seemed like the distant march of some vast army, their harness clanging as they marched, when suddenly there stood by me Xanthippus, the Spartan general, by whose aid you conquered me, and, with a voice as low as when the solemn wind moans through the leafless forest, he thus addressed me:—

"'"Roman, I come to bid thee curse, with thy dying breath, this fated city; know that in an evil hour, the Carthaginian generals, furious with rage that I had conquered thee, their conqueror, did basely murder me. And then they thought to stain my brightest honor. But, for this foul deed, the wrath of Jove shall rest upon them here and hereafter." And then he vanished.

"'And now, go bring your sharpest torments, the woes I see impending over this guilty realm shall be enough to sweeten death, though every nerve and artery were a shooting pang. I die! but my death shall prove a proud triumph; and, for every drop of blood ye from my veins do draw, your own shall flow in rivers.

"'Woe to thee, Carthage! Woe to thee proud city of the waters! I see thy nobles wailing at the feet of Roman senators! thy citizens in terror! thy ships in flames! I hear the victorious shouts of Rome! I see her eagles glittering on thy ramparts. Proud city, thou art doomed. The curse of God is on thee—a clinging, wasting curse, which shall not leave thy gates till hungry flames shall lick the fretted gold from off thy proud palaces, and every brook runs crimson to the sea.' "

This scene of hate and revenge does not make a pretty picture, yet the absolute loyalty to a trust, the ability that it displays to be faithful to one's convictions no matter what the consequence, is one of the greatest of all human character qualities. This is especially true in our day when we so badly need the courage to stand against evil and untruth. William James once said that we need a moral equivalent of war if we are to develop sufficient courage for our lives. This is one of the traits that has always characterized the great prophets, many of whom have also suffered a tortuous death rather than to be unfaithful to the trust that God had imposed in them. And while our total responsibility may be something less than the prophets, yet the importance of being true to our faith is not less. In life, as in battle, it is just as important for the sergeant to be faithful as it is for the general. No army would get very far where only the general could be depended upon. And no country will ever be great where the individual citizen feels free to accept bribes or be untrue, or sell his country to serve his own interests.

Regulus said, "I am a Roman citizen." To him those words stood for something far greater than himself. But we are children of God, destined to become like him, and above everything else we must be good soldiers with the courage of our convictions and an unfaltering determination never to betray his confidence.

Religion

Many years ago Dr. Henry C. Link wrote a very interesting book under the title *The Return to Religion*. The first chapter deals with his own religious experience. Dr. Link grew up in a religious household and received some good religious instruction. But as he climbed the educational ladder he began discarding his religious convictions in favor of what he considered a more intellectual approach to life's problems. And with a Phi Beta Kappa key in his possession he came to scorn what he considered the petty practices of the church. He believed that religion was a refuge for weak minds. He built up his arguments against Christian doctrine until he became what he himself described as a complete and powerfully fortified agnostic.

His wife was something of an intellectual in her own right and fully shared his views of religion. They agreed that instead of sending their own children to church, they would let them settle their religious questions for themselves when they were old enough to know what it was all about.

Dr. Link became a famous psychologist at an early age. In recognition of the many contributions in his field, his name was included in *Men of Science*, the roster of America's foremost scientists, when he was only 32. In his capacity as the Director of the Psychological Service Center of New York City, his job was to help people solve their many difficult problems.

But working in actual contact with personal difficulties, Dr. Link soon discovered that the best solution for almost all problems was to be found in the acceptance and practice of the religion of Christ, as outlined in the Holy Scriptures.

That is, a happy marriage can be most effectively built upon a foundation of real religion; and the problems arising in every other department of life are answered in about the same way. Whether one is seeking occupational success, economic security or social satisfactions, his goal can best be attained by putting the principles of the gospel into actual operation in his life.

Dr. Link and his associates gave psychological tests to thousands of people, and in almost all cases the needed therapy called for the practice of some basic fundamental religious principle. It was found that those whose lives were actuated by religious motives had better social and physical health and significantly better personalities. They were not only happier and more successful, but they were superior in almost every other way.

Dr. Link's discoveries were particularly impressive in the field of child training. It was found that those children who grew up without church teaching never acquired the strong sense of right and wrong possessed by their religiously trained parents, even though the parents left the church after the training had been received.

Referring to his own early experience, Dr. Link said, "We were taught that certain things were right or wrong because God said so. But we could only tell our children that things were right or wrong because we said so. This does not build the same kind of personality strength. Without the pressure of religious training in actual Christian doctrine, children do not acquire the basic moral values in life which the parent accepts automatically even though he no longer credits the divine origin of the teaching itself. The parents who destroy the authority of God in the minds of their children set themselves an impossible task as they themselves must then take over the responsibility.

"Then as the child grows older he comes more and more under the influence of the conflicting authorities of society, the school, the neighbors, the gang, and the community. When the child finds that his own parents are vacillating, uncertain and in frequent error, his defenses are destroyed and he has little left to cling to or believe in. It is pretty difficult for any parent to replace God as an authority on right and wrong."

Dr. Link quotes a striking line from one of Ibsen's plays in which a leading character exclaims, "Without a fixed point outside myself, I cannot exist." In this world of changes and rebellion against authority, God is our only fixed point. He is the unchanging North Star of our universe. The child who early in life accepts God as the supreme arbitrator of good and evil has already acquired the most important basic motive for a good character and good habits.

The strategic time to teach children to subordinate their own impulses to higher values is when they are too young to understand, but not too young to accept. When parents decide not to send their children to Sunday School until they are old enough to know what it is all about, they are adopting a ruinous policy. For by the time the children have learned what it is all about, it is usually too late to do much about it.

It is a dangerous principle to make one's personal likes and dislikes the basis for his action. We need a higher authority on right and wrong than ourselves, our parents, or even the authority of the nation. We have all been disgusted with the irresponsibility and absolute inconsistency and untruth of Mr. Khrushchev, who leans entirely on the arm of flesh and acknowledges no higher authority than his own, either on earth or in heaven. It is a historic communist doctrine that when *they* make war they call it peace, and when we resist they call it war. And they themselves are the only judges of right and wrong. Without a belief in a higher power than themselves, everyone, including the Communists, fail to achieve their own potential. A return to religion is the most important need of the Russian people. It is also our most important need as a nation and as individuals.

Dr. Link says that his return to religion was a highly intellectual as well as a highly scientific return. He discovered that the most effective possible practice of psychology was to live the religion that he had previously discarded as having little value. The greatest of all discoveries is when man discovers God. The greatest of all decisions is when man accepts God as his guide in matters of right and wrong.

Daniel Webster once said, "The most important thought that ever occupied my mind was that of my individual responsibility to God." What a tremendous anchor to our success such a philosophy becomes!

An effective practice of religion can be the most helpful of all of our life's influences. For example, Dr. Link discovered that most of the people who occupied sick beds were there because of some mental or emotional problem that could only be cured by religious therapy. We see this same problem and the same solution in operation all around us.

Some time ago a broken-hearted young woman with her first baby came to talk about her troubles. She had married when she was very young, against the advice of her parents. She had been deeply in love, and she thought that this wonderful feeling that she and this young man had for each other was sufficient in itself to guarantee their happiness. But her husband was lacking in basic moral character and had not been sufficiently grounded in the principles and practices of religion. The only code he knew was that of his own will. God's standards of right and wrong were unintelligible concepts to him. A little drinking with his friends and a few immoral indulgences were not incompatible with the standards set by his bodily urges. Because his wife's life was governed by religious standards and his by his own pleasures, a great void developed between them to make a happy marriage impossible; and what was supposed to be a holy relationship has become one of continual heartbreak and unhappiness.

This splendid young woman has now learned that love alone is not enough. Satisfaction in human relations must have under it a foundation of basic religious character. If this woman's husband cannot be faithful to God, there is little likelihood that he will be faithful to her.

Lord Burleigh once said, "Never trust anyone who is unsound in his religion, for he that is false to God can never be true to man." The purpose of religion is to make men honest and upright in all their dealings and associations. Real religion will make all human conduct conform to the law of God. Can anyone think of anything in the world that is even half as important? Real religion will make a man a better husband, a better father, a better businessman, and a better citizen. Rowland Hill says, "I would give nothing for a man's religion if even his dog and cat were not better off as a consequence."

Dr. Link's return to religion was prompted by his science. But a real return to religion involves much more than psychology. A return to religion is the way we bring about our success as well as the way we save our souls. More than anything else our world and all of us as individuals need to have a return to the religion of Jesus Christ. Nothing else is so important. Solomon sought for wisdom, some seek for education, wealth or personal prestige. Health and strength are priceless assets, but above all other things, religion stands out as the thing most to be sought after.

Near the end of his life, Patrick Henry said, "I have now distributed all of my property to my family. But there is one more thing that I wish I could give them, and that is the Christian religion. If they had that and I had not given them one shilling, they would have been rich. And if they had not had that, and I had given them all the world, they would be poor."

All of us want the good things of life—a good education, a fine home, a happy family, a prosperous business, an honorable name, and material security.   But all of these can be most easily attained on the single foundation of genuine religion.   That is what we believe in, how we think, and what we do.

All education is really about ourselves.   We study medicine to learn how to keep ourselves well physically.   We study psychology and psychiatry to keep ourselves well mentally.   Agriculture is how we feed ourselves.   The social studies teach us to get along with each other.   We study law to learn to keep out of trouble, business is how we deal with each other.

Then we have this great science of religion which teaches us how to keep ourselves well spiritually.   A strong religion makes all accomplishment easy.   Charles Kingsley said that he did not merely want to possess a religion, he wanted a religion that would possess him.   Sometimes we use religion merely as a kind of lightning rod to ward off trouble.   Some use religion primarily for its social or business advantage. But this is not the real purpose of religion, for as Ruskin said, "Anything that makes religion a secondary object makes it no object.   And he who offers God a second place in his life offers him no place."   God and religion should be primary in our lives.

Colton has said that "Men will wrangle for religion, write for it, fight for it, die for it, they will do anything but live for it."   And yet living is our business, and we need some real religious discipline to help us live at our best.   Most people, both children and adults alike, turn away from discipline and make of existence a kind of life-long indulgence. Parents indulge their children and themselves.   Politicians indulge the masses.   The material and scientific advantages of our civilization conspires to make our lives easier and our characters weaker.   We need a stronger portion of the severe standards of right and wrong to make our lives more meaningful.

The great Apostle Paul said, "My son, despise not the chastening of the Lord, nor faint when thou art rebuked of him: For whom the Lord loveth he chasteneth, and scourgeth every son whom he receiveth. If ye endure chastening, God dealeth with you as with sons; for what son is he whom the father chasteneth not? But if ye be without chastisement, whereof all are partakers, then are ye . . . not sons.

"Furthermore we have had fathers of our flesh which corrected us, and we gave them reverence: shall we not much rather be in subjection unto the Father of spirits, and live? For they verily for a few days chastened us after their own pleasure; but he for our profit, that we might be partakers of his holiness. Now no chastening for the present seemeth to be joyous, but grievous: nevertheless afterward it yieldeth the peaceable fruit of righteousness . . ." (Heb. 12:5-11.)

If the gospel of Jesus Christ is true, it is the most tremendous idea ever known in the world, and men who are obedient thereto will enjoy eternal life in the presence of God. But even if the gospel had no divine origin, one would be better off for having lived its principles. Pascal says, "If a man should err in supposing the Christian religion to be true, he could not possibly be a loser by the mistake. But how irreparable is his loss and how inexpressible his danger who should err in supposing it to be false."

The gospel of Jesus Christ is true, and it is the foundation on which all success and happiness must rest. Religion is not the refuge of the weak, but the instrument of those who would be strong. It is the means by which we may become masters of ourselves, rather than slaves of our environment. May each of us personally conduct his own return to the religion of Jesus Christ in such a way that it may possess his life.

The Second Mile

O NE OF the most helpful of all success philosophies was given by Jesus in his story of the second mile. The people to whom Jesus was speaking were subject to a very unpleasant military regulation giving a Roman soldier the right to command a civilian to carry his burden for one mile. This made a very disagreeable situation for those who hated their Roman masters.

It must have been a double shock, therefore, to hear Jesus say, "Whosoever shall compel thee to go one mile, go with him twain." Merely to accompany a Roman soldier was a defiling business. To carry his burdens for any distance was unpleasant. But to voluntarily go even beyond the demands of Imperial Rome was a disgraceful surrender. We can imagine how it would clash with American temperament to be forced to carry the burdens of an oppressive foreign conqueror. It could not have been less distasteful to the Jews.

Over a half century ago Harry Emerson Fosdick wrote a very helpful little book under the title of *The Second Mile*. He challenges our thinking with many interesting applications for this important philosophy of the Master, which we might well utilize to solve our own problems. That is we can also overcome the hates and dreads of life by cheerfully doing more than is required.

To illustrate this point, we recall the interesting fictional story of Ben Hur. Ben Hur, who was supposed to have been a contemporary of Jesus, was made a Roman slave and consigned to work the oars of a Roman galley. Ben Hur's companions accepted their assignments with bitterness and hate, and as a consequence their naked backs were bruised and cut by the lashes of their Roman masters. But Ben Hur adopted the philosophy of the second mile. He did his work as though his oars were taking him on a pleasure cruise to some worth-while objective. Ben Hur knew that no effort is ever lost, and he worked twice as hard as he was asked to work.

His willing attitude and powerful effort greatly pleased his Roman masters, and Ben Hur asked nothing in return except that he be permitted to work on both sides of the galley, that his body muscles may develop equally.

Then came the shipwreck and Ben Hur rescued a Roman Tribune. Then followed the chariot races at Antioch, where those mighty arms developed in the galleys enabled Ben Hur to master the horses, win the chariot race and his own freedom.

History loves to record the names of men who in the spirit of the second mile have conquered the malice of their hate. There is an old Grecian story about one who was chosen in a joke to be the town's scavenger. But he filled the office with such splendid good will and helpful service, that thereafter throughout all of Greece, the office of scavenger was sought as one of great honor.

Military service to one's country is usually not greatly coveted. But we remember that Nathan Hale glorified the offices of patriot, and when his life demanded, went the second mile and said, "I regret that I have but one life to give for my country." But so frequently our attitudes resemble the feelings of the captive Hebrews toward the duties imposed upon them by this hated Roman law.

One of the best ways to avoid bitterness and the slavery caused by life's necessities, is to enthusiastically give more service than is asked for. That super-abundant willingness in life that characterized the service of Ben Hur always marks one for greatness. We can glorify even the most common drudgery by doing it nobly. When we go further than is required, when we do more than we get paid for, only then do we get paid for more than we do.

The second mile philosophy translates duty into privilege. The first mile may be drudgery. But glory always comes with the second mile. This over-abundant willingness to serve must have seemed impossibly difficult to the Jews, and yet it is a basic success principle.

The military might of ancient Rome has long since disappeared, and the hated Roman soldiers can no longer compel reluctant hands to do unwilling service; but the second mile principle remains an important factor in human happiness and success.

All people live on one of three levels of performance. The first level is the *must* level. That is the lowest. Above the must level is the *ought* level. But the highest level of performance is the *want* level. That is the level of the second mile.

If we personify some of the compulsions of our own lives, we will recognize that they are to us about what the hated Roman soldiers were to the captive Jews. Then if we can learn to apply the philosophy of Jesus, we will be able to solve all of our problems on their highest level.

Suppose that we think about that part of the work of the world that we have been given to do. Frequently there is a compulsion involved that may be as disagreeable and demanding as the heavily burdened Roman soldier. Necessity demands that we carry this heavy load for a long, dreary mile. If we accept our work reluctantly and go about its accomplishment like unwilling slaves under the lash of a galley master, begrudgingly performing the barest requirements, then like the rancorous old Hebrew, with resentment in our hearts, we trudge our weary mile in the spirit of bitterness, while failure breeds poison in our hearts. For one mile people are mercilessly beaten by life's cat-o-nine-tails held in the hands of necessity.

But Jesus said, "Whosoever shall compel thee to go with him a mile, go with him twain." To go the second mile requires a different kind of person. We all need some Ben Hur qualifications. The second mile man says, "My work is my best friend. It is my blessing from God, even though it may come in disguise. But even though it shows a stern face, it may be loaded with strength, courage and good cheer. The second mile worker greets his task by saying, "You demand that I travel with you for a long, hard mile. Then take off your scowl and throw away the lash, for I am twice as willing to work as you are to have me. I will go with you to the very limit of my strength. Only let me row on both sides of the ship that I may develop symmetrically."

When thus greeted, any task loses its frown of compulsion, and begins to smile happily upon its devotee.

The attitude of the second mile saves the soul from bitterness and hate. It banishes weariness and makes one's work his very meat and drink. Then he wishes that there were more hours in the day. He dreams of heaven as a greater opportunity to work over a longer period. Then even the slavery of the first mile vanishes and man and his task become good friends as they walk arm in arm to the end of the journey, and are sorry when even the second mile is done.

There is another kind of compulsion that in some degree faces every man, and that is the compulsion of limiting circumstances. Restricted personal powers sometimes narrow one's activities and shuts him up in obscurity. Some people are thwarted by broken health. Some are hedged in by that stern old Roman who compels us to bear the limitations of our own individuality. For a man of one talent to accept himself is difficult business. To noble men the most vexa-

tious handicaps of all, are the limitations found within themselves. It is so easy then to meet our problems and fail by
adopting the one mile spirit. We may grow surly, rebellious
and morose within our narrow limitations.

Then we need to learn from Jesus the philosophy of
the second mile so that we can greet our limitations with a
smiling face and make our own place beautiful no matter
how limited it may be. Fair flowers can grow in small places.
We should remember that limitations are almost always blessings in disguise. Demosthenes became the greatest orator in
the world, not in spite of his speech impediment, but because
of it. John Milton had to be blind for some 20 years before
he could write *Paradise Lost*. Someone said that Milton could
never see paradise until he lost his eyes. The Apostle Paul
was perhaps made great, partly by the thorn that tormented
his flesh.

We have a memory of John Bunyan, glorifying the limitations imposed upon him in Bedford Jail, by writing that
great philosophy of the *Pilgrim's Progress*.

The spirit of the second mile is exemplified by the
young woman who wrote to her friend from her invalid's
bed, and said of her invalidism, "At first I tried to make the
best of it, but now I am going to make the most of it." All
men pay homage to these second mile folks who go the first
hard mile with over-abundant willingness, and then make
the second mile beautiful by their consecration.

Then there are the stern regulations of the duties of our
personal lives. For example, the first mile obligations of
marriage can be enforced. There is an irreducible minimum
of duty which public opinion and state laws insist upon
from wives and husbands, parents and children. Like some
old Roman, the social conscience tells us of the necessary
minimum requirements governing family relationships. We
must do certain one mile things, and sometimes we do just

what we have to do and no more. A household can be run in the spirit of a miser paying his taxes, where the members are concerned only with the minimum duties. Then when a niggardly soul must give a quart of kindness, he measures it out in thimblesful to avoid the risk of an overpayment. The one mile spirit says there must be an overflowing of spontaneous love, or of volunteering any surplus kindness. The law says, only one long, dreary mile, and no one can demand any more. The unnecessary courtesies, the unexpected presents, the uncalled for thoughtfulness, the surprises and kindliness that come over and above what is required cannot be enforced.

However, it is this second mile super-abundance that makes the real home. Any man who has had a real mother knows that the glory of motherhood comes in the second mile. The real mother is faithful to her duties, but she is much more than that. She has an extra radiance that glows through her simple tasks like a quiet dawn in summer. The minimum rules are forgotten. She has an ampleness of love, resembling the love of the eternal God. A mother's ministries go beyond the commonplace, and her spirit far outreaches the requirements of the law. What a delight is a second mile mother, a second mile father and second mile children.

In the religion of Jesus we see the greatest characterization of the spirit of the second mile. But even in religion our conduct divides itself into two parts, the compulsory and the voluntary, the things we *must* do and the things we *want* to do. And only as the voluntary absorbs the compulsory does religion attain its fullest meaning and dignity. Until willingness conquers obligation, even church men fight as religious conscripts instead of following the flag as patriots. Never until our privileges loom larger than our duties do men become truly moral. To be a true Christian one must be more anxious to minister than to be ministered unto.

He must want to go the second mile, to forget seventy times seven, to love his enemies, and make it his meat and drink to do the will of him who sent him.

The essential word in Christianity is love. And a man becomes really Christian when the sense of joy in his religion overflows his rights and duties. The grim moralist doing his duty, or the man who is a slave to necessities, is not equal to him who has an abounding sense of privilege in life. Then we are able to say with the prophet, "My delight is in the law of the Lord."

The Apostle Paul had the spirit of the second mile when just prior to meeting the headsman's axe in Rome he said, "Thanks be to God who counted me worthy, appointing me to be his minister." Paul's second mile zeal took the sting out of death. The love that goes with the second mile is more than a solvent for moral drudgeries. It says, "Whether you are my friend or not, yet I am yours, and will always be." That is the level on which Jesus lived, and that is what he expects from us who follow him.

Jesus said, "If ye love me, keep my commandments." Love is the fulfilling of the law. It makes everything easy, and it embodies that magnificent philosophy of the second mile wherein Jesus says, "Whosoever shall smite thee on thy right cheek, turn to him the other also. And if any man will sue thee at the law, and take away thy coat, let him have thy cloak also. And whosoever shall compel thee to go a mile, go with him twain."

Seeds

W E LIVE IN a day of almost unbeliev-
able miracles and wonders. With
the aid of television our eyes can see across oceans, with
radios our ears can hear around the world. We fly above
the clouds and in perfect comfort ride under the polar icecap. Our rockets have already landed on the moon and
we are now flapping our wings for a flight into outer space.

But a far greater wonder than any of these is outlined
in the first chapter of Genesis. What a thrill we get when
we read of God creating the heavens and the earth. Suppose that we could have been here, when the earth was without form and void, and darkness was upon the face of the
deep. Then picture the joy resulting from those thrilling
words when in the march of progress God first said, "Let
there be light." The vitalizing rays of the sun were made
to shine upon the earth. God covered the earth with some
sixteen inches of a miraculous substance called topsoil. Then
as the key to the existence of all growth, God created that
wonder of wonders called a seed. A seed is a little capsule
containing the secret of life itself. It has the miraculous
power of propagation and multiplication. As one of the
crowning achievements of creation God said, "Let the earth
bring forth . . . the herb yielding seed, and the fruit tree
yielding fruit after its kind, whose seed is in itself." Seeds
are the keys by which we can unlock the great treasure house
of the earth.

Suppose that in imagination we walk through that first
garden which was arranged by the Creator himself. The
Bible says, "The Lord God planted a garden eastward in
Eden." (Gen. 2:8) And he made to grow therein every

tree that is pleasant to the sight and good for food. In the midst of this beautiful garden God planted two special trees — one was "the tree of life" and the other was "the tree of the knowledge of good and evil."

Then out of the ground, capable of producing so many wonderful things, God created the earthly tabernacles of our first parents. And after he had breathed into their nostrils the breath of life, he placed them in the garden. And God said to them, "Behold, I have given you every herb bearing seed which is upon the face of all the earth, and . . . the fruit of the tree yielding seed, to you it shall be for meat." (Gen. 1:29) The Bible says that God created every plant of the field before it was in the earth and every herb of the field before it grew. (Gen. 2:5)

"For," said he, "I, the Lord God created all things of which I have spoken, spiritually, before they were naturally upon the face of the earth . . ." (Moses 3:5)

The other day I visited in a vast supermarket in which were displayed hundreds of varieties and colors of these wonderful products coming from seeds. I thought of the interesting fact that they were first created in heaven by God himself, then he gave us these wonders called seeds whereby we can produce every variety in any color or quantity. From these beautiful godly creations every vitamin can be supplied and every taste can be satisfied. As I marveled I thought what a delight it would have been to have visited in the Garden of Eden as it flourished in that period before man's transgression brought the earth to its fallen condition. As wonderful as the earths productivity is now what must it have been then.

Adding to my own wonder, I recently visited the farm of a very good friend of mine. Each year he supplies the supermarket with hundreds of tons of food to maintain the health of thousands of people. Each spring he plants some of his acres with potato seed. A little later in the year he harvests thousands of bushels of potatoes, all packed with vitamins and every element necessary to nourish the bodies, vitalize the minds, and delight the tastes of people.

If this farmer should pile up the potato crops for a few years that he gets out of this sixteen inches of topsoil, he could soon have potatoes covering the ground twenty feet deep, and still have his sixteen inches of topsoil left undiminished.

But by means of these little miracles called seeds, my friend can also bring out of the ground life-giving grains, delicious fruits and health-packed vegetables of every kind, variety and amount: And in addition to supplying food, there are always an abundance of seeds to satisfy the need of future years. One tomato seed multiplies itself a million times in a single season.

My friend has a most interesting hobby of preparing special plots of ground in which he grows dozen of varieties of flowers, vegetables, fruits and nuts for the mere satisfaction of seeing this miracle of creation repeated before his eyes. Not only does he produce flowers in every pattern of color, design and fragrance but he further re-enacts the miracle of creation by bringing forth strawberries, raspberries, blackberries, grapes, peaches and. apples.

On the morning of creation God looked out upon this wonder and called it very good. My friend does the same thing, and seeing his joy I can imagine the pleasure that even God must have received from these marvelous creations.

My friend showed me his collection of seeds for next year's planting. Some of them are so tiny as to be almost microscopic. No one could ever guess at the fabulous possibilities stored therein. With some feeling near to desecration we broke some of these seeds open and found them as unimpressive on the inside as they were on the outside. We could recognize no sign of life. There were no written directions or formulas to get them going or guide their growth afterwards. There was no hint of the secret of color and beauty of which they were capable nor was there in evidence any machinery to bring about this miracle that was inherent in them.

When seeds are planted in rich black soil, a major miracle can always be depended upon. And each seed will be faithful to God's decree that it shall always bring forth after its kind. Without the aid of scientists or engineers, these little miracles send their unseen fingers among the invisible elements in the soil, the water, the air and the sunshine and pick out exactly the right kinds and proportions of building materials to create the vitamins, fragrance, color, food, vitality and beauty necessary for human health and happiness. All of this takes place in such a way that only God himself can even understand it.

After an excursion around my friend's farm, he read to me from the Bible about the wonders of the heavens and the earth. But one of the parts of creation that thrills me most, is the sunshine and the topsoil and this marvelous invention of Deity called a seed. Man can make airplanes and television sets and self-guided missiles with atomic bombs in their noses. We can even put satellites and astronauts in their orbits in space. But no one has yet come close enough even to hope to understand the mechanism of the most simple seed. My friend had these colorless, unimpressive, lifeless looking seeds all carefully classified, and marked so that at the right time he can drop them into the soil to re-enact at will the exciting story of creation.

For my own pleasure I memorized an interesting poem which says:

> I paid a dime for a package of seeds,
> And the clerk tossed them out with a flip
> "We have them assorted to every man's needs,"

He said with a smile on his lip
"Asters and poppies and pansies and peas
Ten cents a package and pick as you please."

Now, seeds are just dimes to the man in the store,
And the dimes are the things that he needs;
And I've been to buy them in seasons before
But have thought of them merely as seeds.
But it flashes through my mind as I took them this time,
You have purchased a miracle here for a dime!

You've a dime's worth of something no man can create
You've a dime's worth of life in your hand.
You've a dime's worth of mystery, destiny, fate
That the wisest cannot understand.
In this bright little package, now isn't it odd,
You've a dime's worth of something known only to God.

Anyone who can believe in a seed should have no trouble believing in an all wise creator. Mrs. L. M. Child pays her tribute to creation by saying, "How the heart of man blesses flowers. They are wreathed around the cradle, the marriage altar and the tomb. They deck the brow of the youthful bride, they twine around the tomb as the perpetual symbol of the resurrection. They festoon the altar, their fragrance and beauty ascend in perpetual worship before the Most High. Every rose is an autograph from God."

But the Creator has also developed another kind of seed that produces even more miraculous results. Jesus characterized himself as a sower of seeds. He had the world for his field and the minds of men as his topsoil. He planted the seeds of great ideas, wonderful virtues, productive abilities and noble character traits in the lives of people. These are also capable of growing into a most profitable harvest and reproducing themselves through their seeds. Every human accomplishment begins with the seed of a thought.

When young Abraham Lincoln made his first trip down the Mississippi to New Orleans, he attended a public auction and saw a young negro girl on the block being sold to the highest bidder. A vigorous idea immediately took root in his mind. He said, "If I ever get a chance to hit that thing, I'll hit it hard." In a few years this tiny seed had grown into the Emancipation Proclamation, bringing freedom to four million human beings, plus all of their future posterity.

In the Meridian of Time, the Apostle James planted another seed saying, "If any of you lack wisdom, let him ask of God, that giveth to all men liberally, and upbraideth not; and it shall be given him." Eighteen centuries later this seed took root in the mind of a young man named Joseph Smith. The result has already affected the lives of millions and will not only change the history of the world but will help bring eternal life to many of God's children.

Emerson said, "Thoughts rule the world." And Victor Hugo pointed out that "Nothing is as powerful as an idea whose time has come." The right kinds of thoughts arouse our intellects from their slumbers. They give luster to our virtues and dignity to truth. Good thoughts make our souls blossom with a love of goodness. Herter said, "Give me a great thought that I may quicken myself with it."

The Holy Scriptures and life itself are like great seed catalogs where we may find the beginnings of faith, courage, purity, honor, love, devotion, loyalty, and appreciation in all their beauty. When these ideas are planted in the seed bed of a godly human mind, they may produce the most wonderful harvest of satisfactions and eternal benefits.

However, as Jesus pointed out, not all seeds are good seeds. There are some seeds that produce tares and thistles. Jesus said that we should cast away our idle thoughts. (D&C 88:66) Some thoughts produce a poison fruit. Impure thoughts awaken impure feelings, and lead to impure acts. Evil thoughts ripen quickly and if they are not destroyed will crowd out the most worth-while things. Satan himself planted the seeds of transgression and sin in the world and they continue to grow, causing suffering, unhappiness and death. If we take poisonous substances into our bodies, death may be the result. And when we take poisons into our minds and hearts, we may bring upon ourselves a spiritual death.

Sin and evil grow very rapidly in the soil of some people's lives and soon destroy integrity and faith, sometimes without the fact being known. Ere we are aware, the seeds of evil, if given a chance, can crowd everything that is good out of one's life.

One of the greatest of life's privileges is that we may prepare our own seed beds. We may sow our own seeds and reap our own harvests.

There are some people who get their greatest pleasures from creating strains of beautiful music. Others paint inspiring pictures. Some gather the seeds of great literature and transplant them into the rich soil of their own lives. My friend gathers seeds and then reproduces a multiplication of color, fragrance, taste and health for thousands of people. Suppose that we take the seeds of great ideals, ambitions, spirituality and Godliness, and by proper planting produce in abundance the golden fruit of eternal life.

It is a wonderful experience to get an idea. But only when an idea gets us do we make the greatest progress. Ideas can perform miracles. Thoughts are mightier than armies. They go booming through the world louder than cannons. Righteous principles and godly ideas have achieved more victories than all of the tanks, airplanes and missiles of destruction put together.

May God help us to be good husbandmen as we plant the seeds of a godly accomplishment in as many lives as possible.

The Shortest Highway

Some time ago during a General Conference, Elder Harold B. Lee made reference to a road sign at the Point of the Mountain officially marking Utah Highway 187. According to the marker, 187 is the shortest designated highway in the state. It is approximately a quarter of a mile in length and connects Highway 91 with the Utah State Penitentiary.

This day in which we live has been called "The Highway Age." One of the first things that Adolph Hitler did in trying to give power to his country was to build super highways all over Germany to make possible the quick movement of soldiers and supplies from any part of Germany to any other part. At the present time in our own country we also have underway a gigantic highway construction program. At tremendous expense valuable land is being purchased and costly buildings are being torn down and great freeways are beginning to appear in their places. These enable large numbers of people to move quickly with the fewest possible number of stops. We are also making highways under the seas and up into the skies and then on out into space.

But we are also building other kinds of highways. There are highways of thought leading to important spiritual mental and social destinations. The scriptures tell us of a straight and narrow highway that leads to eternal life in the presence of God. It also speaks of a broad road that leads to destruction. Each of these highways has its own individual characteristics. The straight and narrow road is marked by boundaries and limitations. This is not true of the broad road. On the broad way there is plenty of room for turnings and meanderings and everything is permissible.

We have become fairly familiar with the concepts involved in the idea of a straight and narrow way. We also know quite a lot about broad roads and winding roads and crooked roads. We are aware of the uphill and downhill aspects of our thoroughfares. However, Highway 187 furnishes us with a little different kind of concept as *it* is noted for its shortness. Each of these various arteries of travel provide us with interesting parallels for our own lives. That is, life also has its freeways where speed is the chief objective. There are other lives that are noted for their turnings, stoppings, startings, and meanderings. Some of life's travelers are not inhibited by any limitations or restraints and place very few things out of bounds. It is interesting that because of its restrictions the straight and narrow way is traveled by only a comparatively few people.

But one of the most interesting things about any highway is its length. We are greatly interested in shortcuts. Highway 187 is the shortest highway, but in common with some of life's other thoroughfares its length is determined by which direction you are going. Some people have traveled Highway 187 from its eastern beginning to its western ending in just a few seconds, and then have taken the next 25 years to reverse the trip and get from the prison back to Highway 91.

There is an interesting old proverb that says, "There are a thousand steps from hell to heaven, but only one from heaven to hell." Cain took a short cut to hell when he murdered his brother Abel. It probably required only a few minutes to complete the deed, but what a long, difficult, heartbreaking journey the return trip would be.

Judas also took a short cut. At nine o'clock one Thursday night Judas was a member of the Quorum of the Twelve in good standing. Then he spent a few minutes in the deadly business of betrayal, as a result of which by nine o'clock the next morning Jesus was being nailed to a Roman cross and the betrayer himself had already committed suicide. It didn't take very long after Judas left *his* Highway 91 until he had placed himself beyond the point of no return. By suicide he solved his problems so far as this life was concerned, but what about eternity? And what about our eternal lives?

It takes a long time to build up a reputation for integrity and fair dealing. But it can all be destroyed by a ten-minute exception. It requires a long time to build an outstanding business success, but it may be lost in an hour. One may spend a lifetime building up a home with all of its treasures, memories and pleasant influences, but the most priceless home can be burned to the ground in a few minutes by one contact with a tiny little match. A city or a civilization is built to its highest state only when thousands of people work diligently for many years. But then its culture, its people and its wealth can be destroyed by one atomic blast. It takes years to educate a great human being, to build up his body, train his mind and vitalize his spirit, but by one dagger thrust he can be emptied of life.

About the same kind of situation applies in spiritual affairs. The Bible says that "only he that endureth to the end shall be saved." But immorality, crime and sin all provide shortcuts to spiritual death, and the destruction of life's eternal treasures. We understand about the broad road of life being very wide, but we should understand that it may also be very short. We might think of the institution at the end of Highway 187 as a small-scale model of what might be expected at the end of the broad short road spoken of by Jesus. When undertaking any trip in life we should give some advance thought to any possibility or difficulty or heartbreak involved in the return journey, or whether that journey will even be possible.

The people of Noah's day traveled the loose meandering highway of spiritual indifference. The course that they chose brought destruction upon them. However, physical death does not always solve our problems. Eternity has its 187's and its prison houses at the end of the road. For 25 centuries the antediluvians were confined in their eternal prison house to which they were assigned because of their disobedience. Then while the body of Jesus lay in the tomb, his spirit went and preached to them about their possible reformation and deliverance. Peter says: "For Christ also hath once suffered for sins, the just for the unjust, that he might bring us to God, being put to death in the flesh, but quickened by the Spirit; by which also he went and preached unto the spirits in prison; Which sometime were disobedient, when once the longsuffering of God waited in the days of Noah, while the ark was a preparing, wherein few, that is, eight souls were saved by water." (I Peter 3:18-20.)

It is impossible for us to understand either the duration or the extent of this kind of suffering. How intensely the people of Noah's day must have regretted the thought of their looseness and the lack of restraint in their lives! How they must have mourned over the thought of what their lives might have been if they had followed a different highway!

Recently I had the interesting experience of a brief visit among the inmates of the State Prison. I had a few very serious thoughts as I rode down the short length of Highway 187 and went behind strong, well-fortified prison walls. In the following period I met many of the prisoners personally. A number of them told me about their lives in prison and how they happened to get there. They gave an interesting point of view of what life itself meant to them. I had known some of them before as well as some of their families on the outside. What a tragedy this wrong highway procedure can be as it brings shame and unhappiness to so many people! How easy it is to make mistakes when we are on the wrong highway!

On one occasion John Wesley went behind prison walls to witness an execution. The executioner put a hood over the condemned man's head and a noose around his neck.

Then as the trap was sprung which swung this misguided human being out into eternity, John Wesley muttered to himself, "But for the grace of God, there goes John Wesley." Standing among these unfortunate men, deprived of their freedom by the state, one might well say, "But for the grace of God, or but for the instruction of good parents, or but for the inspiration of noble teachers, there go I."

A ride down Highway 187 can be a very interesting experience if you are sure you have a return ticket. Many times I have passed the State Penitentiary along Highway 91 without realizing the problems that had complicated the lives of these prisoners separated from the world only by the short distance of a quarter of a mile. The reasons for the differences in the people's lives living at the opposite ends of Highway 187 might well remind us of W. Somerset Maugham's story *The Razor's Edge*, which Daryl Zanuck made into a four-million-dollar movie, the central theme of which centers around the idea that the difference between failure and success is sometimes as fine as a razor's edge.

One of the best illustrations of this truth was demonstrated during the filming of the picture itself. There were eight principal actors and eight stand-ins. That is, each principal had a substitute to do the hard, grueling, tiresome work. After the film was finished, *Life* Magazine published the pictures of the eight principals on one page and the eight stand-ins on the opposite page. The stand-in for Tyrone Power, for example, was Thomas Noonan, a close associate. They had gone to high school together. They were about the same size, equally intelligent and with equal opportunities. They were dressed about the same and were very similar in appearance. As close a similarity as possible existed between each principal and his stand-in. But in one way they were not similar. The combined salaries received by the eight principals for filming this picture amounted to $480,000, and the combined salaries of the eight stand-ins amounted to $6,534. The principals were just a little bit better, but they received 75 times as much compensation. A little better preparation, a little more attention to right and wrong, and a little more thought as to which road in life we should travel frequently makes the difference between a principal and a stand-in, between life and death, happiness and misery, heaven and hell.

Human progress has not always been steady. It is frequently subject to ebbs and flows. It washes back and forth like waves upon the beach. But history is littered with the bones of dead states and fallen empires because they chose the wrong course. Alaric's Goths poured over the walls of ancient Rome, not because the walls were too low, but because the moral standards of the Romans were too low. Sensuality and corruption had weakened the fiber of these once mighty, highly disciplined people. Their sins had made them unfit to survive and while you can't lock sinful nations up in prisons, yet evil and weakness will destroy them just the same. It was nearly a thousand years after the fall of Rome before the faint light of the Renaissance began to dawn. In between these dates the world endured the long night of the Dark Ages, when nearly all human institutions were inferior to those that had preceded them. The penalty inflicted upon the nations who took the wrong course should prompt us to check up on our own travel philosophy. We are all aware of our own country's crime wave and the rising incidence of human delinquency.

In many cases instead of changing our course, we merely rationalize and say that sin is largely imaginary. We have become believers in what might be called behavioristic psychology. We tell ourselves that we are the product of our heredity and our environment and that our sins are not our fault. When we build our lives upon a foundation of jelly, or when we permit our nation to become an American Sodom and Gomorrah we can depend upon it that we are headed down a short highway with no return ticket.

As a nation and as individuals we are traveling too many of these short roads leading toward disaster. Who of our day does not recognize the dirt and immorality that we are feeding ourselves through the movies, magazines, newspapers and television, or the weakness that we bring upon ourselves by dishonesty? The healthy man who chooses to loaf on unemployment compensation is not strengthening his country. The playwright who would degrade us, the author who would profit from pandering to the worst there is in us are not friends of ours. And when we tolerate personal sins we are buying a one-way ticket on Highway 187. Strong nations are built only by people who are capable of great energy and self-discipline, and so are godly personal lives.

It is time for us to recognize that there *is* such a thing as sin. It is time we brought self-discipline back into style. It is time to revitalize our belief in the doctrine of the eternal judgment, and it is time for us to get on our knees before God and pray that we will have enough strength to get on and stay on that straight and narrow way that leads to eternal life.

Simon and the Cross

THERE ARE many people who live in history mainly because their lives touched the life of Jesus of Nazareth. One woman is remembered because she gave him a drink of water. One because she prepared a dinner in his honor. One poured ointment on his feet. Another woman is remembered because she asked forgiveness at his hands. One man doubted him, one denied him, one betrayed him. Another sentenced him to death, and still another loaned him his sepulchre.

One of these interesting New Testament people who lives in our memories was one whose life apparently touched the life of Jesus by the merest circumstance. After the sentence of crucifixion had been passed, a little group of interested onlookers, led by Roman soldiers, started for Golgotha. The central figure of this interesting company was Jesus, struggling under the heavy weight of his own cross. In the hours immediately preceding this period, he had gone through intense suffering in the Garden of Gethsemane. He had then spent the long, weary hours of the night and early morning hearing unpleasant accusations, enduring a mock trial and suffering an unjust sentence. He now appears to be nearing the point of total exhaustion. And as the solemn procession made its weary way toward Calvary, Jesus stumbled and fell under his heavy burden. From this fall he seemed unable to rise.

But just at the time of his fall, a man named Simon came upon the scene. Simon was a Jew from Cyrene, a settlement in the North African province of Lybia. He had probably come to Jerusalem for the passover, and on this Friday morning as he was going into the city, he met this strange procession. Probably impelled by his own curiosity, he was drawn to where Jesus was having trouble. The Roman officer in charge, impatient to get his job done, specifically selected Simon from the crowd, and ordered him to replace Jesus in carrying the cross.

All of the three Bible accounts make mention of the fact that Simon was *compelled* to carry the cross. Simon was a long way from home, with many things to attend to while in Jerusalem. He had no time to be involved in this distasteful business of crucifixion. But under the compulsion of Roman bayonets, he had no choice; and so Simon the Cyrenian carried the cross of Jesus to the top of Calvary so that the Savior of the world could be crucified.

Being a Jew, Jerusalem was the center of Simon's homeland. His interests focused in the Holy City. In planning this journey, Simon had probably wondered what interesting events would be encountered along the way. Many of our blessings come unexpected and in disguise, and it was Simon's unexpected privilege to walk by the side of the Savior of the world and carry the cross on which the atoning sacrifice would be made for all men.

The lives of most people are made up largely of trifles. Only now and then does one have a really great experience. But it was Simon's good fortune to be forced into what would forever be the outstanding experience of his life. As the passage of time gave the crucifixion importance, Simon must have felt an unusual pride in his significant role of sharing with the Redeemer the spotlight in the central scene in the history of the world. But Simon holds the focus of history's stage only for a moment while his strong, vigorous body is carrying the heavy cross of Christ to the top of Calvary. The moment he laid down the cross, he again dropped from sight never to be heard of again.

Some forty years later a written record was made of the crucifixion. By this time those seeds planted forty years earlier had borne their fruit. Those who had been boys and girls at the time of the crucifixion were now men and women. Young fathers were now old men. Simon himself had probably gone the way of all flesh. But the memory of what he did lived on. The record also calls our attention to the fact that Simon was the father of two staunch loyal followers of Christ by the names of Alexander and Rufus. Paul refers to these sons of Simon as "chosen of the Lord."

Although Simon may have been upset at the time of his enforced service, yet he undoubtedly talked about it with his family, and it is only natural for him to make an effort to learn something about the life of this man whose cross he had carried. Then as the world began to buzz with the fame of Jesus and it became known that he had risen from the dead, Simon's interest must have greatly increased in Jesus and his mission.

Sometimes our chance experiences turn out to have tremendous importance for us. Then we wish that we had realized their real significance at the time they were happening. Certainly Simon's reluctance would have vanished if he had only known whose cross he was carrying.

It would have been only natural later on, for Simon to have tried to compensate for his unwillingness to bear the burden of the Redeemer. In any event we imagine that Simon soon found out a great deal about Jesus and his teachings. The good record of Simon's sons indicates that their father may have set them a good example by being baptized and becoming a faithful follower of him who had already said to his disciples, "Go ye into all the world and teach the gospel to every creature. He that believeth and is baptized shall be saved, and he that believeth not shall be damned." When anyone really understands those tremendous words, a new ambition starts stirring in his soul.

What a thrilling personal meaning Simon must have found in the words of Jesus saying, "If any man will come after me, let him deny himself and take up his cross and follow me." (Matt. 16:24.) I like to think of the Cyrenian as following this instruction in its spiritual as well as its literal meaning.

The term "cross" as used by Jesus was intended to indicate a test of devotion and loyalty to the cause by those who followed him. Certainly the expression "take up the cross and follow me" meant much more than to merely acknowledge his name, or even to be baptized. When Jesus was out in the desert before his crucifixion, he had performed a miracle and fed five thousand from the loaves and fishes. Later Jesus accused some of those who followed him of being more interested in being fed from his loaves than they were in drinking from his cup. There are still those among us who attempt to live by bread alone. Many have a greater appetite for eating of his loaves than for carrying his cross.

On that eventful crucifixion morning as Jesus stumbled blindly toward Calvary, he needed the assistance of a strong, vigorous body to help him carry the load. Because no one volunteered, this great privilege was forced upon Simon. If the foresight of the members of that little group going to Golgotha had been as good as our hindsight, everyone present, including those wearing the Roman uniform, would have fought for the privilege of carrying the cross of Christ. But so frequently we pass up our opportunities until it is too late.

Thirty-five years before Calvary, Jesus had needed a place to be born. But no room could be found for him in the inn. And yet the little village of Bethlehem lives in history merely because he was born in one of its stables. If the people had only known who it was that was about to be born, everyone would have offered him room. At a later date Simon must have felt a very real kind of regret that it had been necessary to use the steel of Roman bayonets to induce him to render this service to the Son of God. I imagine that Simon's regret must have produced in him a kind of over-compensation in his desire to make up for his reluctance and lack of understanding.

But we are also a part of this picture of carrying the cross. The divine need is as great today as it ever was. The work of salvation is not yet finished. One of the greatest lines in Holy Scripture says, "And this is my work and my glory, to bring to pass the immortality and eternal life of man." The work of God continues, and it was not only to those of the first century to whom Jesus spoke when he said, "He that taketh not his cross, and followeth after me, is not worthy of me." (Matt. 10:38)

Things did not go very well for Jesus during those years of his earthly ministry. The people then would not listen and they did not understand. Consequently the world was overrun with unrighteousness. But our world is also working against the cause of Christ. Violence and evil are running rampant through the land. Because there are no Roman bayonets reminding us to do our duty, much of his work is not being done, and the souls of millions of our Father's children are being lost to sin and disobedience. Some day we will surely feel a regret equal to that of those who were content to let Jesus suffer and fall unaided while struggling under the weight of our sins. Or if we can feel the remorse of those who found no room for him to be born, we might understand the bitterness of our future regret if we allow him to bear his present-day burden alone.

What a miserable experience it would have been to have been one of those crowding around the cross as a witness of his suffering for us, and yet to have done nothing about giving him a helping hand! To carry the cross of Christ is our greatest privilege. Jesus used this appropriate figure of speech to specify the willingness of people to work and suffer if need be in this important process of bringing about human salvation. It doesn't do much good to merely support him with our words or our testimonies, and then withdraw our strength and let him carry the cross alone. This idea of carrying the cross represents the test of our Christian patience,

virtue and actual good works. It is also the greatest opportunity in our world of great opportunities.

The Lord is in great need of someone to help him change
the direction of world affairs in our day. Like Simon, we
are strong and possessed of great power. Just think of
what we could accomplish if with one accord we would
set our hearts upon doing his work. Even one man can, if
he will, change the morale of a whole community. Certainly we could change for good the spirituality of that
area in which we live.

The cross has been thought of by many as a symbol
for Christianity. It might also represent the two most important commandments. The gospel has a vertical as well
as horizontal direction. The cross also has its two parts.
The vertical points from the earth up to God. It represents
the first and great commandment and reminds us to do our
duty to our Heavenly Father. The horizontal bar reaches
out toward our fellow men and represents the second great
commandment. The prophet has said that when we are in
the service of our fellow men, we are also in the service of
God. Next only to love for his Father, the life of Jesus is
characterized by his service to men.

What a thrilling thing it ought to be for us to identify
our lives with these two great objectives! The vertical standard of the cross would serve a great purpose indeed if it
made us always conscious of that great commandment that
says, "And thou shalt love the Lord thy God with all thy
heart, and with all thy might, and with all thy mind. And
thou shalt serve him with all thy strength." By obedience
to this commandment we could entitle ourselves to receive
inspiration and direction from the source of all intelligence
and power. But if we really love him we will become like
him and we will serve him. Then we are ready for that part
of our activities that reaches out in horizontal service to
our fellow men.

What a thrilling opportunity Simon had, if he had only taken advantage of it! Even his forced labor is the one thing for which he is remembered. But in addition this incident was undoubtedly responsible for his sons qualifying as "the chosen of the Lord." That is also our opportunity. For the call to service is still before us and we need not make Simon's mistake of reluctance. Jesus is still saying to us, "Take up your cross and follow me." (D&C 112:14) Jesus said: "Take my yoke upon you, and learn of me; for I am meek and lowly in heart: and ye shall find rest unto your souls. For my yoke is easy, and my burden is light." (Matt. 11:29-30) But we must do something about it while the opportunity is still available.

Members of one organization were recently shocked when their secretary read to them a list of 46 resolutions that they had passed during a certain year, on which no action had been taken. We also make a lot of resolutions. But nothing is settled by merely passing resolutions, however excellent they may be.

In war they refer to this "fractional devotion" as foxhole religion. There are people who turn to God only in the pinches or in their desperation. However, the most healthy kind of God-seeking is not like the man who neglects his friend until he needs a loan, or like Simon who carried the cross only before the point of a Roman bayonet. Today we have the greatest of opportunities to serve God. Jesus himself gave us the formula when he said, "Deny yourself and come, take up the cross, and follow me."

Sohrab and Rustum

IN 1853, Matthew Arnold wrote his great father-and-son poem, entitled "Sohrab and Rustum." Rustum, a powerful young Persian war Lord, had met and wed the daughter of the King of the Koords. Before their son Sohrab was born, Rustum was called to a far-away field of battle; and because his wife feared that he might seek out their son to train for war, she sent him word that the child which had been born to them had been a sickly girl.

But Sohrab's warrior inheritance and the stories of his father's heroism and might led him to adopt the profession and develop the abilities of his great father. But Sohrab was called into the military service of the Tartars among whom he lived, although they were the enemies of Persia. But above everything else Sohrab longed to know his hero father. Everywhere he was sent he was possessed by only one thought and that was to find Rustum.

One day the Tartars met the Persians by the River Oxus. Sohrab gained consent to challenge the Persians to seek out their greatest champion to be matched with him in a single combat. Because of Sohrab's fame among the Tartars he hoped that the Persians would not dare to match him with anyone but the mighty Rustum himself. This proved to be the case, and not knowing that young Sohrab was his son, Rustum was persuaded to take the challenge up, though he insisted that he fight unknown. As Rustum watched Sohrab's approach he felt a strange liking for this heroic young challenger. So slender Sohrab seemed, so softly reared, like some young cypress as in the queen's garden, and Rustum—

Beckon'd with his hand and said:
"O thou young man, the air of Heaven is soft.
And warm, and pleasant, but the grave is cold,
Behold me: I am vast, and clad in iron,
And I have stood on many a field of blood
And I have fought with many a foe;
Never was that field lost, nor that foe sav'd.
O Sohrab, wherefore wilt thou rush on death?
Quit the Tartars and come
To Iran, and be my son
And fight beneath my banner till I die.
There are no youths in Iran brave as thou."
Sohrab heard his voice,
The mighty voice of Rustum; and he saw
His giant figure planted on the sand,
His temple streaked with the first touch of gray
And he ran forward and embrac'd his knees,
And clasp'd his hand within his own and said:
"Art thou not Rustum?"

But Rustum feared what the motive of this young man
might be, that maybe he was being tricked into giving up the
challenge, and thereby the Persian Lords might be shamed
through him. So Rustum turned and sternly spake and said:

"Rise! Wherefore dost thou vainly question thus
Of Rustum? I am here, whom thou hast call'd
By challenge forth
Is it with Rustum only thou wouldst fight?
Rash boy, men look on Rustum's face and flee,
For well I know, that did great Rustum stand
Before thy face this day
There would be no talk of fighting then
But I tell thee this;
Either renounce thy vaunt, and yield;
Or else thy bones shall bleach upon the Oxus sands."
He spoke: and Sohrab answer'd, on his feet:—
"Art thou so fierce? Thou wilt not fright me so.
I am no girl, to be made pale by words.
Yet this thou hast said well, did Rustum stand
Upon this field today, there would be no talk of fighting then,
But Rustum is far hence, and *we* stand *here*.

Begin: thou art more vast, more dread than I,
And thou art prov'd, I know, and I am young—
And though thou thinkest that thou knowest sure
Thy victory, yet thou canst not surely know.
For success sways with the breath of heaven.
And only the event will teach us in its hour."
He spoke, and Rustum answer'd not, but hurl'd
His spear: Sohrab saw it come, and quick as a flash
He sprang aside and the spear
Hiss-d, and went quivering down into the sand,
Then Sohrab threw in turn
And his spear struck Rustum's shield;
The iron plates rang sharp, but turn'd the spear.
Then Rustum seized his club, which none but he
Could wield.
He struck one stroke; but again Sohrab sprang aside
And the club leapt from Rustum's hand
And thundered to the earth.
And Rustum follow'd his own blow, and fell
And now might Sohrab have unsheath'd his sword,
And pierc'd the mighty Rustum while he lay dizzy
And on his knees, and chok'd with sand:
But Sohrab smiled nor bar'd his sword,
But courteously drew back and said:
"Thou strik'st too hard.
But rise, and be not wroth; not wroth am I;
No, when I see thee, wrath forsakes my soul.
Thou say'st thou art not Rustum:
Who art thou then, that canst so touch my soul?
Boy as I am, I have seen battles too;
Have waded foremost in their bloody waves,
And heard the hollow roar of dying men;
But never was my heart thus touch'd before.
Old warrior, let us yield to Heaven!
And plant here in the earth our angry spears,
And make a truce, and sit upon the sand,
And pledge each other in red wine, like friends,
And thou shalt talk to me of Rustum's deeds.
There are enough foes in the Persian host
Whom I may meet, and strike, and feel no pang;
Champions enough Afrasiab has, whom thou mayest fight
Fight them, when they confront thy spear.

But oh, let there be peace 'twixt thee and me!"
He ceas'd; but while he spake, Rustum had risen,
And stood erect, trembling with rage: his club
He left to lie, but had regain'd his spear,
Whose fiery point now in his mail'd right-hand
Blaz'd bright and baleful
His breast heav'd; his lips foam'd; and twice his voice
Was chok'd with rage: at last these words broke forth.
"Girl! Nimble with thy feet, not with thy hands!
Curl'd minion, dancer, coiner of sweet words!
Fight; let me hear thy hateful voice no more!
Thou art not in Afrasiab's gardens now
With Tarter girls, with whom thou art wont to dance;
But on the Oxus sands, and in the dance
Of battle, and with me, who make no play of war
I fight it out, and hand to hand.
Speak not to me of truce, and pledge, and wine!
Remember all thy valour: try thy feints and cunning
All the pity I had for thee is gone:"
He spoke: and Sohrab kindled at his taunts,
And he too drew his sword: at once they rush'd together
And crashing blows Rustum and Sohrab on each other hail'd.
And you might say that the sun took part
In that unnatural conflict; for a cloud
Grew suddenly in Heaven, and dark'd the sun
Over the fighters' heads; and a wind rose
Under their feet, moaning swept the plain,
And in a sandy whirlwind wrapp'd the pair.
The on-looking hosts on either hand
Stood in broad daylight, and the sky was pure,
And the sun sparkled on the Oxus stream.
But in the gloom they twain fought on with bloodshot eyes
And labouring breath, first Rustum struck the shield
Which Sohrab held stiff out; the spear
Rent the tough plates, but fail'd to reach the skin,
And Rustum pluck'd it back with angry groan.
Then Sohrab with his sword smote Rustum's helm,
Nor clove its steel quite through; but all the crest
Was shorn away, and that proud horsehair plume,
Never till now defil'd, sank to the dust;
And Rustum bow'd his head; but then the gloom
Grew blacker; thunder rumbled in the air,

And lightnings rent the cloud.
But Sohrab rush'd right on
And struck again; and again Rustum bow'd his head
But this time all the blade, like glass,
Sprang in a thousand shivers on the helm,
And in Sohrab's hand the hilt remain'd alone.
Then Rustum rais'd his head; his dreadful eyes
Glar'd, and he shook on high his menacing spear,
And shouted, "Rustum!" Sohrab heard that shout,
And shrank amaz'd; back he recoil'd one step,
And scann'd with blinking eyes the advancing form:
And as he stood bewilder'd; he dropp'd
His covering shield, and Rustum's spear pierc'd his side.
Sohrab reel'd and staggering back, sunk to the ground.
And then the gloom dispers'd and the wind fell,
And the bright sun broke forth, and melted all
The cloud; and the two armies saw the pair;
Saw Rustum standing, safe upon his feet,
And Sohrab wounded, on the bloody sand.
Then with a bitter smile, Rustum began:
"Sohrab, thou thoughtest in thy mind to kill
A Persian Lord this day, and strip his corpse,
And bear thy trophies to Afrasiab's tent.
Or else that the great Rustum would come down
Himself to fight, and that thy wiles would move
His heart to take a gift, and let thee go.
And then that all the Tartar host would praise
Thy courage or thy craft, and spread thy fame
Fool! Thou art slain, and by an unknown man!"
And, with a fearless mien, Sohrab replied:—
"Unknown thou art; yet thy fierce vaunt is vain.
Thou dost not slay me, proud and boastful man!
No! Rustum slays me, and this filial heart.
For were I match'd with ten such men as thou,
And I were he who until today I was,
They should be lying here, I standing there.
But that beloved name unnerv'd my arm—
That name, and something, I confess, in thee,
Which troubles all my heart, made my shield to fall
And thy spear transfix'd an unarm'd foe.
And hear this, fierce Man, tremble to hear
My father, whom I seek through all the world,
The mighty Rustum shall avenge my death!"

And with a cold, incredulous voice Rustum replied,
"What prate is this of fathers and revenge?
The mighty Rustum never had a son."
And, with a failing voice, Sohrab replied:—
"Ah yes, he had! and that lost son am I."
Sohrab spoke of many things and as he ceas'd he wept aloud,
Thinking of her who bore him and his own untimely death.
Rustum listen'd, plung'd in thought
Nor did he yet believe it was his son who spoke
Although he call'd back names he knew;
For he had sure tidings that the babe,
Which was in Aderbaijan born to him,
Had been a puny girl, no boy at all:
And so he deem'd that either Sohrab took,
By a false boast, the style of Rustum's son;
Or that men gave it him, to swell his fame.
So deem'd he; yet he listen'd, plung'd in thought;
Tears gathered in his eyes as he saw
His own youth; saw Sohrab's mother, in her bloom;
And that old King, her father, who lov'd well
His wandering guest, and gave him his fair child
With joy; and all the pleasant life they led,
They three, in that long-distant summer-time—
And Rustum gaz'd on him with grief and said:
"O Sohrab, thou indeed art such a son
Whom Rustum, wert thou his, might well have lov'd!
Yet here thou errest, Sohrab, or else men
Have told thee false;
For Rustum had no son: one child had he
But one—a girl: who with her mother now
Plies some light female task, nor dreams of us—
Of us she dreams not, nor of wounds, nor war."
But Sohrab answer'd him in wrath; for now
The anguish of the deep-fix'd spear grew fierce,
And he desired to draw forth the steel,
And let the blood flow free, and so to die;
But first he would convince his stubborn foe—
And, rising sternly on one arm, he said:—
"Who art thou who dost defy my words?
Truth sits upon the lips of dying men,
And falsehood, while I liv'd, was far from mine.
I tell thee, prick'd upon this arm I bear

That seal which Rustum to my mother gave,
That she might prick it on the babe she bore."
He spoke: and all the blood left Rustum's cheeks:
His knees totter'd and he smote his hand,
Against his breast
And in a hollow voice he spake, and said:—
"Sohrab, that were a proof which could not lie
If thou shew this, then art thou Rustum's son."
Then, with weak hasty fingers, Sohrab loos'd
His belt, and near the shoulder bar'd his arm,
And shew'd the sign of Rustum's seal
And then he touch'd it with his hand and said:—
"How say'st thou? is *that* the proper sign of Rustum's son,"
He spoke: and Rustum gaz'd, and gaz'd, and stood.
Speechless; and then he utter'd one sharp cry—
"O boy—thy father!"
And then a dark cloud pass'd before his eyes,
And his head swam, and he sank down to earth.
But Sohrab crawl'd to where he lay, and cast
His arms about his neck, and kiss'd his lips,
And with fond faltering fingers strok'd his cheeks,
Trying to call him back to life; and life
Came back to Rustum, and he op'd his eyes,
And they stood wide with horror; and he seiz'd
In both his hands the dust which lay around
And threw it on his head, and smirch'd his hair,
His hair, and face, and beard, and glittering arms;
And strong convulsive groanings shook his breast,
And his sob's chok'd him; and he clutch'd his sword,
To draw it, and forever let life out.
But Sohrab saw his thought, and held his hands,
And with a soothing voice he spoke, and said:—
"Father, forbear.
I meet today the fate which at my birth
Was written down in heaven,
And thou art heavens unconscious hand
But let us speak no more of this:
Let me feel that I have found my father.
Come, sit beside me on the sand, and take
My head betwixt thy hands, and kiss my cheeks,
And wash them with thy tears, and say: 'My son!'
Quick! Quick! for number'd are my sands of life."
So said he: and his voice releas'd the heart

Of Rustum, and his tears broke forth; he cast
His arms round his son's neck, and wept aloud,
And kiss'd him, And awe fell on both the hosts
Because of Rustum's grief:
Then Rustum said—"Sohrab my son,
I will burn my tents,
And quit the host, and bear thee hence with me to Seistan,
And I will lay thee in that lovely earth,
And heap a stately mound above thy bones,
And plant a far-seen pillar over all;
That men shall not forget thee in thy grave.
And I will spare thy host:
What should I do with slaying any more?
I would that all whom I have ever slain
Might be once more alive; my bitterest foes,
And those through whose death I won the fame I have;
That thou mightest live too, my Son, my Son!
Or would that I myself,
Might now be lying on this bloody sand,
That I might die, not thou;"
He spoke; and Sohrab smil'd on him, and took
The spear, and drew it from his side, and eased
His wounds imperious anguish: but blood
Came welling from the open gash, and life
Flow'd with the stream;
His head droop'd low, his limbs grew slack;
Motionless and white, he lay—
His eyes fix'd lovingly upon his father's face:
Till all his strength had ebb'd, and all
Unwillingly his spirit fled away,
So on the bloody sand, Sohrab lay dead.
And the great Rustum drew his horseman's cloak
Down o'er his face
And father and son were left alone upon the Oxus sands.

It is thought that the sentiment of this great poem may
help to develop our own wonderful Father-and-Son relationships.

The Statue of Liberty

|T HAS been said that a thing is important not only for itself alone, but for what it stands for, and what it projects into the lives of others. We have a very helpful way of investing a symbol with meaning, so that it can present ideas to the mind with greater power. For example, a flag in the sky or a light in the window or a ring on the finger may have a significance to us far beyond the meaning of the actual thing itself. A uniform or an insignia of office may lift up our thoughts and center them on great principles and ennobling ideals.

One of the greatest symbols of our world stands on Bedloe Island at the gateway of America. We refer to this symbol as the Statue of Liberty. It towers majestically over the New York Harbor, extending a welcome to all of those who seek freedom and equal opportunity in a great, free, and divinely established land. The Statue of Liberty represents to the world the great ideas embodied in the American Declaration of Independence, the Constitution of the United States, and the American way of life.

All of America and much of the world looks up to this great statue as it symbolizes the American purpose with the American mission to keep freedom alive in the world. It is the mission of America to provide equal opportunity, fair play and free agency for all men. The full and official name of this "Lady of the Harbor" is "Statue of Liberty Enlightening the World."

This important symbol was presented as a gift to the American people on July 4, 1884, by the people of France. The statue itself was the creation of Frederic Auguste Bartholdi, sculptor and fighter for freedom. At the conclusion of the Franco-Prussian War in which he fought, he sailed for the United States. And as his ship came into the New York Harbor, Bartholdi stood on the deck and drew in his sketchbook the figure of a great lady holding aloft a burning torch as the everlasting symbol of freedom. Its purpose was to commemorate Franco-American friendship and to send the light of liberty out across all of the lands of the earth implanting in the hearts of all men the idea of the liberty and brotherhood as it existed in a great, free people under a free form of government.

On Thursday, October 2, 1886 a large welcoming celebration was given to commemorate this great lady's arrival upon our shores. There was a typical New York parade formed with 70 bands, and thousands of people with many nationalities participating. The flag of the United States with its 28 stars floated beside the French tri-color. Bells rang, whistles blew, and fireworks were shot in the air. Harbor boats clanged a greeting, and ocean liners signaled their salutes, as the Statue of Liberty assumed her permanent place of honor at the gateway to America.

President Grover Cleveland watched the statue being placed in position, and then in a welcoming speech said, "This token of the affection and consideration of the people of France demonstrates the kinship of our two republics, and conveys to us the assurance that, in our efforts to commend to mankind the excellence of a government resting upon the popular will that we still have a firm friend and steadfast ally beyond the American continent."

The statue itself is the largest one ever erected by man. The torch rises 305 feet above the base of the pedestal. Eighty tons of hammered sheet copper covers the steel base. The statue itself is large enough that forty people can stand comfortably in its head, and a long stairway runs through the 42-foot arm up to the torch held in a hand measuring 16 feet 5 inches. The index finger is 8 feet long. The length of the statue's nose is 4½ feet. The right arm holds aloft the great torch which at night gleams abroad with a powerful fluorescent light. This historic figure casts its symbolic light across the world and many men are guided and inspired by its rays. Floodlights shine upon the statue from its base. The left arm holds a tablet which bears the date of the Declaration of Independence—July 4, 1776. A crown with huge spikes representing the sun's rays rests upon the head. At the feet where it is seldom seen, lies a broken chain symbolic of the bonds broken by a peace-loving people in their struggle for liberty.

In 1908 a tablet was placed on the pedestal containing the sonnet of Emma Lazarus, entitled "The New Colossus." It says:

> Not like the brazen giant of Greek fame
> With conquering limbs astride from land to land,
> Here at our sea-washed sunset gates shall stand
> A mighty woman with a torch whose flame
> Is the imprisoned lightning, and her name
> Mother of Exiles. From her beacon hand
> Glows world wide welcome; her mild eyes command.
>
> The air bridged harbor that twin cities frame.
> Keep ancient lands, your storied pomp! Cries she
> With silent lips, "Give me your tired, your poor,
> Your huddled masses yearning to be free,
> The wretched refuse of your teeming shore.
> Send these, the homeless, tempest tossed to me.
> I lift my lamp beside the golden door."

America was founded by, and for, those seeking liberty and freedom from oppression. And America continues in her purpose. Emerson, who has been referred to as America's spokesman, said, "The office of America is to liberate, to abolish kingcraft and priestcraft, to pull down the gallows, to take in the immigrants, and uplift all of mankind."

Again he said:

> For of what avail
> Is plow or sail
> Or land or life
> If freedom fail.

Through all our generations, Americans have been in the vanguard of freedom. We cherish our national image as the citadel of democracy, morality and a living defiance of despotism everywhere and at all times.

In our day the ancient tyranny of enslavement and force has reappeared among us in its newest and most insidious form called communism. Many peoples have already succumbed to this influence. In all countries this new tyranny, like those of the past, is abetted by ignorance, poverty, conflict, and a widespread belief that freedom and morality were not meant for people generally.

America remains the world's chief home, and chief hope of freedom. A present refusal or inability on our part to defend it could demoralize the cause of liberty and justice for a thousand years. This would have been quite a different world if there had never been a United States of America.

Prior to July 4, 1776 and in many cases since, the national purpose of nations has been and is to dominate. Alexander and Cyrus, Caesar and Napoleon, Hitler and Khrushchev have all dreamed of world dominion with themselves at the head. This philosophy of domination has been openly and vigorously proclaimed by communists from the days of Lenin down to Khrushchev, Mao and Castro. "It was never intended by God that man, created in his image, should live with somebody else's foot on his neck or someone else's hand over his mouth." Even before this earth life began God decreed that men and women everywhere should be free. However, the forces of evil have always sought, sometimes with considerable success, to overthrow the freedom of the world and the free agency of man.

What a thrilling thing it is to have a part in carrying out the divine commission to liberate, to educate, to set men free! How appropriate to look up to our national symbol and rededicate ourselves to our national responsibility! Every good American strengthens the nation. Neither those who wrote the Declaration of Independence, nor the patriots of our own day are acting for themselves alone, but for the whole human race. What a great mistake to think of dedication as a sacrifice. Rather we should feel the stimulating exhilaration that always comes when devoted effort is applied toward the accomplishment of our country's highest aims.

A little girl was once taken by her father on a visit to New York City. The most impressive part of all their experience was the trip to Liberty Island. They made the long climb to the very top of the statue. But that night after returning to their hotel, the little girl could not sleep. When her father asked her what the trouble was she replied, "I have been thinking of the great lady with the lamp standing out there on her island alone. She must get awfully tired. Don't you think that somebody should help her to hold up her light?" The little girl had a great idea. There are 185 million somebodies that need to help her hold aloft the lamp of freedom and this can best be done by all of us individually deserving to be free.

In one of our most honored songs we sing, "God Bless America." What kind of an America do we have in mind? Surely not a drunken America nor an immoral America nor a shiftless America, nor a godless America. This nation was established under God by wise men raised up to that very purpose. Freedom itself comes from God. Bondage and slavery are the instruments of Satan. No one has a *right* to do *wrong*. No man can really be free until he chooses to do God's will. Seneca once said, "To obey God is perfect liberty. He that does so shall be free and all his actions shall succeed."

A degenerate state of morals or a corrupted public conscience is incompatible with freedom. No free government can be preserved except by a firm adherence to justice, temperance, frugality and virtue. And the blessings of liberty can only be maintained by a constant adherence to the fundamental principles of righteousness.

If we wish to be free we must *love* God and *serve* God and *be* godly. Only as we make ourselves unworthy of God's gifts will they be lost to us. The Lord has said, "Abide ye in the liberty wherewith ye are made free; entangle not yourselves in sin, but let your hands be clean until the Lord comes." (D&C 88:86.) Again he said, "Wherefore hear my voice and follow me, and you shall be a free people." (D&C 38:22) "I the Lord God make you free, therefore, you are free indeed." (D&C 98:8)

". . . Governments were instituted of God for the benefit of man; and . . . [God] holds men accountable for their acts in relation to them, both in making laws and in administering them, for the good and safety of society. . . . No government can exist in peace, except such laws are framed and held inviolate as will secure to each individual the free exercise of conscience, the right and control of property, and the protection of life." (D&C 134:1-2)

We can be sure that our prayers will be answered if, when we sing "God Bless America," it is a righteous, godly America on which his blessing is sought. Nations in the past have fallen only when they have forgotten God. We will lose our promised blessings if we mislay our national purpose, or go to sleep while our Founding Fathers' dream of American destiny is taken from us. We who live in this choice land might well feel a kinship to the ancient Israelites who were also chosen of God for a holy experiment on a new soil, where righteousness and free agency were its cardinal principles.

We should also set up in our own lives something akin to a Statue of Liberty, thereby keeping ourselves from becoming enslaved individually. Political slavery is not the only dangerous variety. We can be enslaved by sin. We can lose our freedom to negative attitudes. We can be taken prisoner by our own bad habits. We can bind ourselves with our own ignorance. Epicetetus said, "No man is free who is not master of himself."

Jesus gave us the best formula when he said, "Ye shall know the truth, and the truth shall make you free." The way to freedom for the mind is to know the truth, and the way of freedom for the soul is to live righteously.

The world needs a free America. The world needs a righteous America. The world needs a purposeful America made up of godly citizens, each doing his part to hold up the torch of freedom.

To this end may God bless America and may God bless Americans.

The Sword of Damocles

IN 400 B.C. the ancient city of Syracuse in Sicily was ruled by a famous king named Dionysius. One of the prominent members of his court was called Damocles. Damocles was one of those interesting folks who could always see the greener grass on the other side of the fence. He was always talking about what a great job Dionysius had in being king. According to Damocles, the king had everything to make him happy. He had power, security and a soft life without the worries that bothered other people.

Then one day the king gave Damocles a magnificent banquet. Damocles was seated in the place of honor at the king's right hand. He was given the recognition of royalty, regaled with gifts, provided with the finest entertainment and served the best fare in the kingdom. Nothing was lacking, and Damocles was making the most of it with his friends. But in the midst of his great enjoyment Damocles looked up and saw that a naked sword was suspended directly above his head, held in place by a single hair. Damocles knew that any false move could cause the sword to fall and slice him in two.

The king used this visual aid in trying to teach Damocles and the other members of his court that there were also some hazards going along with the responsibilities of kingship. He felt that Damocles should know that a king's job consisted of something more than attending banquets, giving orders, and having fun. And many kings have lost their thrones as well as their heads merely because they made a few mismoves. It is not the easiest thing in the world to be a king in any field. If one desires a high place in life he should not only be prepared to pay the price but he must also learn to shoulder the responsibility.

It is one of the laws of existence that as the rewards of life get bigger, the size of the problems are also increased. Someone has said, "The higher up the mountain you go the harder the wind blows."

No matter what one's field may be, the king is usually required to do the most work, pay the biggest price, and be the most careful. This ancient banquet took place in Syracuse over 23 hundred years ago, but the experience of Damocles has lived through the ages because everyone who gets very close to the king row of success, usually finds a sword or two hanging over his head. And it doesn't take very many wrong moves to break the thread and bring the sword of consequence down upon him. Incidently there is a postscript attached to the Damocles story to the effect that the hair that held up the sword was one that Dionysius had found on the tunic of Damocles which he recognized as belonging to the queen. This may indicate that there had already been some false moves that were responsible for the sword hanging over the head of Damocles in the first place.

But, be that as it may it seems that the times have not changed very much, as there are still some problems and a lot of swords hanging over our heads, just waiting for something to happen. It is also still true that those that enjoy the greatest privileges, and sit in the places of greatest responsibility, must also be the most careful of mismoves. This idea is illustrated by the story of a prize fighter who wanted to be the king of the heavyweights. The path leading to this particular accomplishment took him into the ring with the great Jack Dempsey. The contest hadn't gone very far before the fighter complained to the referee that Dempsey had hit him when he wasn't looking. The referee said, "No one has any business being in the fight ring with Jack Dempsey who doesn't pay attention." And whether our problem comes from the left hook of a prize fighter or from our own sins, or from the way we handle our responsibilities, we had better pay attention, for any of these mismoves are likely to break the only hair that can keep the sword of Damocles from severing us from our future.

We should remember that if we are going to maintain our place among the champions we had better keep on our toes and be able to look out for ourselves. Even the referee can't protect our jaws if we are looking in some other direction when the blow lands. And besides, if we plan to win the battle of life and sit in the king row of success, we had better stay on the job and keep our eyes on the ball.

The biggest job that anyone ever has in his life is that of building his own personal success, and that is pretty difficult unless we always keep our wits about us. We can depend upon it that seen or unseen there are some swords hanging around over our heads held in place by some very fragile connections which can be easily broken.

We might get some good ideas for ourselves by taking a few notes from some of those around us, who are having their success destroyed by this Damoclean process. The boom is being lowered on someone every day for some reason. For example, I know of a very intelligent young salesman who is capable of being the president of his company. In his first few years he looked like a sure winner, but he became so hungry for praise and so anxious for promotion that he became a little careless with the truth and a little neglectful of his own honor. He began taking a few out-of-bounds privileges with morality. He didn't actually mean to do anything bad; he just got too interested in short cuts.

Because he was irritated with the restraints his company imposed upon him, he changed companies, but he didn't change himself, and his carelessness increased, because of what seemed to him like his immunity from consequences. To him his success was apparent and the king row was in sight. But once he had removed the boundary line between right and wrong he didn't quite know where to stop and he finally got to the point where he himself was unsure of what was right and what was wrong. He successfully covered up some of his misdeeds for a while, and he fully intended to make everything right in the end after he had become the king. Then these little misdeeds would no longer be necessary, and it seemed to him that the end justified the means. But once when he wasn't paying attention a wrong move broke the hair, and with great finality down came the sword. My friend is now licking his wounds in the state penitentiary.

Dishonesty is a Damoclean sword that hangs over the head of every individual. Sometimes we do wrong and then compound the felony by attempting concealment. Phillip Brooks once said, "Beware of concealment. . . . It is an awful day in one's life when he has to hide something." But no matter how well a thing may be hidden, there is always someone who can spot the telltale hairs of wrong, gathering on our tunics. When the hair is broken, the jig is up. Concealment is a process far too complicated for anyone to carry on with safely. As has been said, "Oh, what a tangled web we weave when first we practice to deceive."

Another Damoclean sword is complacency. One of the best ways to make a false move is to just sit still. With an attempt at combining humor and truth someone was once praising a certain church group. He said, "They don't lie, they don't steal, they don't cheat, they don't smoke, they don't drink, they don't go to church, they don't pay their tithing, they don't say their prayers." Without sufficient works the Damoclean sword always strikes to kill our faith.

I know a young man who several years ago was probably the most promising church man that I had ever known. He worked very vigorously in doing his duty. He was always conscientious in doing what was right. He was courageous and enthusiastic and his strong desire to succeed was supported by a vigorous, well-planned industry. The fact that he was intelligent, faithful and on his toes indicated that he had tremendous future possibilities. The roadway ahead showed great promise, and the spiritual king row was in clear view. Of course, his excellence soon began to bring him great honors and high praise and as with so many other people this diverted his attention, and little by little the dry-rot of complacency began to do its deadly work. The ability which he had developed, his new-found confidence in himself, and the honor that people lavished upon him encouraged him to relax his drive while he enjoyed his success. He was now sitting right in the middle of the king row. He got the same idea held by Damocles that once you were the king, any success became almost automatic. But no success comes as a permanent endowment. Success must be continually won. Instead of acting like a king and doing twice as much work as anybody else, he made the same mistake that dozens of others have made. He let his ego become so inflated that it choked off his industry. He believed that any failure was now practically impossible. He subscribed to the old doctrine, that "the king can do no wrong." Like King Nebuchadnezzar he said to himself, "Is not this great Babylon, that I have built . . . by the might of my power, and for the honour of my majesty?" But, soon the great sword of Damocles had cut him in two.

The story is told of a great wrestler who, while he was not as strong as some others, won many wrestling matches against stronger men by a rather questionable stratagem that life sometimes employs against us. When the other wrestler nearly had him down, he would reach up and pat the near-champion on the back. The wrestler on top, thinking that the referee was giving him the decision, would relax his hold and turn off his effort. Then it was a comparatively easy thing for the other wrestler to exert his greatest effort and win the match. That is, before his opponent knew what was happening he would find his back on the mat and the prize lost.

That is what complacency often does to us. This was the trick that fate played on King Nebuchadnezzar. The king had built up the greatest empire ever known in the world. He was the mightiest monarch on the earth. Then life began patting him on the back and he thought that he had won the fight on a permanent basis. But as soon as he relaxed his hold he found that he had lost his kingdom. He was driven from among men and ate grass like the oxen.

Nebuchadnezzar learned by sad experience that the battle is never permanently won. He learned that the Damoclean sword is always in its place just waiting for someone to make a few mismoves.

Some of the results of our personal defects are about as devastating as if the sword had actually cut our heads off. Certainly our brains are of little use when complacency gets control of our muscles and our personality. Then we try to be leaders without leading. We try to have faith without works. We try to have success without merit. For these reasons a great number of failures and successes are trading places every year. Someone has said that we should be very considerate of those we pass on our way up to success, as we may pass them again on our way down. In any event we should remember that a pat on the back is not necessarily the signal to turn off the effort. The one thing that we may be sure of is that no king ever stays in the king row for very long if he doesn't stay on the job and keep pitching. As a nation we have found that a little bit of complacency can easily bring the threat of a total destruction down upon our heads.

There is a moving picture going around showing how by their sins some of the ancients living in Sodom and Gommorah brought fire and brimstone down from heaven upon themselves. Sin always does that to nations and to individuals. Every sin is a Damoclean sword. And life can be pretty cruel both here and hereafter to those who violate the laws of righteousness. Whenever we violate the laws we had better be prepared to pay the penalties. One of the disturbing things about life is that very few reach their goals in safety. Just think of the large numbers who intend to get a college education or try for success in one of the occupations or in life itself; as compared to the very few who are ultimately successful. Jesus pointed out this hazard in its most significant aspects when about the greatest of all prizes in life he said, "Strait is the gate, and narrow is the way, which leadeth unto life, and few there be that find it." (Matthew 7:14) And yet any of us can be outstandingly successful in anything we undertake if we just fully follow the rules. Of course, it is a good thing to keep in mind that only those who endure to the end shall be saved. And we can't make too many false moves along the way. It has been said that endurance is the fifth principle of the gospel. As important as the other principles of the gospel are, none of them amount to very much without endurance. We must learn to hang on to the end. And as we work our way toward success, like the prize fighters and the kings and those seeking eternal life itself, we had better pay attention, for we usually lose our crowns either because we aren't on our toes, or we make some mismove, or quit our training, or lose our industry, or make love to the wrong kind of ideas. Then we break the thread of our success and bring down the Damoclean sword of failure upon ourselves and we may even miss the greatest of all prizes, which is to find a permanent place for ourselves in the eternal king row.

The Ten Commandments

O NE OF the most important of all of the great world movements was set in motion 3,400 years ago. The posterity of Abraham, Isaac and Jacob, who for many years had been held in Egyptian slavery, had just been released from their bondage. With a great demonstration of power the Lord had brought them out of Egypt under the promise to make them the greatest nation in the world. And they were now awaiting the Lord's direction at the foot of Mount Sinai in the desert of Arabia.

To assure the success of this project, it was necessary that a clear understanding of the fundamental principles involved be had by all the parties concerned. To make sure that there was a complete meeting of the minds, God called Moses up to the top of Mount Sinai and explained what the people must do in order to reach the high destiny that had been marked out for them. Moses then went down and presented the Lord's program to the people, and they unanimously accepted it. They indicated their enthusiasm for making a covenant with the Lord to keep all of his commandments. Then at the proper time God descended to the top of Mount Sinai and to the accompaniment of lightnings and thunders gave them that law which if followed would make them the most successful and the most happy people upon the earth. They were to be an outstanding generation, a royal priesthood, a holy nation.

As the central part of this law, God wrote Ten Commandments on tables of stone. These ten fundamental principles have been held up as the basic law of the world ever since. During these 34 past centuries, the world has undergone great changes. The camel no longer serves as our primary means of transportation. Systems of communication, processes of manufacture, and methods of warfare have been radically modified. Most text books on science that are even a few years old have been discarded as obsolete, and yet the importance of these fundamental, timeless laws themselves are as completely up-to-date today as they were 34 centuries ago in that far-away Arabian desert. Obedience to these laws represents our world's greatest present need.

When Moses came down from the Mount and saw his people dancing around the golden calf, he became angry and broke the tables containing the commandments. But in our day of weakness and transgression, we are breaking the commandments themselves; though in a more real sense, as pointed out by Cecil B. DeMille, we cannot break the Ten Commandments, we can only break ourselves against them. No proof is required in our day that we are fulfilling the scriptural declaration "that all have sinned and come short of the glory of God."

It is unnecessary for anyone to point out our degradation to us. Our sins are plainly manifested in every town and hamlet throughout the land. We see the evidences of our delinquency and crime all about us. Our sins are reported in the daily press. We hear them announced over the radio, and when we meditate a little we can feel the sting of our own reproving conscience.

It has been said that in all probability there is not one person who does not break every one of the Ten Commandments. For example, in the sixth commandment God said, "Thou shalt not kill." But Jesus reminds us of the larger concept of this law by saying neither should we hate. He made it clear that a person who gives himself over to anger is already committing a sin. The murderous hand is always impelled by the hateful heart. It is true that there are many who have never committed the gross murderous deed of actually destroying life itself, but who is free from the sinful approaches that must always precede the actual dagger thrust? The law provided a severe penalty for the visible act, but the gospel rebukes the evil passion that leads to it by first setting the thought to motion.

Likewise the law forbade the awful sin of adultery. But Christ pointed out that the sin actually began with the lustful glance, the sensual design, and the evil thought by which it was supported. How God must hate this unnatural, soul-destroying emphasis presently being placed upon sex! We are feeding our minds and stimulating our passions with this poisonous fruit of sin as we find it on the newsstands, in the movies and in our own evil inclinations. The violation of this great commandment both in the spirit and in the letter is presently ruining the sanctity of thousands of homes, and causing the spiritual decay of tens of thousands of individuals. Satan clothes his goddess of lust as an angel of love to lead away our souls. Jesus pointed out that it was better to go through life blind than to have eyes devoted to seeing evil. He said it were better to have our hands cut off than to use them to work iniquity.

No nation can ever be great unless it keeps these statutes given from the top of Mount Sinai 3,400 years ago.

During the Civil War someone inquired of Abraham Lincoln if he didn't think the Lord was on our side. President Lincoln replied that he was not so much concerned about whether or not the Lord was on our side. What he wanted to know was whether or not we were on the Lord's side. We never need to worry very much about whose side the Lord is on. He is on the right side, and we can always be certain that he will be on our side if we are always on his side.

One of the reasons that we are so frequently on the wrong side is because we fail to recognize or will not acknowledge wrong itself. Some time ago a minister pointed out that some of our forefathers walked through the world haunted by their sins and tormented by their fears of the judgment. Then with an apparent sense of relief he said that these things didn't bother us much any more. We have eased our consciences by merely failing to recognize our sins. Instead of worrying about improving our lives we merely refuse to acknowledge the transgression.

This attitude of irresponsibility so prevalent in our world is represented by the answer a young woman from Pennsylvania gave to the reporters of *Look Magazine* who were conducting a survey on this subject. When asked if she thought she was doing wrong in a particular thing she said, "Who am I to say what is right or wrong?" So many people say that sin is a part of the times, and that the individual is not to blame. We say it doesn't matter what we believe, that we are all going to the same place anyway. We feel that one belief is as good as another, that one set of activities is as good as another, and that one religion is as good as another.

Although these are popular beliefs, they are the doctrines of evil. It matters a very great deal what we believe. One religion is not as good as another. Falsehood is not as good as truth. We are not all going to the same place. If we were, we might just as well scrap the scriptures, forget all moral considerations, and turn the calendar of history back to the Dark Ages. The most serious problems have always resulted when nations or individuals have lost their sense of sin, and this particular hazard is one of the most destructive evils of our own day.

In spite of their overwhelming importance, we do not like to think or talk about our sins. And if we do speak of them, we usually modify the meaning of the term so that it will not offend us. We refer to our sins as experience or as something of little consequence for which we have no individual responsibility. However, we cannot reduce the deadliness of a poison merely by changing the label on the bottle. Throughout the scriptures God probably talks as much about sin as about any other thing. He has said that it is tremendously destructive. Instead of saying that it doesn't make any difference, he has said, "The soul that sinneth, it shall die." (Ez. 18:4) That is plain enough and forceful enough that everyone should be able to understand it.

There is a very dangerous so-called psychology that says that the way to develop oneself is to give expression to one's feelings. Some say that parents should not say "no" to their children for fear of dwarfing their spirits or inhibiting their personalities. They say that desires should be expressed, not suppressed. If a child feels like slamming the door, he should slam it, otherwise he might become inhibited. For the same reason, if one feels like sowing some wild oats, he should sow them. They say we only live once. We should shoot the works. They say "live it up," "eat, drink and be merry, for tomorrow we die." Though popular in some places, this is the philosophy of death. Such attitudes have caused more crime and misery than all of the wars in history. In fact, this is the attitude that has caused the wars themselves. It also causes sin, crime, death and eternal misery.

The people who are afraid of becoming inhibited by curbing their sinful inclinations should remember that God is the same yesterday, today and forever; that he hates all sin and that no one is permitted to violate his law without placing a serious demerit upon his own soul.

The murders described in our daily newspapers are just as sinful as the murder of Abel by his brother Cain. The sex perversions on which we are fed by the radio, the movies and the magazines are only modern-day copies of those sins for which God rained fire and brimstone upon Sodom and Gomorrah. We are horrified when we read of the deadly transgressions of Noah's day. But Jesus himself pointed to Noah's time as the period most resembling our own. We should occasionally take a careful look at our own situation.

It has been said that in some of our modern-day households the word "father" has come to mean a person with a highball in one hand, a cigarette in another, and spiritual indifference in his heart. We may try to pass these things off with a shrug, yet five million alcoholics with millions of other people on their way to becoming alcoholics represents a lot of sin for our great Christian nation. But the worst of our problem is that our trend in the use of alcohol, tobacco, delinquency, crime and immorality are headed in the wrong direction and pointed upward at an alarming angle.

It is our solemn duty to remind ourselves that all of our accounts with God must some day be settled, even though the conditions may not be to our liking. The same inspired scripture that proclaims the wonders of heaven also describes the tortures of hell and the abject misery involved in eternal banishment from the presence of God. Ten thousand years from today we will all be living somewhere, and right now is the time given to us to determine where that place will be. The important questions of our lives will be answered by how obediently we listen to the voice of God coming down to us out of the thunders and lightnings of Sinai, saying:

1. Thou shalt have no other gods before me.
2. Thou shalt not make unto me any graven image.
3. Thou shalt not take the name of the Lord thy God in vain.
4. Remember the Sabbath Day to keep it holy.
5. Honor thy Father and thy Mother.
6. Thou shalt not kill.
7. Thou shalt not commit adultery.
8. Thou shalt not steal.
9. Thou shalt not bear false witness.
10. Thou shalt not covet.

We must never weaken the influence of these great commandments by thinking they are negative or in bad form. One of the first and most important steps in any success is to get our minds definitely settled about those things that we must never do under any circumstances. Only when these decisions have been made once and for all, are we in a position to enthusiastically go to work on those things that we should do. Neither should we smart under the positive, authoritative form in which these commandments were given.

One man once said that this harsh word "commandment" should be modified to some word like request or suggestion. But we will never get very far until we love God's word as he gave it. Certainly he has not left us in any doubt as to exactly where he stands. And on this point, Dr. Henry C. Link says, "Nothing does so much to put order into a man's life as do sound principles. They are worth more than a library full of books or a den decorated with diplomas. Principles and standards clarify and simplify our thinking. They are points of reference which help us to avoid complexity and confusion. They rescue us from the necessity of prolonged and useless debate. They give us a base for decision and action.

Suppose then that we set these ten great laws up in our hearts and accept them as the unchanging will of God. When we determine to live by their every word we will also be "a chosen people." And may we take full advantage of the power of these great laws to this end.

The Time We Save

RECENTLY I read a very provocative article about a certain distinguished Chinese gentleman visiting in this country. Among other things, he was shown through the new home of a well-to-do American friend. He was very interested in what he saw and listened attentively as the many labor-saving devices were explained to him, and he was told about the saving in time that they made possible. After the tour was over the guest said to his host, "And what do you do with all of this time that you save?"

That is a pretty good question and one that everyone should give some attention to. It has often been pointed out that more than about anything else, the quality of our lives is determined by what we do in our free time. We now save one-half of the time formerly spent in earning a living. Modern transportation has saved us a lot of time in getting from one place to another. The fact that our food is produced by giant machinery and then pre-mixed, packaged and delivered to our door saves us more time.

Even our life expectancy has been increased from 35 years in George Washington's time to 48 years in 1900 and to 70 years in our day. That is, in the first part of this century 22 years has been added to our lives. This brings us back again to the important question of how are we using this extra time.

Following are four suggestions that may be helpful. First, it is thought that we might well spend a little more of this saved time reading good books. By and large we are not as well informed about some of the important things in life as we should be. Someone has said that "The great

American Desert is not west of the Mississippi as was at one time supposed, but it is underneath the hat of the average man." A little of this desert condition has also gotten into our hearts and spirits. This in spite of the fact that one of the most profitable, pleasant and inexpensive of all the forms of entertainment and personal uplift may be had in absorbing the helpful ideas of our great literature. There is a source of tremendous wealth easily available to us in books. And how could one more pleasantly or profitably close each day than to spend an hour in a comfortable chair with a good book?

It has been recommended that we read with a pencil in hand, so that we can write down our own ideas in the book's margins. A book may be extremely valuable for the ideas it contains but it is sometimes even more valuable for the things that it stimulates us to think about. Once your own thinking processes have been set in motion, don't be in too big a hurry to get back to the book. Follow your own ideas at least until you discover where they are leading you. Let them stimulate your resolutions and as they do, write your notes in the book's margins or on its blank pages.

Some of the primary uses of books are to help us to think, make decisions, and take action. When the particular thought you are following has been exhausted, go back to the book and take up where you left off. High speed in reading may be all right under many circumstances, but there are times when we should proceed carefully and let the ideas thoroughly infiltrate our minds. Reading furnishes us a good opportunity to plant new seeds of thought and establish profitable springboards for action. How wonderful when some of our wisest men are willing to spend a lifetime in writing a great book we may absorb in a few hours!

Sometime ago there was a prominent radio program entitled "You Were There." In imagination, this program took you back to some actual scene of great significance while you relived that important event. And if you are a good reader, "You Also Are There," you can refeel and relive the greatest ideas, you can march with Napoleon or sail with Columbus, or converse with Socrates, or study with the Prophets, or live with Jesus. You can absorb the best from the greatest lives. If you feel that you can't spare an hour for such an employment, check on how much time you spend watching television or just doing nothing at all.

Not long ago a man told me that during the last five years he had not read a single book. That would have been unfortunate even in the Dark Ages, but it is stark tragedy in this great age of wonders and enlightenment that we know as the dispensation of the fulness of times.

Another tragedy is seen in the case of a fine young woman who recently dropped her education upon completion of high school. Her parents have tried to urge her to go to college but she just isn't interested. Night after night she watches television and is completely missing the thrill hopelessly awaiting her in an enlightened mind. Her mind and soul are being starved for the great mental and spiritual nourishment that is going to waste right under her nose.

What a calamity to see the pores of a human mind close so tightly that the spirit is forced to live in the darkness of spiritual night!

Suggestion number two is that some of this time that we have saved can profitably be spent in memorizing choice bits of philosophy, scripture, poetry, etc. It is a well-established fact that a great deal of our success is put together by that part of the mind that lies below the level of consciousness. Many of the things that we do, like walking, talking, eating, etc., are carried on by the subconscious mind with very little conscious effort on our·part. This is also the source of some of our most enlightening flashes of inspiration, we are also powerfully influenced by the ideas and ideals that are under the control of the subconscious mind. Recently a friend told me about some advice given to him by his father when he was just a boy. He had accepted the idea without question and it had become such an important part of him that it now governed his life. In fact, every part of him would rebel even at the thought of going contrary to this philosophy that had become so well established in his character.

This general situation reminds us of an interesting sight sometimes, seen at sea, where the winds, the waves and the surface ice were moving in one direction at the very time and place that a great iceberg is sailing serenely in the opposite direction. This phenomenon is explained by the fact that the motion of the iceberg is controlled by the powerful currents in the ocean's depths where the bulk of the iceberg is based. This same kind of a phenomenon operates in our lives. In fact, the mind has often been compared with an iceberg, 80% of which lies below the water level. Sometimes the influence on the surface of life may prompt us to do one thing. But the control of our lives is based in the depths of our souls where early training, well-established ideals and fundamental character qualities and even our training in our pre-earth life gives us the power to sail against the wind. What then could be more important than to use this power below the water line by memorizing wise sayings, inspiring poems, helpful bits of philosophy, and powerful scriptural passages!

I know of one man who keeps a valuable collection of these gems of thought in well-ordered idea books. Then he writes some of them out on cards and carries them with him and commits them to memory while he is waiting, or walking, or traveling. We can even memorize the words of God himself and store up his attitudes in our souls to give us this power in depth and direction.

The third recommendation for profitably spending a little of this time we have saved is in the development and effective use of our imaginations. Someone has said that the greatest gift that God has given to man is an imagination. The human imagination was given to man for a very good purpose and is like a great beam of light searching the skies. Like a giant radar beam, it penetrates every field and when properly directed it always brings back to us some valuable thing.

I know of a man who has been remarkably successful in his business and personal life. He always has the best ideas and the most up-to-date methods operating in his business and his life. He never seems to overlook anything. Many people have asked him how he thinks up all of these good ideas. He appears to them to be a genius, but he merely formed the habit of setting aside thirty minutes each evening devoted to imaginative research. This is when he sums up his day's work and tries to determine where he has made his mistakes and how they can be corrected for the future. This is the period when he makes his plans for tomorrow and sends his mind out on an expedition of discovery to explore every possibility of success.

During this thinking and planning period he sits alone and centers his mind on his objective. He asks himself searching questions trying to determine whether or not he is overlooking any opportunities, and, if so, what they are. What is he doing wrong? And how can they be corrected? He tries to determine if there are any new procedures that he should be introducing into his business or into his life. We place ourselves under a severe handicap when we fail to develop our powers of imagination. Many books have been written containing suggestions as to how to use the imagination so as to make money, to strengthen personality, to increase happiness and to save the soul.

The last and most important of these recommendations as to the use of the time we have saved is to use it in worshipping God. The fundamental purpose of life is to build greatness into human beings. Recently I received a letter

from a man in his eighties. He has worked hard all of his
life. He is probably worth ten million dollars. His life has
always stood for honor and he has tried to build character
into other people. He said, "I am an old man. I have wit-
nessed the folly of people neglecting their Christian faith
while practicing dishonesty, immorality and laziness." He
said, "I want to see people practice only goodness, fairness
and the other Christian virtues." What a thrill it is to see
a really great Christian, a really great human being with
the qualities of godliness firmly established in his soul. Food,
clothing, and other necessities of life are important, but of
what good is even ten million or ten billion dollars except
as it can be used to build the only real values, which are
human values?

All good comes from God. And by our worship we
can build a kinship with him that will make us like him.
To this end, God has set aside one day per week or one-
seventh of our total allotment of time while on this earth to
be spent in his worship. He has set aside the first day of each
week as a day of study and prayer, and planning and righteousness. This is the day when we get the philosophy of
the scriptures down into our subconscious minds and give
them the power to guide us to God! What a tragedy when
we desecrate this day and pervert its purpose to profane uses!
Sometimes we are so anxious for more time that we appropriate the Sabbath Day to be used for making money, or for
fishing or hunting, or recreation. Sometimes people lacking
in basic righteousness sail with the surface winds directly
against the word of the Lord. They rationalize themselves
into believing that their lives will be just as productive and
happy if their Sabbaths are spent out in the mountains or
at the lake. Some use the Sabbath Day as a time to get
drunk. They say it relaxes them and they like the feeling
that comes as a consequence. But we may be sure that the
family that goes to church and fulfills the Lord's require-

ments for the Sabbath will be a better kind of family than the one that desecrates the Sabbath for their own pleasures.

One of the first steps in our search for immortality is to learn how to use the time of the Sabbath Day. Even with the additional 22 years of extra time we have been given, and counting all the time that we have been saved by our inventions and gadgets, our supply is still exhaustible. But these four recommendations if followed will greatly increase the effectiveness of our lives, and that is the one thing that is important.

The Trojan Horse

HOMER was a blind Greek poet who lived in the ninth century B. C., and wrote the great epic poems known as the Iliad and the Odyssey. The first of these great literary classics tells the story of the Trojan War, which began when Paris, a Trojan prince, eloped with Helen, the wife of Menelaus, king of Sparta. To get Helen back, Menelaus enlisted the support of several kings of neighboring Greek states. Among them was the great Greek warrior, Agamemnon, king of Mycenae, and brother of Menelaus. This aggregation sailed a thousand ships across the Agean Sea, and laid siege to Troy, a large and well-fortified walled city near the Hellespont.

The Trojans were noted for their industry and ability as warriors. They successfully resisted this overwhelming Greek force for ten years, and it appeared that they would be able to hold out indefinitely. One thing was certain, and that was that they were safe as long as they kept the Greeks outside their walls.

On the other hand, ten years of failure had seriously demoralized Greek courage, and they were about to pack up and go home. But one of the Greeks by the name of Prylis had an interesting idea about how they could win the war. Following the strategy of Prylis the Greeks built a giant wooden horse, and into the hollow interior they hid a large number of heavily armed Greek soldiers. Then the rest of the Greeks got into their ships and sailed out of sight of Troy as though they were giving up the siege. However, they left one Greek behind them, who told the Trojans that this giant horse was built under the direction of the war goddess Athene, and that it had a magic power with an evil significance for the Trojans. As long as this great horse stood outside the walls of Troy it would bring continual misfortune to the city. He told the Trojans that the Greeks had purposely built it large to make it impossible to get through their gates. It was pointed out, however, that if in some way the Trojans were successful in getting this magic horse inside their city it would lose its power to harm the Trojans. Instead it would then bring them good fortune and stand as their guarantee from the gods that Troy could never be captured. Therefore, in order to thwart Greek strategy, the Trojans took down a section of their wall and dragged the giant horse inside the city. Then they held a great feast to celebrate their good fortune.

In the meantime a signal was flashed to the Greek ships waiting at sea. The main army returned in the middle of the night. Then the hidden Greeks came out of the wooden horse, overpowered the Trojan guards, and opened the city gates to the conquest-hungry Greek soldiers. Once the Greeks were inside the city walls, the intoxicated, celebrating Trojans were helpless in their hands. The city was robbed of its treasures. The great men of Troy were slain and the city itself was burned to the ground. Menelaus got his wife back, and with their job done the Greeks loaded their ships and set sail for home.

In the first place, this is a very interesting story. In the second place, it is about as good an example of military infiltration or fifth-column activity as we know anything about. But probably more important than either of these, it serves us with a very interesting parallel for our own accomplishment. Life has always been a kind of battle. The Apostle Paul said, "We wrestle not against flesh and blood, but against principalities, against powers, against the rulers of the darkness of this world, against spiritual wickedness in high places." To help us protect ourselves he said, "Wherefore take unto you the whole armour of God, that ye may be able to . . . withstand in the evil day." (Eph.

6:12-13) Paul knew that we would be safe only if we could keep the evil outside our walls.

There is no question but that the powers of darkness are presently laying a life-and-death siege to our lives. So far as we are concerned everything, including eternal exaltation itself, depends upon the outcome. The Trojans held out against the combined strength of one of the greatest group of warriors ever known in the world for just as long as they could keep them outside their walls, whereas the city fell in a single night once the enemy got its fifth-column inside the gates.

This strategy of infiltration always has and always will be the most effective way of overcoming an enemy. This is the source of the present success of communism. When the original communist leaders first announced their plans to dominate and enslave the world they were weak and few in number. They were then unable to launch any kind of a successful frontal attack against those they proposed to conquer. Even today they carefully avoid any use of military strength except when their advantages are so overwhelming that there is no possibility of defeat. Yet with almost no actual fighting they have brought under their dominion and control a very large part of all of the peoples of the earth. They have won this tremendous victory by getting their fifth-columnists not only inside our gates but also inside our minds.

But this technique is not new to the communists. Homer wrote about it nine centuries B. C. Then in 538 B. C., Cyrus the Persian captured the almost all-powerful city of Babylon by this same process. Babylon had prepared herself in every way to indefinitely resist the force of any aggressor. But while King Belshazzar was giving a feast to a thousand of his lords making them drunken with wine, Cyrus was a few miles north of the city turning the river Euphrates from its course, which ran under the walls of Babylon. Then

Cyrus marched his army into the city on the empty river-bed and overthrew the most powerful world capital, without the loss of a single soldier.

This technique has also been used successfully by Satan since time began. And it is still the process by which the eternal destruction of people is brought about. The ruler of darkness knows all of the tricks of infiltration and he knows that if he can first get his soldiers inside our gates, everything else will be easy.

If we could analyze the records of those who have gone or will go to their destruction down that broad, heavily traveled road mentioned by Jesus, we would certainly find that very few of us are ever destroyed by any force from the outside. Every case of spiritual downfall is an inside job. God never forces anyone to do right, and Satan has no power to force anyone to do wrong. We fall only when we first open our gates to evil and give the enemy a control in our lives. Every individual could hold out indefinitely against any frontal attack that could be launched by all of the powers of sin and evil put together. We go down in defeat only when we relax our guard and close our eyes to the evil that lies hidden inside some beguiling Trojan horse. And once Satan gets his fifth-column inside our gates, then like the Trojans and the Babylons we frequently go to our doom without even a struggle. For example, no one is ever forced by someone else to become a drunkard. If someone tried to compel us to live the life of an alcoholic, anyone in his right mind would and could resist with complete success. But that isn't how the attack comes. The adversary first sends out his propagandists, like the single Greek left behind at Troy for that purpose. Satan sends us to the movies or gets us to read the glamorized liquor advertisements, and we see the supposed pleasures of drinking and imagine the fun we could have pouring this poisonous stuff down our throats. The Greek that is left behind helps us to think that drinking will help to make us successful and happy. Then we tear down the protecting walls of our sense of right and wrong and drag this pleasant, many-advantaged, Trojan horse of alcohol inside our lives. Then in the middle of the night, its belly is opened and we are overpowered by the armed soldiers of immorality, irresponsibility, and every other kind of sin that is hidden inside of what Robert G. Ingersol refers to as "that damned stuff called alcohol."

But Satan has a far greater number of Trojan horses than the Greeks ever thought about. He has a Trojan horse to fit every situation. For example, ignorance is a Trojan horse, and the worst ignorance is that ignorance that is conscious of no ignorance. So many people go through life with very little study or prayer or meditation or attempt to make up their minds about objectives or standards or what the real values in life are. God is far wiser than we are, yet we leave his word untouched and see little that is of value in the holy scriptures. A survey recently indicated that most people own a Bible but almost no one ever reads it effectively. Thirty-four percent of all of those interviewed could not give the name of even one of the Gospels. What a shameful ignorance and what a terrible loss it brings upon us! God has given to the world this tremendous philosophy of success that we refer to as the gospel of Jesus Christ, through which, if we will, we can save our souls. Dozens of people have borne testimony to us about God and truth, but mostly we don't even investigate. Rather we hang on to our ignorance for dear life.

Like alcohol, the Trojan horse of ignorance is made to look very attractive. It offers us freedom from spiritual effort, freedom from making moral decisions, freedom from problem-solving, and freedom from an accusing conscience. For these glittering inducements we drag this destructive Trojan horse inside our walls. Then its belly opens, releasing spiritual incompetence and the failure to understand the very purpose of our lives. With ignorance in control our faith never develops, our attitudes become distorted, and our lives miss the objectives of eternal exaltation. The Lord himself said, "No man can be saved in ignorance." That is, no man can be saved who has this Trojan horse inside his walls, for then he has the soldiers of apostasy, negative attitudes, and lack of understanding continually attacking this spiritual vitality and destroying his chances for eternal life.

Every kind of sin is a Trojan horse. Sin breaks down the walls of morality, faith, integrity, religious standards, personal ideals, and ethical considerations. We cannot afford to tolerate wrong practices or partial truths in our lives. There is a very good reason why no sin is permitted in the presence of God and there is an equally good reason why none should ever be tolerated inside our gates.

The Trojan horse of sin has in its belly dozens of evils which when turned loose upon us leaves us no chance for success. The soldiers of sin afflict us with a guilty conscience, a bad reputation, destructive internal moral conflicts, and causes us to lose our own self-respect.

A man once applying for a job wrote in his application that he had quit his previous employment because of illness. "What kind of illness?" asked the interviewer. The applicant replied, "The boss got sick of me." That is a common complaint of our present day. Not only do we make others sick with our evil, but we get sick of ourselves. We might try to imagine what it would be like to have God get sick of us.

There are a lot of other Trojan horses outside our walls waiting for an opportunity to get in. As long as we keep them outside we are safe. As long as we are only exposed to a frontal attack from an enemy that we can see and understand, we can make ourselves invulnerable. But when these forces of damnation are made to seem so pleasant that we start the wrecking crews tearing down our protecting walls, then we never know what unseen enemy soldiers will run a knife into our backs, killing our success

We should not be misled by the fact that some of these dangers seem small to us. It is one of life's impossibilities to keep the problems of sin small once they get on our insides. We should remember that it was just a little handful of Greeks that sent the great city of Troy into oblivion. It is good to remind ourselves occasionally that Babylon, the strongest power of the ancient world, vanished overnight without the loss of one of the attackers. Our eternal glory may be similarly destroyed, for once the wrong influences get a toe-hold inside our fortifications, we never know what evil will be pouncing upon us.

One of the best ways to keep the Trojan horses of Satan outside our walls is to avoid being deceived by the propagandists that are left behind for that purpose. Then we should work like Trojans, doing those things that will keep our inside fortifications strong and safe. Joseph Addison once gave a great success formula to his friend. He said:

> Tis not for mortals to command success,
> But we'll do more, Sempronicus,
> We'll deserve it.

That is a great idea and it will guarantee our eternal glory.

The Same Jesus

M ANY years ago someone published a picture Bible, in which it was attempted to make the great scriptural messages more memorable by presenting them in visual form. Our natural tendency is to see things more clearly when they are presented in pictures. Mere ideas are often too abstract for the mind to deal with effectively.

One of the visual portrayals in this interesting Bible was a colored picture of the ascension. It showed the resurrected Jesus standing in the air above the Mount of Olives as he was ascending to his Father. And standing slightly below the master were two angels dressed in white clothing. Over the years I have drawn great strength from the thrilling ideas represented by this picture. Christ's ascension to heaven marked the end of an important period. He had finished one part of the work assigned to him in the grand council of heaven. He had organized the church and had left ordained apostles to carry on its work. He had taught them the doctrines of salvation and had given them the Priesthood with the power to bind in heaven what they did on earth. He had shed his own blood to pay the penalty of our sins. Then in the last words spoken just before his ascension, Jesus said to the twelve, ". . ye shall be witnesses unto me, both in Jerusalem, and in all Judea, and in Samaria, and unto the uttermost parts of the earth."

The ascension picture is completed by the interesting scriptural statement which said, "And when he had spoken these things, while they beheld, he was taken up; and a cloud received him out of their sight. And while they looked stedfastly toward heaven as he went up, behold, two men stood by them in white apparel; which also said, Ye men of Galilee, why stand ye gazing up into heaven? This same Jesus, which is taken up from you into heaven, shall so come in like manner as ye have seen him go into heaven." (Acts 1:9-11)

During the second World War, I added another impressive mental picture to my collection. This one shows General Douglas MacArthur about to take flight from Corregidor under the military pressure of Japanese conquest. To those who were forced to remain behind General MacArthur said, "I shall return." I like to imagine the hope that this promise must have brought to the people of the Philippines during those long months in which they awaited their liberation from the bondage of the Japanese. They knew that Mac-Arthur would not forget They knew that just as soon as possible he would come back to set them free and punish their oppressors. His promise may have had more than ordinary significance to me, inasmuch as some of the members of my own family were among those awaiting Mac-Arthur's return. They hid in the hills, until they were captured and sent to a Japanese concentration camp in Manila.

The General's promise to return must have had a disturbing significance for the invaders themselves, for they must have known that MacArthur would never rest until they had been driven from the islands, or annihilated during their resistance. This "I shall return" picture was given its happy ending some two years later, when the General's promise was finally and fully kept.

However, the world still awaits this more significant "I shall return" promise that had been made some nineteen hundred years earlier from above the Mount of Olives. It is very important to remember that the Savior of the world was only bidding the earth and its people a temporary farewell. Many times before his death, he himself had foretold his own glorious second coming to judge the world.

On that last Tuesday before his death on Friday, Jesus had been teaching his followers about his second coming. Near the end of the day he left the temple and led the twelve across the Mount of Olives. As he sat down to rest near the summit his disciples said to him, "Tell us, when shall these things be, and what shall be the sign of thy coming, and of the end of the world?" (Matt. 24:3) Then Jesus told them of the wars and contentions that should characterize the last days, and as one of the important signs that should precede his second coming he said, "And his gospel of the kingdom shall be preached in all the world for a witness unto all nations; and then shall the end come." (Matt. 24:14)

As the people of the Philippines waited their liberation, they probably wondered whether or not General MacArthur had the ability to fulfill the conditions involved in his promise to return. There are also a great many in our world who discount both the possibility and the probability of the second coming of Christ. Yet we may be certain that God's program has never been abandoned and will not be forgotten.

In those last sad hours just prior to his death, Jesus said to his disciples, "Let not your heart be troubled; ye believe in God, believe also in me. In my Father's house are many mansions: if it were not so, I would have told you. I go to prepare a place for you. And if I go and prepare a place for you, *I will come again,* and receive you unto myself; that where I am, there ye may be also." (John 14:1-3) What a thrilling, frightening thought when we understand the conditions under which he will come again! And what tremendous consequences are involved in the message of ascension day! As the resurrected Son of God stood there between the heavens and the earth, holy angels from God's presence made a firm promise, that he would personally return. The angels said, "This same Jesus . . . shall so come in like manner as ye have seen him go. . . ."

Since ascension day, some nineteen wide centuries have come and gone and many important events have taken place. Tradition has it that with one exception, the apostles that Jesus appointed to carry on his work were all subjected to violent deaths. The report has it that Peter, Philip, Simon and Andrew were crucified; James and Paul were beheaded; Bartholomew was flayed alive; Thomas was run through with a lance; James, the son of Alphaeus, was beaten to death; Thaddaeus was shot through with arrows; Barnabas was stoned; Matthew was slain with a battle axe in Ethiopia, and Mark was dragged to death in the streets of Alexandria. Then John, the sole survivor, was banished to the lonely isle of Patmos in the Aegean Sea. Jesus had built his church upon the foundation of apostles and prophets. When the foundation was destroyed, the building crumbled. In time what had once been a divine organization became merely human institution. The great Christian doctrines were misinterpreted, the ordinances were changed, the authority was lost, the apostasy grew, and the world slipped gradually into the long black night of the Dark Ages. Then some said that the heavens were forever sealed, that the canon of scripture was full, and that no voice from God would ever again be heard upon the earth. The spirit of those who crucified Christ, destroyed his organization and disbelieved his doctrines, still have a numerous following among us.

One of the most serious problems of our present world is that there are so many people who disbelieve in a Supreme Being. To some, man is the highest authority and the greatest intellect in the universe. Others believe that God has gone out of business and that the last words that we will ever hear from the Savior of the world were spoken at the ninth hour of that awful Friday afternoon, when from Calvary's cross the dying Christ said, "It is finished." The last memory that some have of their Redeemer pictures him hanging upon the cross. The world has been flooded with the crucifix, but Jesus did not remain upon the cross. Some

remember him lying in the garden tomb of Joseph of Arima-
thaea, but Jesus did not remain in the tomb. Nothing in
the scriptures could be plainer than the fact that the life of
Christ did not begin in Bethlehem, neither did it end on
Calvary. He said, "I came forth from the Father, and
am come into the world: again, I leave the world, and go to
the Father." (John 16:28) In his prayer in Gethsemane
while contemplating his own death he said, ". . . And now,
O Father, glorify thou me with thine own self, with the
glory which I had with thee before the world was." (John
17:5)

Long before our earth was created, Jesus lived and
ruled with his Father as a part of the presidency of the
universe. Under the direction of the Father he was the
Creator of the earth. In the first chapter of Genesis, God
is recorded as saying, "Let *us* make man in *our* image, after
our likeness." The use of these plural pronouns indicates
that the Son also took part in the creation. But even then
he was no novice as a creator. In one of the great revelations
given to Moses and revealed anew in the latter days, God
said, "And worlds without number have I created . . . and
by the Son I created them, which is mine Only Begotten."
(Moses 1:33)

We think of greatness partly in terms of what it has
already accomplished, and partly in terms of what it promises for the future. As I rerun my mental picture of ascension
day, I like to think of the Redeemer in terms of his tremendous background. Not only had he created worlds without
number, but in his pre-mortal existence he was that magnificent personage of great authority and power known in the
scriptures as Jehovah, the God of Abraham, Isaac and Jacob.
He was the first begotten Son of God in the spirit, and was
chosen to be the Savior of the world because he was the best
qualified for that important calling. Then, as a part of his
own progression, he took upon himself a body of flesh and

bones, and became the only begotten Son of God in the flesh. There are those who even seek to deprive God of his body. Many do not believe in their own resurrection, but next to the human spirit the human body is the most marvelous of God's creations. If the body was not necessary, God would never have created it in the first place. If it were not necessary for eternity, God would never have instituted the resurrection. If a body was not necessary for God the Father, certainly there would have been no reason why God, the Son, should have been resurrected. The spirit and the body inseparably connected constitutes the soul. The spirit could never be perfect without the body. There can never be a fullness of joy until the spirit and the body are inseparably joined together.

The resurrected, glorified Jesus, like Elohim, his Eternal Father, has a body of flesh and bones as tangible as man's. (D&C 130:22) When Jesus appeared to the eleven, after his resurrection, they were frightened and supposed that they had seen a spirit. Jesus corrected them by saying, "Behold my hands and my feet, that it is I myself: handle me, and see; for a spirit hath not flesh and bones, as ye see me have." (Luke 24:39) Jesus did not lose his body after his resurrection. It did not evaporate in some mysterious way, neither did it expand to fill the immensity of space. Jesus had his body as he ascended to his Father from the Mount of Olives, and the record is perfectly clear that he will still have that same body when he comes in glory to judge the world.

In addition to the information given in the Bible we now have some new evidence of universal importance which has been given to the world on this subject in our own day. In the early spring of 1820, in upper New York state, God the Father and his Son Jesus Christ reappeared upon the earth to re-establish among men a belief in the God of Genesis, a belief in the God of Abraham, Isaac and Jacob, and a belief in the God of Mount Olivet. The Prophet Joseph Smith describes his part of this experience by saying, "I saw two Personages whose brightness and glory defy all description, standing above me in the air. One of them spake unto me, calling me by name and said, pointing to the other . . . *This is my beloved Son. Hear Him.*" (*Joseph Smith* 2:17) Then there followed the great message of the restoration.

The same Jesus who healed the sick and walked upon the waves has spoken again in our day, and has reaffirmed the fact that he is still interested in our success. The same Jesus who said to his disciples, ". . . Go ye into all the world, and preach the gospel to every creature. He that believeth and is baptized shall be saved; but he that believeth not shall be damned." (Mark 16:15-16) This same Jesus has informed us anew that he has not changed his mind about the importance of this and the other great Christian doctrines.

The same Jesus who upon the Mount of Olives said, "and this gospel of the kingdom shall be preached in all the world as a witness unto all nations, and then shall the end come," has, under the direction of his Father, restored *that* gospel, in preparation for *that* day. He himself looked forward to that day saying, "For the Son of man shall come in the glory of his Father with his angels; and then shall he reward every man according to his works." (Matt. 16:27) What a tremendous day that will be! That is also the day foretold by Malachi, who said, "For behold, the day cometh that shall burn as an oven, and all the proud, yea, and all that do wickedly shall burn as stubble; for they that come shall burn them, saith the Lord of Hosts, that it shall leave them neither root nor branch." (*Joseph Smith* 2:37) That tremendous event is fast approaching and we must work while it is called today, for the night cometh, wherein no man can work.

I would like to bear to you my personal witness that God has not gone out of business; that the heavens are not sealed, that the Redeemer of men has not forgotten his promises, nor is he any less interested in our welfare now than when in Gethsemane, and upon Mount Calvary he suffered for our sins. And in conclusion I would again like to take you out to the sacred top of the Mount of Olives, and again hear the angels say, ". . . This same Jesus, which is taken up from you into heaven, shall so come in like manner as ye have seen him go into heaven." (Acts 1:11) May the importance of this event challenge us to be ready.

Thou Shalt Not Covet

IN THE tenth commandment the Lord said, "Thou shalt not covet." The dictionary says that to "covet is to long inordinately for something that belongs to someone else." It is an overdose of selfishness or an excess of avariciousness. The covetous person lives more or less as though the world was intended only for him.

The first sin recorded in the Bible after the fall of man was centered in covetousness. The first verse of the fourth chapter of Genesis tells of the birth of Cain. Cain's mother was delighted with her new-born son and said, ". . . I have gotten a man from the Lord." The second verse tells of the birth of Cain's brother, Abel, and gives his occupation as a keeper of sheep, whereas Cain was a tiller of the ground.

"And in process of time, it came to pass, that Cain brought of the fruit of the ground an offering unto the Lord. And Abel, he also brought of the firstlings of his flock, and of the fat thereof. And the Lord had respect unto Abel and to his offering: But unto Cain and to his offering he had not respect. And Cain was very wroth, and his countenance fell. And the Lord said unto Cain, Why art thou wroth? and why is thy countenance fallen? If thou doest well, shalt thou not be accepted? and if thou doest not well, sin lieth at the door. . . . And Cain talked with Abel his brother: and it came to pass, when they were in the field, that Cain rose up against Abel his brother, and slew him." (Genesis 4:1-8) Then Cain gloried in that which he had done saying, ". . . surely the flocks of my brother falleth into my hands." (Moses 5:33)

There are only six brief Bible verses separating the announcement of Cain's birth from that of his eternal condemnation as the first murderer. How quickly this little sin of covetousness changed his life! After his sin had run its course God said to Cain, "Where is Abel, thy brother? And Cain said, I know not. Am I my brother's keeper?"

Cain's experience points out the pattern usually followed by evil. One sin leads us on to another, and more serious sin, until we may pass the point of no return. A little selfishness gave Cain a bad attitude and made his offering unacceptable. Avariciousness grew within him until he could not resist the temptation offered by his brother's flocks, and thus he was led on to the awful sin of murder. But even this was not the end. In trying to cover up his terrible deed, Cain tried to deceive God. What a tremendous price everyone must pay when even a little covetousness is allowed to sink its deadly roots into our souls to start this chain reaction. As the poet has said:

> Oh what a tangled web we weave,
> When first we practice to deceive.

We begin weaving a tangled web the minute we break any of God's commandments, for in one way or another they are all tied up together, and when we violate one, we involve ourselves in the danger of other violations. Yet, it is very probable that most of our crimes are born of covetousness. Many forms of evil grow out of our desire to get something for nothing. Most of the stealing, lying, cheating, deceiving and even killing takes place because we long inordinately for something that doesn't belong to us. Covetousness also tends to cause the death of character, ability and creativeness. The boy who covets instead of working, or longs for the things he hasn't earned, or the man who seeks an increase of pay without increasing his effort is actually wasting the time and resources that might otherwise be used in creating his own wealth. Covetousness curtails the very habits that produce wealth. Most people expend more effort in going to hell than it would take to get them to heaven. If

Cain had merely given his effort a little different direction, he could have had a fine attitude, offered an acceptable sacrifice and made himself an outstanding and successful man. We can also create great material and personal wealth with the effort we use up longing for those things that belong to someone else.

In the 12th chapter of Luke we read of one man saying to Jesus, ". . . Master, speak to my brother, that he divide the inheritance with me. And Jesus said unto him, Man, who made me a judge or a divider over you? And he said unto them, Take heed, and beware of covetousness: for a man's life consisteth not in the abundance of things which he possesseth." A great many of us appoint ourselves to be dividers of the goods of others. We have an equal need to beware of covetousness, as it can easily wreck our lives here and hereafter.

We should all understand the declaration of Jesus that life is more than meat, and the body is more than raiment. One of the greatest of all success formulas says, "Seek ye first the kingdom of God, and his righteousness; and all these things shall be added unto you." (Matt. 6:33-34) It is good to covet if we covet the right things. Paul said, "Covet earnestly the best gifts." (I Cor. 12:31) He said, "Covet to prophesy and forbid not to speak with tongues." (I Cor. 14:39) These good gifts were intended for us and only good can come from their possession. Jesus' warning was against selfishness and those things that destroy our souls.

In spite of the fact that "covetousness" is so deeply involved in our present-day problems, yet this destructive little word has practically disappeared from our present-day vocabulary and conscious thinking. However, it is still present in our activities and destroys the good things of our lives. A good measure of covetousness is at the root of all of our wars, crime and sin. Anyone who reads the daily newspapers is aware of the constant effort on the part of both nations and individuals to get possession of things that belong to someone else. We like to receive favors even though we render none. Nations, like individuals, like to borrow money but they seldom like to pay their bills. Strong nations gobble up weak nations. In our own land, political leaders try to outdo each other in finding new shortcuts to the more abundant life that requires no effort. Cities, states and even churches sometimes conduct lotteries as a means of raising money. The popularity of the slot machine bears testimony of our insane hope to get something for nothing. A drive was recently launched in the great state of Idaho attempting to legalize gambling, even though it would mean corrupting the people and destroying much that is best in any community. Chain letters and other lunatic programs have reached proportions that classify them as a major phenomenon of our time.

Sometimes we say that our economic system has broken down. It is not the system that has broken down, rather our human character has disintegrated under our desire to get something for nothing. The speculative mania causing disturbing booms, busts and lack of confidence in our economy grows out of our frantic attempts to produce the more abundant life by a political sleight-of-hand performance. The desire to get something for nothing is the dominating cause of our stock market upsets. It also brings us a false security, unreasonable installment buying and the constant specter of a destructive inflation.

On a national scale we are speculating in unsound practices of social welfare, social security, horse races, lucky numbers, old age pensions, and other devices calculated to produce wealth for a particular group without work on the part of the recipients. We have over-emphasized the American standard of living and under-emphasized the American standard of character and the sound religious principles on which morality is based. Cain was setting the short-cut pattern to wealth by killing his brother and taking his flocks

by force. We have made some refinements in our procedures
since Cain by using the ballot box to get our brother's property. We merely vote ourselves into prosperity, and a more
abundant life. However, instead of calling the procedure
covetousness, we use such phrases as "the redistribution of
wealth." We tax "the haves to pay the have-nots." We
assess the "wills" to provide for the "won'ts." We make
social security laws, build up relief rolls, and do many things
for special classes to be paid for by the money taken from
someone else. Of course taxation is entirely proper in many
ways, but we should beware how we exercise our office of a
divider of other men's goods, for many of our programs are
based on covetousness and the insidious popular appeal to
get something for nothing. Someone said that if the Founding Fathers thought taxation without representation was bad,
they should see what it is like with representation.

It seems that we are becoming more and more reluctant
to accept the old-fashioned virtues of thrift and individual
responsibility under which both character and wealth are
most effectively created. In its many guises what has been
called the redistribution of wealth has often been a more
potent political slogan than a program involving the creation
of wealth.

We had an interesting demonstration of this a few years
ago when it was reported that ten million people had enrolled
under the Townsend banner with demands for immediate
pensions and other benefits to be paid for by someone else.
The importance of this philosophy in our minds is indicated
by the fact that when someone wins a quiz program or a
sweepstakes to which millions of others have made contributions, we make an event of national importance out of it
and give it a big play in the newspapers, glamorizing it with
pictures and stories. And yet many people fail in life because
of their preoccupation with this kind of success. Probably
more people today suffer from the delusion that the world
owes them a living than at any other time. They claim the

good things of life as a right. And somehow we feel it is a little unfair if we are asked to work for what we get. Even the great Church welfare program has had great difficulty in teaching people the importance of their own labor as a basis for their daily bread.

Very largely covetousness destroys our sense of responsibility and obligation. And the evil traits that grow in their places sometimes makes us as Cain, unfit to live successfully and happily either in this world or in the next. It is a great ability to be able to see in advance the consequences of this important sin. Unfavorable situations almost always arise when we have too many things done for us. Then we fail to develop the habits of doing things for ourselves. When we covet the wrong things we set influence in motion that prevents us from developing the abilities to get the right things. Like Cain, we can start a chain reaction that eventually leads us to destruction.

The government can easily pauperize its citizens by doing too much for them. There have been occasions when even those on government relief have gone on strike for higher pay. Suppose that we make a list of troubles that we can bring upon ourselves by indulging in covetousness. Parents and schools often weaken the children by indulging them. Parents indulge themselves. The politicians indulge the people. The people indulge each other. There are so many easy material advantages in our day that conspire to make our lives easier and our characters weaker. The idea of something for nothing always works against our own interests. As Oliver Goldsmith has written:

> Ill fares the land, to hastening ills a prey,
> Where wealth accumulates and men decay.
> Princes and lords may flourish or may fade,
> A breath can make them as a breath has made.
> But a bold peasantry, their country's pride,
> When once destroyed can never be supplied.

The condition that makes effort unnecessary or the attitude that makes it seem undesirable often does us an irreparable harm. The sins of the father's prosperity and the bad attitudes that sometimes come from inherited wealth are often visited upon the children, and the children's children under the third and fourth generation. The children of poor parents who have good attitudes toward life usually start out with a tremendous advantage in the struggle for character. And one of the most important aids to our success is to learn the lesson taught by the Lord from the top of Mount Sinai when he said, "Thou shalt not covet." He said, "Thou shalt not covet thy neighbour's house, thou shalt not covet thy neighbour's wife, nor his ass, nor any thing that is thy neighbour's." (Exodus 20:17) And that includes thy neighbor's job, his home, his personality and his opportunity.

The safest way to success is to follow the Lord's program and seek first for the kingdom of God and his righteousness, then all other necessary things are added. *Things* always follow *talents*. We need only develop the *talents*, and the *things* will follow. But when we covet the *things* first, we destroy the *talents*, which in turn make the *things* possible.

In his inaugural address, President Kennedy gave us a good anti-covet procedure when he said, "Fellow Americans, ask not what your country can do for you, but rather ask what you can do for your country." Our primary concern should be what we can do for others, not what they can do for us. It is always more blessed to give than to receive. It is always better to serve than to covet. The abundant life comes not from the things that we get, but from the things that we give. And giving helps us to avoid the awful sin, and giant evil of covetousness.

The Unknown God

THOMAS CARLYLE once pointed out that a man's religion is the most important thing about him. That is what he believes in and thinks about and fights for and lives by. Of course, all true religion centers in God, and makes up our relationship to him. To know God and to obey his commandments is the most important responsibility of our lives. And as has often been pointed out, the greatest difficulties of our present-day world come because of false religion. When we live by wrong principles, we develop wrong attitudes and attain wrong goals.

Some time ago a survey indicated that 95% of all Americans believed in God, but a very small percentage had any clear conception of the kind of God they believed in. One woman included in the survey said "I don't know what God is. I haven't given it very much thought." Her neighbor said, "I believe God is something existing somewhere, but I don't know very much about him." One church officially describes its God by saying, "There is but one living and true God who is infinite in being and perfection, a most pure spirit, invisible, without body, parts or passions, immutable, eternal, and incomprehensible." How can one believe in something that he can never hope to understand, or what advantage could possibly be derived from a belief in a mysterious, incomprehensible, impossible God?

One prominent minister recently expressed himself by saying, "It is impossible to know about God. He is absolutely unknowable, indiscernible and undiscoverable. He is not limited to boundaries, and we can be certain that he has no body or shape." According to Jesus, that would make salvation impossible, as he said, "This is life eternal that they might know thee, the only true God and Jesus Christ whom thou hast sent." This minister says it is *impossible to know about God.* Then he proceeds to say that God has no body or shape. How did this minister discover this if God is undiscoverable? This same minister said, "God is one person, but is manifested in three persons." He said, "Don't ask me to explain it, I can't. It is impossible for me to explain. It is impossible for me to understand. I can only believe." No wonder that such a belief does not produce the same great power that characterized original Christianity.

Great harm is done to many people when their religion encourages them to abandon their reason and take refuge in the argument that they can't understand. How inconsistent to live in this great scientific age where we are flapping our wings for travel into space, and at the same time say that we can't understand. The Gospel of Jesus Christ was designed to be understood by the most unlearned of those living twenty centuries ago. God has made personal appearances on several occasions, and Jesus and the prophets have outlined the Christian doctrines with such great clarity that "even a fool need not err therein." To describe God as a formless, shapeless, sexless, incomprehensible mass without body, parts or passions, reminds us of the declaration of one who said, "I believe in the dogmas of the church, in spite of the fact that they are absurd."

Inasmuch as we were created in God's image, how would you personally like to fit the sectarian specification so often used to describe God? So many people speak of the Creator only in terms of what he is not. They say he does not have a body, a form, dimensions, faculties, feelings or personality. How much more helpful to have him described in terms of what he is! To further add to our difficulty, many theologians confine God to the past tense. They say there can never be any more revelation, that God's lips are forever sealed, and that eternal silence must reign forever so far as God is concerned. This false religion says

THE LAW OF THE HARVEST

that all revelation is in the past, that angels no longer minister to men, that no more messages of truth can ever come from God. What a hopeless situation to imagine that God has gone out of business in the very time that we need him most.

Mr. Khruschchev has subscribed to a false religion, but he came out forthrightly and closed up the churches. In his opinion, God's retirement left the communist leaders as the highest authority in world affairs. It has been false religion that has caused every one of the world calamities, including the flood, the confusion at Babel, the crucifixion at Calvary, plus all the wars and sins of history, including those of our own day.

The Apostle Paul found a false religion in operation when he visited Athens. The city was completely given over to idolatry. The people had erected images to every conceivable kind of deity and had created a theology to match. Paul said to them, "Ye men of Athens, I perceive that in all things ye are too superstitious. For as I passed by, and beheld your devotions, I found an altar with this inscription, TO THE UNKNOWN GOD. Whom therefore ye ignorantly worship, him declare I unto you." (Acts 17:22-23)

Then trying to make them understand, Paul quoted one of their own poets as saying that they were the offspring of God. Paul reasoned that inasmuch as they were God's offspring, they ought not to think that God was like these man-made creations that they had set up. What a difference it would make if we all accepted Paul's logic that the offspring should sometime become like the parent.

It is a very serious thing in any age to believe in false gods or subscribe to a false religion. God talked with Moses face to face and said, "Thou shalt have no other gods before me." If God was offended by the graven images of Moses' days, how disturbed he must be when we deprive him of his body, deny his faculties and personality, and then destroy his reality itself by saying that he is merely an influence or an eternal principle, or something that we need not be concerned about because no one can understand him anyway!

One minister said that no two theories or ideas of men agree. He said that most of the popular ideas about God are products of someone's imagination, and he said, "Your guess is as good as anyone's."

If these popular ideas about God are accepted, then we are still at the feet of the unknown God. How could this formless, shapeless, incomprehensible mass, reason, or speak, love, teach, rebuke, show anger, or beget offspring. How could any reasonable person accept such as the Father of Jesus Christ, or the all-powerful Creator of the universe and our own worshipful Heavenly Father? Certainly we would not expect the parent to be less than the offspring. If the Father is incomprehensible and fills the universe, if he has no body, parts or passions, how do we account for the fact that the children do not fit this description? Think how difficult it would be to believe in any person without boundaries, or without a body, or without parts or passions. Or try to determine how he could be benefited by believing in a God who was incomprehensible and impossible.

A young man once said to an older friend, "I don't believe in God. I am an atheist." His friend said, "Will you describe the kind of God that you *don't* believe in?" The young man gave the usual sectarian description. His friend said, "If that is a proper description of God, then I am an atheist also."

Then the older man tried to do for his young friend what Paul attempted to do for the Greeks on Mars' Hill when he said, "Whom therefore ye ignorantly worship, him declare I unto you." God is a person in whose image man was created. He is not merely an essence, or an agent, or a force, or a shapeless mass. He is not a *thing*, and should never be referred to as an "*it*."

God is the greatest intelligence in the universe and he has endowed us with his potentialities. The Book of Genesis clearly tells us of two creations. In Genesis 1:27 we read, "So God created man in his own image, in the image of God created he him; male and female created he them." But in the second chapter of Genesis we read, "Thus the heavens and the earth were finished, and all the host of them . . . but there was not a man to till the ground." (Gen. 2:1-5)   In the second chapter we are told of the second creation as follows: "And the Lord God formed man of the dust of the ground, and breathed into his nostrils the breath of life; and man became a living soul." (Genesis 2:7)

This double creation is explained by the fact that the first was the creation in heaven when our spirits were formed in God's image. The second creation was when our bodies were created in the exact image of our spirits. The writer of Genesis says that even the plants were first created spiritually. He said, "And every plant of the field before it was in the earth, and every herb of the field before it grew." (Genesis 2:5)

In a modern revelation the Lord makes this passage complete by saying, "And every plant of the field before it was in the earth, and every herb of the field before it grew. For I, the Lord God, created all things, of which I have spoken, spiritually, before they were naturally upon the face of the earth. For I, the Lord God, had not caused it to rain upon the face of the earth. And I, the Lord God, had created all the children of men; and not yet a man to till the ground; for in heaven created I them; and there was not yet flesh upon the earth, neither in the water, neither in the air; . . . and I, the Lord God, formed man from the dust of the ground, and breathed into his nostrils the breath of life; and man became a living soul, the first flesh upon the earth, the first man also; nevertheless, all things were before created; but spiritually were they created and made according to my word." (Moses 3:5-7)

What a thrilling doctrine that we are literally of the same species as God, our Heavenly Father, and what a disservice is the false religion that says otherwise! Suppose that some of those who say that God is unknowable had confronted Moses as he came down from the Mount where he had talked with God face to face and had said to him, "No one can possibly know about God." Or suppose such a one should have said to Jesus that God was merely an influence that no one could understand, that he had no body of his own, or that he was diffused throughout the area of many billions of light years making up the immensity of space. Or supposing that these people had said to Jesus that his Father was merely an eternal principle. If the Creator is not less than the created then how could he be merely an eternal principle? How would you like to have a wife and family who were only influences or forces of eternal principles? Jesus said, "I ascend unto my Father and to your Father, and to my God and to your God." To Jesus, God was a real personage, his literal Father, who was in form and feature as he himself was. Paul said, "Ye are also his offspring." (Acts 17:28) and David said, "Ye are gods and all of you are children of the most High." (Psalm 82:6) And to the Hebrews Paul explained that God is the father of spirits. (Hebrews 12:9) What a tremendous fact and how important that we understand it!

Some time ago one of the great ministers of the world wrote a book in which he compared the great Christian doctrines as taught in the Bible with the doctrines taught by the popular ministers of the present day. In making his comparison he said, "The God of the Bible is a personal God, there can be no question about that." And then he said, "But we don't believe that any more." Then he quoted from the answers he had received from present-day teachers of religion, explaining what they believed God to be. One said that he was like a giant electronic brain. One said that God was anything that you couldn't explain. He said he was atheism to the atheist. Another said that God was a mobile, cosmic ether. This man said, "Imagine Jesus praying to a mobile cosmic ether." Jesus prayed, "Our Father which art in Heaven." What did he mean? Can we accuse Jesus of double-talk and an attempt to deceive? Did Jesus believe that he was the Son of an incomprehensible, shapeless influence without body, parts or passions? Jesus talked with his Father and his Father replied.

Some not only say that God has no body, but that we will also lose our bodies. If bodies were not necessary, why were they ever created in the first place? If they are not necessary for the hereafter, why did God go to all the bother to establish the resurrection? If a body was necessary for God the Father why should God the Son have been resurrected? Next to the spirit, the human body is God's greatest creation. And none of his works are temporary.

Jesus did not lose his body after the resurrection. It did not evaporate. It did not expand to fill the immensity of space. At the resurrection his spirit and body were inseparately joined together, never again to be separated. When he ascended into heaven he had his body and the angels who stood at his side said, "This same Jesus, which is taken up from you into heaven, shall so come again in like manner as ye have seen him go into heaven." Paul said that Jesus is in the express image of his Father's person. If a body is necessary for Jesus, why isn't it necessary for his Father? Or if it isn't necessary for the Father, why should it be necessary for the Son. There are some people upon the earth who know beyond any question of doubt that God has a body. He has appeared to man in our own day and has left indisputable evidence and a powerful written testimony about himself. Men in our own day have seen God even as Moses did, face to face. A modern revelation says, "The Father has a body of flesh and bones as tangible as man's; the Son also; but the Holy Ghost has not a body of flesh and bones, but is a personage of Spirit." (D&C 130:22.)

We can know the truth of this for ourselves. It is not necessary for us to believe in a false religion and base our faith in an unknown God. God has not gone out of business. God still lives and is interested in us. And every human being upon the earth will some time know this for himself, for many of the wonderful works of God are still in the future. Angels do minister to men upon the earth, and if we would make our lives successful, we must learn about the true God and establish his religion securely in our lives.

The Unprofitable Servant

ONE OF the very constructive lessons of the scriptures is taught in the parable of the talents. In this interesting experience related by Jesus we learn of the individual responses made by three men to the same opportunity, and based on their reactions the Master appraised their lives.

He said, "For the kingdom of heaven is as a man traveling into a far country, who called his own servants, and delivered unto them his goods. And unto one he gave five talents, to another two, and to another one; to every man according to his several ability; and straightway took his journey. Then he that had received the five talents went and traded with the same, and made them other five talents. And likewise he that had received two, he also gained other two. But he that had received one went and digged in the earth, and hid his lord's money.

"After a long time the lord of those servants cometh, and reckoneth with them. And so he that had received five talents came and brought other five talents, saying, Lord, thou deliveredst unto me five talents: behold, I have gained beside them five talents more. His lord said unto him, Well done, thou good and faithful servant: thou hast been faithful over a few things, I will make thee ruler over many things: enter thou into the joy of thy lord. He also that had received two talents came and said, Lord, thou deliveredst unto me two talents: behold, I have gained two talents beside them. His lord said unto him, Well done, good and faithful servant; thou hast been faithful over a few things, I will make thee ruler over many things: enter thou into the joy of thy lord.

"Then he which had received the one talent came and said, Lord . . . I was afraid . . . and hid thy talent in the earth: lo, there thou hast that is thine."

The third servant had not improved his situation during the lord's absence and in condemning him for his wasted opportunity the Lord made one of the most vigorous denunciations of his entire career. He said to the man who showed no gain, "Thou wicked and slothful servant." Jesus then gave directions that the unused talent should be taken from him and given to the one who had best demonstrated his ability to handle the situation most advantageously.

The Lord closed the case by saying, "Cast ye the unprofitable servant into outer darkness: there shall be weeping and gnashing of teeth."

We feel very sorry for this unfortunate man. His loss was not because he did anything wrong, but rather because his fear had prevented him doing anything at all. Yet this is the process by which most of our blessings are lost.

Immediately following the account of the unprofitable servant Jesus gave us that great basic success principle which says, "For unto everyone that hath shall be given, and he shall have an abundance; but from him that hath not shall be taken away even that which he hath." (Matt. 25:14-30)

We see this principle in operation around us in all of its physical, mental and spiritual aspects. We know that when one fails to use the muscles of his arm he loses his strength. The mole didn't use his eyes, and so nature took away his eyesight. When we don't develop our abilities, we lose our abilities. When the people in past ages have not honored the Priesthood, it has been taken from them. When we don't obey the gospel, we lose its benefits and apostasy possesses us. Neither spiritual, mental nor physical talents develop while they are buried in the earth.

As if to reinforce the thought of this great idea, Jesus gave another parable with about the same meaning. He said, "A certain man had a fig tree planted in his vineyard, and he came and sought fruit thereon and found none. Then said he unto the dresser of his vineyard, Behold these three years I come seeking fruit on this fig tree and find none; cut it down; why cumbereth it the ground?" (Luke 13:7)

It would be pretty difficult to miss the Lord's meaning. He intends that his children should make their lives productive. Everywhere we go in life we come face to face with the Lord's meaningful question, What doth it profit? Only a godly parent can understand the Lord's desire that his children make something of themselves. And one of the greatest yearnings that we know is that our children develop their ability and their righteousness.

One of the most pathetic of all experiences is to have a child whose body does not develop, or whose mind does not mature. However, in most of these situations no one is to blame, and the shortage can be made up in the resurrection.

But what must be the yearning and sorrow of a Heavenly Father whose children allow wickedness, sloth and fear to destroy their spiritual growth and forever disqualify them for the great blessings of the celestial kingdom. Our lives must be made to show a profit.

One of the basic laws of the Lord and one on which our eternal welfare depends is the law of stewardship. In the Doctrine and Covenants the Lord makes this idea clear by saying, "For it is required of the Lord, at the hand of every steward, to render an accord of his stewardship, both in time and in eternity." (D&C 72:3) "And whoso is found a faithful, a just and a wise steward shall enter into the joy of his Lord, and shall inherit eternal life." (D&C 51:19) What a tremendous opportunity!

All sin is displeasing to God because he understands the great damage it does in the lives of people. But one of the traits that has seemed to most incite his displeasure is for one to let his personal gifts go unused. These are the sins of people who bury their talents in the ground, or hide their lights under a bushel, or allow their salt to lose its savor. By far the most important values in the world are human values, and the Lord has indicated that the worst of all of the sins is that of turning away from righteousness in the face of great knowledge.

At one time Satan was high in the councils of heaven and was called Lucifer "the light bearer," a son of the morning. But Satan sinned and became a son of perdition. His sin made him the chief of the unprofitable servants. This was not alone for the damage he brought upon himself, but for the resulting destruction to others of God's children. Everyone is relatively unprofitable to the extent to which he is performing at less than his best. And Satan like we then help the lives of others to show a loss.

Mr. H. G. Wells tells how any person may determine whether or not he is succeeding in his life. He says, "Wealth, notoriety, place and power are not measures of success. The only sure standard of judgment is the ratio between what we *might have done* and what we *might have been,* on the one hand; and what *we have actually done,* and what *we have actually been* on the other.

Certainly the greatest waste there is in the world is not the devastation that goes with war, nor is it the cost that goes with crime; it is not the erosion of our soils, nor the waste of our raw materials. The greatest waste there is in the world is that human beings, you and I, live so far below the level of our possibilities. We are therefore re-enacting in our own lives the parable of the unprofitable servant, by burying our talents in the ground.

The treasures that God has placed in human personality are greater than all other kinds of wealth combined. Wealth cannot produce personality, but personality can produce wealth. All of the primary values in the world are in human beings, and to the extent that these human values are wasted and lost, we are made poorer. That is, wealth is not so much what you have as what you are. We don't work merely to acquire but to become. Success in life isn't determined by what we can get out of it, but by what we can become by it. And one of the most common ways of becoming an unprofitable servant is to join with this poor, unfortunate one-talent man and say, "I was afraid."

Fear has probably caused more problems than almost anything else in the world. We are afraid of failure, we are afraid of other people. We are afraid of ourselves. Fear is the absence of courage. It is an important part of discouragement. It destroys industry. It saps our strength, wastes our enthusiasm and brings our effort down to zero. That is, a discouraged man is always a weak man, and weak men fall down in their stewardship and become unprofitable servants.

Just think how much talent is lost to the world for want of a little courage. Every day sends to their graves obscure men whom fear and timidity prevented from making the first effort. If these people had only had the courage to begin, they may have gone a long way in whatever career they may have chosen. To do anything worth doing, we must not stand back shivering and shaking and thinking only of the cold and danger, we should dive into our job and scramble through as best we can. One who is perpetually calculating fine risks and overworrying about the possibility of failure will usually not get very far in life. Sometimes a man waits and doubts and fears, while he consults his neighbors and his friends until one day he wakes up and finds out that life has passed him by, and that he has lost so much time in worry and consulting cousins and uncles, that he now has no time to follow their counsel.

One of the greatest enemies of any progress is an overdose of what might be called too much caution. For example, we remember the reason that the children of Israel were kept wandering for forty years in the Arabian Desert. Shortly after they had left Egypt, they found themselves with Moses at their head, standing at the very door of their promised land. The Lord had promised them the land of their fathers, and was now ready to give them occupancy. Prior to their entry Moses had sent twelve spies, one representing each tribe, to gather information about the present inhabitants, their fortifications, etc. Just before they left, Moses said to them, "Be ye of good courage." But this important instruction they failed to observe. When they returned ten of the twelve, under the influence of their fears, made an "evil report." They said, "We be not able to go up against the people; for they are stronger than we. . . . [they] are men of a great stature. . . ." They said, the land is full of giants, and then added, ". . . we were in our own sight as grasshoppers. . . ." (Nu. 13:31-33)

Joshua and Caleb, who favored following the command of the Lord, said, ". . . Let us go up at once and possess it; for we are well able to overcome it." But the ten were afraid and they so incited the fears of the people that they also rebelled against Moses and God. Then in their fear and rebellion the people said, ". . . Would God that we had died in the land of Egypt . . . wherefore hath the Lord brought us unto this land, to fall by the sword? . . ."

Fear in ten men started a stampede in the whole camp and they all became unprofitable servants. The ten frightened leaders lost their lives and the entire group were kept wandering for forty years in the wilderness. Of those over twenty years old, only the courageous Joshua and Caleb lived long enough to enter the promised land forty years later.

Panics caused by fear are still taking their toll. In the great financial depression of the thirties, President Roosevelt said, "The only thing we have to fear is fear itself." That is still our problem. We are afraid of failure. We are afraid of the future. We are afraid of the present. We are afraid of what people will say. We are afraid of ourselves. We are afraid to stick to our convictions. We are afraid to live at our best.

One of the most valuable Christian traits is courage; the courage to try, the courage to be different, the courage to live up to our possibilities. We should develop more self-discipline and the courage of righteousness. Listen to the inspiring words of the Master as he went around saying to people, "Fear not, be not afraid, why are ye troubled? Why do thoughts arise in your hearts? Rejoice and be exceeding glad."

Most occupational failures come because of discouragement, doubt, worry, dread, fear and lack of self-confidence and for about the same reasons we fail in the larger field of life. We are afraid to be righteous. We are afraid to serve God and follow our own convictions. What a calamity it will be if when we ultimately come before God in final judgment, we then find that we are labeled as unprofitable servants, and then hear the Lord say "take his talent from him and give it to him who had demonstrated his ability to use it."

We may eliminate the destructive effects of fear in our lives if we trust and obey God. He has said, "Lo, it is I, be not afraid." May we follow this important instruction as we make the greatest possible use of our God-given talents until we may sometime hear the Lord say to us, "Well done, thou good and faithful servant. Thou hast been faithful over a few things, I will make thee ruler over many things: enter thou into the joy of thy Lord."

INDEX